What People Are Saying About
Why Good People Make Bad Choices

"I find this to be a very valuable framework for therapy, and for living a good life generally. It is a challenging book that can lead one to a new, more satisfying life. It does not minimize the difficulties encountered in growth toward maturity, but rather provides useful signposts for the journey." —Robert Rich, PhD, author of *Cancer: A Personal Challenge*.

"*Why Good People Make Bad Choices* is an incredible tool to aid in the transcendence of the ego and to initiate the establishment of a personal belief system in order to live life with integrity. Strongly recommended for anyone interested in improving their life."
—Richard A. Singer Jr., psychotherapist, author of *Your Daily Walk with the Great Minds*

"*Why Good People Make Bad Choices* answers the question in its title by borrowing ideas from an impressive range of psychological theories, expanding or re-defining them, and integrating them into a cogent and useful whole. Thought-provoking and well worth the time, this book should be read once throughout and then repeatedly and in small doses. It is bound to trigger a lot of introspection, something we sorely lack in modern life."
—Sam Vaknin, author of *Malignant Self Love: Narcissism Revisited*

"*Why Good People Make Bad Choices* offers a unique and much needed synthesis of cognitive-behavioral therapy and values clarification. In sharing the practical wisdom learned by reflecting on his own life and the decisions that shaped it, Charles L. Allen creates a path from confusion and conflict to integrity, insight and control." —Pamela Kaden, Psy.D.

"I found the book simple to read yet profound in its depth. By clearly explaining the Ego Agenda, getting readers to visualize the psychological as 'cycle-logical', and even drawing on the laws of thermodynamics, the author leads readers to recognize ineffective patterns in their lives and provides sound suggestions for creating new templates."
—Debra Cruickshank, MSW

"Even after years of experience as a Mental Health Counselor it provided me some 'ah ha!' moments in understanding why things happen the way they do. I am going through a major loss and this book provided me with a lot of insight and empowerment. I needed to read this book right now and I thank you for the opportunity to provide input into the final edition."
—Bonnie White, LHMC, M.S.

D1604757

Loving Healing Press is dedicated to producing books about innovative and rapid therapies which redefine what is possible for healing the mind and spirit.

Why Good People Make Bad Choices

How You Can Develop Peace Of Mind Through Integrity

CHARLES LAWRENCE ALLEN, MSW

Why Good People Make Bad Choices: How You Can Develop Peace Of Mind Through Integrity

Book number five in the New Horizons in Therapy Series

First Edition: January 2007

ISBN-13 978-1-932690-25-5
ISBN-10 1-932690-25-5

```
              Library of Congress Cataloging-in-Publication Data

Allen, Charles Lawrence, 1962-
  Why good people make bad choices : how you can develop peace of mind through
integrity / by Charles Lawrence Allen. -- 1st ed.
        p. cm. --  (New horizons in therapy series ; 5)
  Includes bibliographical references and index.
  ISBN-13: 978-1-932690-25-5 (pbk. : alk. paper)
  ISBN-10: 1-932690-25-5 (pbk. : alk. paper)
 1.  Decision making--Moral and ethical aspects. 2.  Ethics. 3.  Emotions. 4.
Human behavior. 5.  Integrity. 6.  Peace of mind.  I. Title. II. Series.

  BJ1419.A45 2007
  158.1--dc22

                              2006015550
```

Distributed by: Baker & Taylor, Ingram Book Group, New Leaf Distributing

Published by:
Loving Healing Press
5145 Pontiac Trail
Ann Arbor, MI 48105
USA

http://www.LovingHealing.com or
info@LovingHealing.com
Fax +1 734 663 6861

Loving Healing Press

The New Horizons in Therapy Series

- **Got parts? An Insider's Guide to Managing Life Successfully with Dissociative Identity Disorder, by ATW**

- **Got parts? Companion: A Workbook of Understanding and Hope**

- **Coping with Physical Loss and Disability: A Workbook, by Rick Ritter, MSW**

- **Enfrentando la Discapacidad y el Deterioro Físico: Un Manual, by Rick Ritter, MSW**

- **Why Good People Make Bad Choices: How You Can Develop Peace Of Mind Through Integrity, by Charles Allen**

About our Series Editor, Robert Rich, Ph.D.

Loving Healing Press is pleased to announce Robert Rich, Ph.D. as Series Editor for the *New Horizons in Therapy Series*. This exciting new series plans to bring you the best of person-centered therapies in practical application, theory, and self-help formats.

Robert Rich, M.Sc., Ph.D., M.A.P.S., A.A.S.H. is a highly experienced counseling psychologist. His web site www.anxietyanddepression-help.com is a storehouse of helpful information for people suffering from anxiety and depression.

Bob is also a multiple award-winning writer of both fiction and non-fiction, and a professional editor. His writing is displayed at www.bobswriting.com. You are advised not to visit him there unless you have the time to get lost for a while.

Three of his books are tools for psychological self-help: *Anger and Anxiety: Be in charge of your emotions and control phobias*, *Personally Speaking: Single session email therapy*, and *Cancer: A personal challenge*. However, his philosophy and psychological knowledge come through in all his writing, which is perhaps why three of his books have won international awards, and he has won many minor prizes. Dr. Rich currently resides at Wombat Hollow in Australia.

Table of Contents

Preface

Why Good People Make Bad Choices takes you on a journey of self-discovery by way of insights about the human condition. It describes the dynamic interplay between the instinctualized ego and a consciously developed belief system. It uniquely defines an ego-dynamic problem yet provides a cognitive-behavioral and existential solution.

The ego is "following an instinctual set of instructions for survival." Clearly and specifically delineated, these instructions are called, the ego's agenda.

Due to the ego's agenda, we experience problematic feelings, maintain maladaptive thoughts, and engage in behaviors that we know are not in our best interest. As a solution to the problem of the ego's agenda, this book describes the components of, "a consciously developed belief system." As we consciously establish a belief system, which includes a sense of prioritized values and a moral code, we are compelled to think and behave in a manner that is reflective of our own best interest.

This book explains how inner turmoil is inevitable as instinctual ego desires and conscious belief system values become conflicted. A simple yet effective method of understanding and reducing this inner conflict is described. It also specifically shows how to understand and manage feelings and moods, develop new and valued behaviors, and develop a belief system that will create personal integrity.

This work began many years ago with my own quest to become an effective psychotherapist. I have a formal graduate school education where I studied the usual fanfare of theories and approaches to psychopathology, neuroses, and the treatment of mental health conditions. While I was content in the early years of my career to provide this standardized style of psychotherapy it became increasingly clear to me that there was something lacking; it was possible for me to regurgitate that knowledge base, yet produce marginal results. Marginal was not good enough for me, or the clients who would count on me to bring them out of a quagmire of distress.

I came to believe that there must be a missing piece that would explain basic human suffering, and that through a determined effort I could find this missing piece. A search ensued and I looked toward eastern philosophy, western religion, mysticism, and a study of basic physics. Having spent several years in search of the holy grail of treatment approaches, I decided in frustration that I had had enough.

In 2000 I stopped reading other texts of any kind, and began a writing process in January 2003. Instead of looking to outside authorities for answers, I wrote down my questions about basic human suffering in journal form, and then I answered them. In the following two years, the theory and content for *Why Good People Make Bad Choices* was born.

About the Author

Charles Lawrence Allen is a licensed psychotherapist working in private practice in Tampa, Florida. This book is based on his two decades of experience in transforming lives. Over the years, he has treated individuals from all walks of life with a wide variety of mental health concerns. He is in his fifth decade of life, happily married, and has two wonderful children.

You can learn more about Charles Lawrence Allen, his philosophy, and methods at:

www.CharlesLawrenceAllen.com

Photo credit: James McHenry.

Introduction

Mr. Dross, my sixth grade principal, had a reputation that preceded him. I knew that he was tough, strict, and unforgiving. I also knew him to be my mom's boss. She was the librarian for the same grade school. Derek, my partner in crime on one particular fateful day, was my best friend from pre-kindergarten. He and I were passing some time in the grade school library. Boredom set in and we were soon looking for some peer attention. While my mom was out of sight, we decided to engage in some serious spitball target practice. That was a bad choice. It was after a few great shots at our target that Mr. Dross happened to walk through the hallway and saw what we were up to.

When I realized that we were caught, I nearly sucked a spitball down my throat. While being escorted down the hall by Mr. Dross, I swear I could hear some kind of dreary funeral music playing in the background. As we continued to head toward his office I could feel my heart thud more quickly with each step taken. When we arrived, my buddy and I took our seats in two chairs directly in front of Mr. Dross's desk, while he turned and headed for his closet. At that time, he pulled out the 'board of education', which was the sawed-off flat paddle end of a rowing oar, and carefully laid it out on his desk for both of us to ponder upon. In moments, I felt a strange sensation come over me. It was every nerve ending in my scalp and face tingling simultaneously, while my heart began to pound out a new round of thumping as if to signal out S.O.S. to any hero that might swoop in and save the day.

This kind of intense fear was a new sensation for me. Mr. Dross then indicated to us that he did not like the spitball incident he had just seen, and that further instances of this behavior would be met with the board of education. It took a few seconds to sink in, as I realized that on this particular day, I would not feel that paddle on my backside. This was a feeling of relief that I cannot easily put into words, although if the victims of the Titanic disaster had seen empty lifeboats coming toward them, I guess the magnitude of my relief would have been similar. After telling us a story, Mr. Dross led us back through his office door, and stated that we would now rejoin our classmates.

My sense of guilt was tremendous. In what may have been a few seconds, but seemed like an eternity of fear, I made a decision to turn back and come face to face with my principal, and speak the truth. "I'm sorry Mr. Dross, I'm sorry about what I was doing, I thought I could get away with it because my mom works here. It won't happen again." In that moment of choice, and on that day I learned about integrity: I learned about what was important to me, what was right for me, what I expected of myself, and the kind of person I had become in that moment. I learned that it was important for me to honestly and directly face my fear of people with courage. I decided that I would hold myself up to *that* standard; it would become the right thing for me to do. I decided that from then on I would expect myself to face these and other challenges in my life. I decided that I would become *that* kind of person. *Still, there was fear.*

Part 1. THE PROBLEM

1 The Agenda

The Ego's Agenda

Bad Choices and Good Choices

Why do we behave in ways that we don't want to? We overeat, stay in relationships that are no longer good for us, hurt the people that we care about, or say things we wish we had never said. We become obsessed with and sometimes addicted to eating food, smoking cigarettes, relationships, sexual activities, shopping, the internet, gambling, alcohol, drugs and various other pleasurable experiences. We engage in these and many other types of problem behaviors even when it is clearly no longer in our best interest to do so. We say to ourselves, "I want to stop, but I just can't." If there was just one simple theory to explain all of these problems and other common personal and relational human problems, we could perhaps move toward resolving them.

Most of these problems have obvious and quite logical solutions that almost any reasonable individual of average intelligence could suggest—solutions such as: "Just stop eating so much." "If the relationship isn't working, just end it." "Be nice." "Don't say mean things." "Just stop smoking, stop drinking, and stop spending six hours a day on the computer." "Just stop making bad choices." This is good advice, certainly not rocket science—easy to say, difficult to do.

These and other problematic behaviors are all matters of choice. We choose to eat, drink, and be merry way beyond what is in our best interest. When we attempt to change these behaviors, we discover that there is a part of us that does not want to change. Still, there is also a part of us that would perhaps like to put an end to these problematic behaviors once and for all, and experience a different life. The internal conflict of interest, which exists with each of these problems, must be resolved in order for you to experience a life that is less depressing, less anxious, more fulfilling, more joyful. In such a life, you may also get to know peace of mind.

Fortunately, you have the means to create that life, because, you are at the center of your universe. Furthermore, you are in control of your universe. These statements may appear to be arrogant at first glance, or perhaps it's just a matter of perspective.

What is your perspective, or your belief, about how your universe works? I'm not talking about how the planets and stars move in space and collide into space drama. I'm referring to your personal universe, your perspective of life—your belief system. Your perspective includes beliefs about: who you are, why you are here, what you should be doing in life, what's really important, what's the right way to live, why do things happen the way they do, and what should you expect of the people and things around you. There may be a big difference between your own perspective of the universe, and the way that it actually works. The bigger the difference, the more frustration, or anger, you might experience. If you believe that everyone should drive on the road like a saint, you are going to be angry most of the time you drive. Perhaps true wisdom means developing a belief system perspective of the universe that is a peaceful match to reality, and then living that way.

Ultimately, you will live with your perception of the universe, along with your choices, your joys, your pains, your problems, and all of the resulting feelings. If you see your universe as a negative place, you will very likely experience a lot of negative feelings. A perception of the world as a dangerous place will produce vast amounts of fear. If you see your universe as an opportunity for learning, you may experience much gladness through discovery. To a great degree then, I believe that the amount of joy that you can experience in life is a perceptual challenge. The notion of a challenge suggests an inherent and fundamental conflict. The conflict exists between an ego perspective and a consciously developed belief system perspective; this is an internal conflict of interest. Your ego has an interest in survival through a means of following an instinctually based agenda. Beyond that instinctual agenda lies the potential for a consciously developed belief system. These fundamentally different and conflicted perspectives will be clearly identified and fully explained throughout the remainder of this book. To the extent that you know, understand, and recognize these two perspectives, you can begin to reduce the conflict, reduce your problematic behaviors, and create your own peace of mind.

Regardless of the difficulty or challenge, you are at the center, and are in charge of your universe. You already have all that you need to experience peace of mind, but reducing inner conflict and creating peace of mind in a predictable way requires a specific method of doing so. One such method is described in this book. Before moving on, here is a concise summary of the remainder of this book in terms of *The Problem, The Solution, The Method, and The Choice.*

> Your ego is a fundamental aspect of who you are. Following your ego's instinctually based agenda is not always in your best interest. Following it blindly and habitually is the cause of most personal and relational problems. You must be able to know, understand, and recognize the ego's agenda when and where it is playing out in your psychological functioning. Then you will need to do something else instead—make a different choice. This requires you to establish and develop a belief system of your own conscious choice. Then, instead of reacting according to your ego's agenda, you act on the basis of your belief system. Occasionally, you will encounter your ego's resistance—this is the internal conflict of interest. When you encounter this conflict (and you will encounter it) you will need to recognize it, and have an effective method of resolution available to you. To resolve in accordance with your belief system creates integrity and is always a matter of choice.

The Ego

Tom Anderson was my first psychotherapy client for the day. He and his wife Laura sat in the waiting room, with an empty chair between them. I indicated that we were ready to start, and Tom got up alone. As we walked toward my office, Tom said he wanted to do the first session by himself. "I'm kind of guessing we might be talking about my past. Laura really doesn't know much about it, and I think that she might be bored with all the historical stuff." We both sat down and Tom continued, "I'm mostly here today because she's really frustrated with me. And I don't blame her…I'm pretty frustrated with myself. For some reason, I'm finding that I fly off the handle for no reason at all. I just don't understand it, I've never been like this before." Tom continued on to explain how over the past several months he had been experiencing a great deal of emotional fluctuation. Also, he was having trouble with making decisions, wasn't getting much sleep at night, and was spending less time with his wife and kids. "I think sometimes I'm going crazy, I used to have better control over my life, now it seems like it's all coming apart at the seams."

Tom continued, "I know my behavior hurts Laura, and it's killing me that I do this, but I just don't know what to do. Also, there's another problem that she doesn't know anything about. It started several months ago as just something to do to take up my extra time. I've been going to this local casino to play cards. It helped to get my mind off of things. I just started out spending pocket change, and then it gradually picked up to a few hundred dollars a month. At first I told myself that it was better than burning up gas and driving so many miles on my truck. There were times when it was really exciting, and I could hardly wait to get there.

But now I've gotten myself into a mess." Tom paused and sighed deeply. "After a few months of going to this casino I started to use a credit card to take out some money, and so now I'm looking at about ten thousand dollars of debt that Laura knows nothing about."

Tom is a good guy, making bad choices. His ego is leading the way. What is the ego? The basic concept of the ego has been around for many hundreds of years. A full study of the history of the term or the concept is not necessary for the purpose of reading this book. It is enough to know the simple Latin origin of the term, which is "self". My own expanded version of this definition for ego is, "Your instinctual identification with the needs of your body." The ego, as a conceptual manifestation of you, is generally concerned with survival. For the most part it is operating subconsciously behind the scenes of your thinking and perceptions of life around you.

Your ego develops from the time of your birth as you recognize and identify with the needs and wants of your body—"I am this body." At some time during childhood development, as language ability is acquired, what you might call an ego voice develops in your conscious awareness to tell you what is needed and wanted, what is good and what is bad. This ego voice, or perspective, which represents the body's needs and wants, follows an instinctual agenda. The body does not like or want physical pain, including the painful stress of some emotions, such as anger, sadness, guilt, or fear. As a result, the ego voice instinctively intervenes by developing strategies to manage, manipulate, or reduce this pain. By contrast, the body wants pleasurable gratification, immediately and in unlimited amounts if possible. Again, the ego voice instinctively intervenes by developing strategies to increase these gratifying physical sensations and emotional experiences. Essentially, these strategies involve getting what you want through the manipulation and control of the environment, including the people in the environment. Whenever you hear the newborn that cries, the two-year-old who is having a temper tantrum, the teenager complaining, or the adult who yells or pouts, you are a witness to these ego strategies.

The ego is not the enemy. To a great extent, you owe your life to it, and its survival strategy. However, when this agenda is carried to an extreme, there can be problems—there can be bad choices. Indeed, the personal and relational problems referred to earlier result from following the agenda to extreme lengths. Too much avoidance, too much pleasure, wanting too much control, caring too much about appearance—these are the extreme problems related to the ego's agenda.

Integrity

When I was ten years old, my grandmother gave me one of those glass globes with the fake snow inside. It depicted a winter snow scene, and of course it would snow when I turned it upside down and shook it around. Each and every time, snow would fall all over the fake landscape, all over the fake house, and all over the fake little boy on his fake sled. The scenario outcome for that globe was highly predictable. There was a stable set of circumstances, with a cause and effect that you could count on. It presented no holes, no flaws, and no doubt that the little boy would see his snow fall each and every time. That system had integrity.

So, how do you know if something has integrity? I recognize integrity by the following qualities: 1) it has predictability, 2) there is intra-connectedness, and 3) there is containment. You can count on integrity. You can predict its functioning. You can say with a high degree of certainty that if this happens, then that will happen. You can trust integrity. With some systems, such as a glass globe, a car engine, or a television set, there is a high likelihood of predictable outcome or functioning. If you put gas in the car's gas tank, the car will probably run. If you put water in the tank, it will probably not run. If you plug the television into an electrical outlet, and turn it on, it will probably present you with some television show. If you plug it into a loaf of bread, you should find something else to do. Integrity also means that a system functions with connection from one system component to all other system components in a meaningful way. The fake snow depends on gravity and the water to propel it slowly through the fake atmosphere to the fake ground. Each part depends on the function of the other parts, and when one of the components is not working properly, the entire system is affected. And finally, with integrity, there is some degree of containment of the system; there is a recognizable boundary, or perimeter—outside circumstances only affect the contained system as the system allows. A glass globe is well contained, as is a car engine, or television set. In general then, more system integrity means more potential for trust of the system, and less system integrity means more drama. So, while the glass globe does have integrity, you might say that it is also pretty boring. No matter how many times you shake that thing, it's not ever going to turn into a sunny day, "One hundred percent chance of snow every day."

How do you know if someone—a person—has integrity? You look for predictable behavior that is reflective of their expressed values and morals. In other words, you watch and see that when they say something is important to them, it is then expressed in their behavior consistently over time. Your own integrity is based on the same premise:

> Personal integrity is characterized by: 1) predictability "my trustworthy behavior, you can count on me, I can count on me," 2) intra-connectedness, "There is a connection from my behavior to my values to my moral code to my expectations to my self-image and back to my behavior," and 3) containment, "My choice to establish boundaries for me and limits for others—I have belief system containment, I am in charge of how I am influenced and how my belief system evolves."

None of us will be able to follow even our own consciously established belief systems perfectly. We are going to experience a certain amount of what you might call system failure—bad choices. In other words, sometimes we don't follow our own rules. We still eat that half-gallon of ice cream while watching junk television after a bad day. We still engage in the shopping sprees to feel better. We drink too much alcohol, can't stop smoking, engage in infidelities, and the list goes on. Indeed, the ego is a force to be reckoned with. So, why even bother going to all of the trouble of consciously developing a belief system if we're not going to follow it? If you don't take the lead in your approach to life, your ego will.

Again, your ego is not necessarily your enemy. You may decide that you want to recognize and understand it. In order to live according to your own best interest, you may need to essentially make friends with your ego. That is, recognize its agenda, and meet some of its needs in a realistic, reasonable, and relationally fair manner. In other words:

> "My belief system has integrity; I know because there is predictability, intra-connectedness, and containment. Still, I am going engage in pure self-indulgence at times, just because I can. I can do that, as long as I'm not hurting others, and I know I will continue on the "right" path for me. I'm going to be open to life's changes. I will value appropriate adaptation, growth, and development. My belief system can evolve with integrity."

The Ego's Agenda

The following four objectives represent an instinctual agenda to achieve survival. These objectives become the ego's agenda. Your ego directs you to carry out these objectives:

> ➤ Minimize physical and emotional pain.
> ➤ Maximize physical and emotional gratification.
> ➤ Seek out, establish, and maintain control and power over environments and people.
> ➤ Seek out, establish, and maintain an ego-ideal.

According to the ego, the order in which these objectives are pursued is not necessarily important as long as the overall agenda goal is maintained. The goal is—survival. Physical survival is obviously important. However in this day and age, for most of us it is virtually guaranteed. On the surface, this agenda can be very effective at producing survival. Indeed, human beings have remained on this planet through great adversity because of this instinct to survive. However, this agenda is also at the heart of most human problems. Bad choices are born in this agenda.

Let's return to the story of Tom Anderson. Tom was a young-looking forty-six year old gentleman. He was dressed in professional attire for his work day, appeared to keep himself in good physical shape, and wore a neatly trimmed graying mustache. He seemed to struggle emotionally at times to tell his story, occasionally pausing briefly to fumble with a credit card that he held in his hands. There was a look of pure anguish in his eyes, as he made his way through telling his tale of the past couple of years of his life.

About a year and a half ago, Tom's father began a struggle with emphysema, a condition that had been diagnosed several years previously. His father was a life long smoker, who never quit the habit in spite of his serious medical condition. Tom offered to have his father move into their home to be cared for rather than to go into an assisted living facility or nursing home. After just a few months, he was on oxygen twenty-four hours a day as the quality of his health continued to steadily decline. "In a way it's hard for me to see him going through this. I lost my mom about ten years ago, that was one of the saddest times in my life. So I feel sorry for my father, I know one day soon I might lose him too, but it's hard to feel my own sadness about that.

Tom continued, "This is why I'm here, I'm so angry all the time. And then, I seem to start crying at times for no reason. I think maybe I just need to put my father in a nursing home now. I can't take him being in our house anymore, and it's driving me nuts seeing him smoking on the back porch with that clunky old oxygen tank right by his side like it was the only friend he had in the world. It's ruining our family. And, he just sits around and barks out orders to my wife and my kids. I had enough of that when I was growing up, and I figure just I don't have to take it anymore."

"I know this sounds bad, but sometimes I've been driving home from work and I think maybe today he could have died…and that wouldn't be so bad. I can't believe that I'm saying that out loud, but it's true. My wife has always said, 'Tom would never hurt a fly, he's the most gentle man I've ever known.' But she doesn't know the kind of stuff I've been thinking about lately. That son-of-a-bitch controlled every bit of the house and the people who lived there when I was growing up. He made us all nuts, and I'll be damned if I'm going to let that happen again."

This is the subconscious voice of the ego, "Take control…follow the agenda." The ego's agenda is instinctual, subconsciously based, and *old*. Genetically speaking, the human body has remained virtually unchanged over the past hundred thousand years or so. Those many years ago, before we had a spoken language, we relied upon the body to communicate to the brain in a very direct type of language; this was essentially an instinctual, or innate language of feeling. It was this feeling language that we can all thank for our very existence today. You might say that we have an old biological imperative to survive, and that your feelings are a mechanism for that survival. Very early, in our own lives, prior to the development of sophisticated spoken language, we begin to develop a system of beliefs with a focus on the most effective ways of getting our needs and wants met. The influence and impact of the ego's agenda in these early years is powerful. The ego follows a very old set of simple instinctual rules for living. If it were possible to see these subconscious survival rules in written form, this is what they might look like:

➢ Drink.

➢ Eat.

➢ If some*thing* feels bad, avoid it.

➢ If some*thing* feels good, do it.

➢ Whatever feels bad, is bad.

➢ Whatever feels good, is good.

➢ If you perceive something that is unfamiliar, it may be bad. Be prepared to fight it, or run from it.

➢ If something tastes, smells, or looks bad, don't eat or drink it.

➢ Food satisfies; eat it—lots of it.

➢ If there is food available, eat it until you are quite full because you never know when food will be available again. When you are able to eat again, do it. Do the same with liquids that taste, or feel good.

➢ When some*thing* feels good, try to get control of it so you can maintain the gratification predictably.

Later on in life…

➢ Copy the behavior of the group you are dependent on.

➢ Safety feels good. There is safety in numbers, stay in the group, observe the group, and act like the group.

➢ Cooperate with the group. This increases the safety and security of the group of which you are part.

➢ The observation of sexual behavior produces a sexual feeling/desire/tension of your own. Reducing this tension (sexual behavior/orgasm) feels good, do it.

➢ Sexual behavior/orgasm feels good, do it whenever you can and when it is available, preferably with someone who has a healthy appearance, or with someone who clearly exhibits power and control.

➢ When some*one* feels good, try to get control of him or her so that you can maintain the gratification predictably.

➢ If you are not getting what you want, exert physical and/or emotional power to get it.

➢ If someone else exerts more power, size up the situation quickly, be prepared to back-off, or attack.

➢ Appear powerful and controlled. When you appear powerful and in control, you stand a better chance of getting more of what you want—what you want is predictable gratification and safety.

➢ If someone else appears to be powerful and in control, there is a good chance that if you join up with that person, you will survive too, and establish more predictable gratification. If you are not getting what you want with them, exert physical or emotional power. If they exert more power, size up the situation quickly, be prepared to cooperate, or attack.

➢ If necessary or possible, take control of the group.

These are indeed ancient instinctual rules. Our way of living now compared to life thousands years ago is of course incredibly different. On some level, the ego is apparently unaware of this time passage. We could look at the agenda of the ego as a simple but highly effective four-step instinctual pre-language belief system. This belief system would be established by the ego, through observing life, and by providing for the obvious needs of the body. From the ego's belief system, we can extrapolate the ego's values. In other words, this is what the ego values:

> ➤ Survival.

> ➤ A supply of food and water.

> ➤ Avoidance of physical or emotional pain.

> ➤ The immediate gratification of the bodily organs in need, i.e., stomach, sexual, skin/muscles.

> ➤ Safety.

> ➤ Security.

> ➤ Attention/admiration/acceptance.

> ➤ Gaining control and appearing in control.

> ➤ Gaining power and appearing powerful.

> ➤ Conquest over life (guaranteed survival).

According to the ego's agenda, priority number one is—survive. On a subconscious level of awareness, we believe that the agenda of the ego will lead to our survival. In other words, we think that if we feel good, decrease our emotional pain, and stay in control today, we will survive until tomorrow. This drive to stay in control can lead you to try to control other people, especially in close relationships. When things don't go as you want them to, your mad or sad ego might tell you, "You don't need anyone else [to survive]." Realistically however, we do need each other to survive. You know this on a subconscious level of awareness. This need starts from infancy and continues though childhood when you are dependent on others for your literal physical survival and emotional well-being. These needs gradually decrease in the teen years. As an adult, you greatly rely on societal structure and institutions for your day-to-day comforts. The car you drive, the road you drive on, the gasoline that makes your car go, the food that makes you go, and the doctoring that makes sure that you continue to go, are all available to you as conveniences of society. We do depend on each other, and actually have a great amount of trust in each other. Maybe if you found yourself stuck on a deserted island you could learn to physically survive without anyone else or their help. Over time however, your psychological survival would likely suffer a much different fate. Long-term isolation from other people can produce some pretty disturbing results, hardly resembling human functioning. So, the mad or sad adult ego may be correct; we may not literally need each other to survive, but it seems that we survive more efficiently when we cooperate together.

When it comes right down to it, human relationships can be extremely challenging, but the alternative can be worse. Your ego is obviously right; you do need to survive. Again however, we will survive in this day and age. We don't need to be so concerned with it any more. We survive better when we work together cooperatively. The above outlined examples of ego rules and ego values are in many ways incompatible with working together cooperatively. If you are interested in having quality relationships and experiencing peace of mind, then living out the ego's agenda is not in *Your Own Best Interest (YOBI)*.

Essentially, there are four main components that make up a belief system: values, morals, expectations, and self-image. At this point, half of the ego's belief system has been revealed in terms of its values and survival rules (morals). The expectation component of a belief system would represent your beliefs about what you have come to expect from yourself, other people, and the world around you. Here are some, but not all, of the ego's expectations:

> ➤ The ego expects that things should always go "my way." If not, something is wrong.

> ➤ The ego expects that you, others, and the world should help to reduce or eliminate its emotional/physical pain. Emotional/physical pain can and should be eliminated, immediately if possible. "Take away my pain."

> ➤ The ego expects that you, others, and the world should help create and increase its immediate emotional and physical gratification. Emotional/physical gratification can and should be gotten immediately if possible, "Make me feel good."

> ➤ If you, others, or the world do not participate in my agenda, they are bad. If they do, they are good.

> ➤ The ego expects that everyone else should see things "my way," if not, they are wrong, and that is a threat.

> ➤ The ego expects that everyone else is seeking out power and control, and so, everyone else is potentially "the enemy." "Be aware of others out there."

> ➤ The ego expects that you, people, places, and things can be controlled, if it just applies the correct approach.

> ➤ The ego expects that the ideal situation is "out there," (as opposed to within one's self).

> ➤ The ego expects that when something feels good, "More is always going to be better."

> ➤ The ego expects that people, places, and things will respond best to power and control.

Everyone has an ego that operates according to a specific set of instinctual instructions. Many of us maintain a primary focus on these ego needs and wants and behave accordingly resulting in bad choices. The results of such an ego-maintained life can be quite satisfying for some and quite frustrating for others. One possible reason for this is that when you begin to chase after power and control, keeping up with the Jones', and the gratification of the body, you can never get quite enough. In the chase, you get caught up in a never-ending pursuit for more, more, and still more. It is the bias of this book that peace of mind is experienced through a belief system that is defined by values of your choice and is well established in reality. Obviously, the values of your choice may be, or include, power, control, and an abundance of immediate physical gratification. Thanks to the ego's agenda, we all pursue some aspect of these things on some level. Therefore, it is in your best interest to at least pursue them realistically, reasonably, and with greater awareness of the process behind the scenes of the chase.

2 The Instinctual Management of Feeling

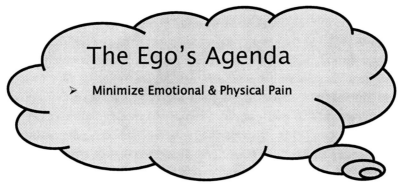

The Ego's Agenda

➢ Minimize Emotional & Physical Pain

Minimize Pain

Laura attended the next session with Tom Anderson. "I worry about him, he's just not himself these days. It seems like this all started when his father came to live with us about a year ago. Before that, Tom was the most pleasant guy to be around. He loved playing with the kids and kept himself busy fishing. Most weekends he'd be working around the yard, and he went jogging at least a couple of times a week. Now, I don't think he's been fishing in over six months and the yard is falling apart. When he is at home, I usually see him lying around on the couch watching television. This is not my husband anymore, I don't understand what is going on, but I'd really like to have my husband back."

Tom had begun to spend more time away from home. He also reported an increase of alcohol consumption, "I've started to drink a few more beers at night than my usual, which used to be maybe one or two, a couple of nights a week. Now, some nights I'm probably putting away a six-pack or so. After I leave work, sometimes I just drive around in my truck, sort of going nowhere. I just don't feel right in my own home anymore." As he grabbed the box of tissues beside the couch in my office, Tom began to wipe off the tears that were streaming down his face, "I feel so bad about this, but that man has ruined my life again, and I'm so angry about it."

This is the subconscious voice of the ego, "Pain is pain, get rid of it, it's dangerous, it's wrong...carry out the agenda." Following this directive can lead to bad choices. Emotional pain and physical pain are at times entangled and therefore difficult to differentiate. Your ego simply knows that if you are experiencing pain, it cannot be good, and this must be avoided whenever possible. "If something feels bad, avoid it. Whatever feels bad, is bad." Realistically however, there is an important difference between physical pain, and the experience of emotional pain; painful feelings cannot cause your death.

It is quite possible that the emotional pain you want to avoid the most is what you must face the most regularly. The experience of emotional feeling is a phenomenon of the human being. The rest of the animal kingdom is set apart from us in that respect. Much, if not all, of their functioning is related to instinct and biological imperatives to reproduce and protect territory. They are simply behaving in accordance with internal instructions that increase their chances of survival. We humans also have survival instructions. We function according to these biological imperatives, drives, needs, and wants. However, human functioning includes some added components. We engage in a higher form of cognition (or thinking), and we experience feeling (or emotion). Those feelings are an efficient and valuable point of reference for problem solving. Unfortunately, we have an instinctual directive to avoid, minimize, or eliminate any pain. While this may make sense from a survivalist perspective, there are potential problems when this directive is taken to an extreme. Emotional pain is the next subject to be explored. Your ego will urge you to avoid the stressful pain of anger, sadness, guilt, and fear. Each one of these feeling categories is associated with a particular type of thinking. Let's start by taking a look at the feeling category related to anger—mad.

Mad

We experience the feeling of anger when we think about unmet expectations. The kind of thinking, either consciously or subconsciously, that produces the feeling of anger is: "things aren't going in a way that I want them to." This can be a painful experience for your ego. Following the ego's agenda for managing anger can lead to bad choices.

We maintain expectations with regard to the following three points of reference: self, other, and the world. We remember our life experiences, and as certain experiences repeat, they become expected. Over time, we expect ourselves to behave in certain ways. We expect others to behave in certain ways. We expect the world around us to operate in a certain way. We all have expectations of how things should be related to those three points of reference. Having expectations is unavoidable and is a vital aspect of your natural inclination to attempt to predict the future, and to attempt to establish control over your environment. In other words, having expectations is part of your instinct to survive. Because you are old enough to read this book, you have undoubtedly developed an enormous storehouse of expectations created out of your many experiences.

We generally use many other words to describe the feeling of anger: irritated, miffed, livid, annoyed, hot, upset, enraged, irate, fuming, infuriated, incensed, outraged, or just plain "ticked-off." These words are helpful in that they are a language for assigning different levels of intensity to feeling mad. However, it is important to understand that for the purpose of problem solving, they all have a common thought origin: "things are not going my way."

It has been my experience as a therapist that many people do not like to think of themselves as being angry at either themselves or others. They would like to think that they rarely, if ever, get mad or angry at anything. These individuals generally have a moral belief that says, "Anger is bad." Unfortunately, because they avoid anger, they are likely to engage in other forms of trying to get their way rather than the direct approach of recognizing their own anger and expressing it in an appropriate way. At the other side of the personality spectrum is the individual who over-utilizes anger as a means of getting what they want. This may describe the angry-bully-tyrant type who lives next door to you. No matter where you are on this spectrum, there will be times when things don't go your way. It is important to recognize this perception and thinking when it happens to you. Here are some examples of how the ego experiences anger either consciously or subconsciously: "I want it now." "I want to have control over this now." "I want to have power over this now." "I can't stand it when I don't get my way." "You are making me mad." "You are not doing it my way."

Sad

We experience the feeling of sadness when thinking, either consciously or subconsciously, about loss. We feel sadness in anticipation of loss, with the perception of loss, and in the experience of loss. We experience loss of people and things in numerous ways over the course of our lives. Jobs, friends, cars, houses, and even our family and loved ones will eventually come and go. As we age, physical agility, mental acuity, memories, and sexual functioning are all experienced as gradual losses. Of all the feelings we encounter, sadness may be the most difficult due to its very nature. There is generally a strong sense of helplessness associated with sadness, which runs contrary to our basic instinct to control and maintain what we have. This is a painful and intolerable experience for your ego. So we tend to fight against the feeling, manipulate it, ignore it, pretend normal, get angry about it; do almost anything we can to avoid it. Try as we may, more than likely reality will eventually catch up with us and our efforts will be for naught. Loss is an unavoidable part of life, and to the extent that we are unable or unwilling to deal with it, we can make ourselves miserable. Following the ego's agenda for managing sadness can lead to bad choices.

Sadness can be a complex emotional experience. When dealing with an identifiable and confirmed loss, we can go through certain predictable thinking/feeling phases starting with a type of shock and shifting toward realization, acceptance, adaptation, and readjustment. Each of these phases is associated with a feeling that must be resolved in order to be able to process the loss in a healthy manner. These phases may be experienced over a matter of many months, or within minutes. We might alter the sequence, cycle though them repeatedly, and even possibly skip some. Elisabeth Kübler-Ross is well known for having identified these phases, or "stages of grief" in her book, *On Death & Dying* (1969). Her theory represents one way of understanding the adjustment to loss. Below, I will identify the traditional Kübler-Ross stages and then add what I believe to be the associated feeling, thinking features, and the healthy resolution thought.

The first phase is denial, which is fear-based thinking. In grieving there is a fear about a "bad outcome or situation" that has been brought to awareness. For example, Jill was just told by her husband that he wants a divorce, and Bill was just told that he is being fired from his job for chronic absenteeism. They are both essentially thinking, "This is not happening." Jill thinks, "You must be kidding, is this some kind of joke?" Bill thinks, "This must be a bad dream, after all the good work I do here, there's no way I could be fired." Over time, the eventual healthy resolution thought is essentially, "This is happening, and I am facing the outcome of this real loss."

Next phase is anger, which is of course associated with the feeling of mad. The thinking is, "This is not going my way." Jill says, "Why in the hell are you doing this, you can just never be happy can you, you are always making my life difficult, I've had it with you too!" Bill says, "How can you do this to me, I'm going to speak to my lawyer about this." The eventual healthy resolution thought is, "I can't change this," or, "This will not change."

Next comes what has been identified as the bargaining phase. It is associated with the feeling of bad, or guilt. In this phase one goes about the business of attempting to change the undesired (bad) outcome. There may be a feeling of panic/fear, or need to negotiate as a last resort. The bad (guilt) feeling is characterized as, "Have I done something wrong, I'm sorry, I can change, I can do better, please, I'll do anything, this is all my fault." Jill says, "Isn't there some type of therapy we can get. I'm sorry if I've hurt you. God, please give me back my life, I'll do anything." Bill says, "Okay, I know I've been late, I'm really sorry. Can't I go to another department, or maybe I can be put on a probationary phase so I can improve." Much of this phase can be associated with the idea of self-blame, or guilt. The healthy resolution thought is, "So…you won't change this," or, "We won't/can't change this." And after an honest appraisal, "I did/did not, do something wrong according to my morals." "I did/did not do the best I could at the time." "Right or wrong, I will face this change and learn from it."

Now comes despair or sad. This is at the heart of grief. The thought reference is, "This loss really hurts and this is change." Jill says, "So, what you are saying then, is there's nothing we or I can do, I need to learn to deal with this, I am going to lose you." Bill says, "Okay, will there be a severance package…this really sucks. I lost my job." The healthy resolution is, "This really did happen, and this is a real loss."

The final phase according to Kübler-Ross is acceptance, which is most closely associated with glad. The thought element is, "I have emotionally survived this real loss." Acceptance of loss may not literally equate with gladness. Perhaps there is merely a reduction of other painful feelings, you are no longer stuck, and you are ready to move on. Jill concludes, "We did have some good years together, I've learned a lot and I have a lot of life to live. It's time that I started to reconnect with a social network, and when I'm ready to date I can have some fun with it." Bill concludes, "I was looking for a job when I found that one. Maybe the next job I get will be better than this one anyway. I can get a hold of that headhunter guy I met at the conference last year." The healthy resolution is, "Things have really changed, I have readjusted, although I have experienced a loss I have also experienced a gain which is _____, I'm moving on, and I'm looking forward to_____ now in my life." Theoretically, with acceptance of the reality of the loss, the grieving cycle is then complete or resolving. There has been a loss experienced and it has been fully processed. If any of these phases has not been completed with a healthy resolution thought, the feeling may remain an obstacle to moving on. Sometimes we can move through readjustment relatively easily. On other occasions, due to ego interference, we can become stuck for years or possibly a lifetime. The circumstances, personality style, and relative value of the object of loss are relevant factors. In other words:

➤ Was this an expected loss or a "surprise" loss?

➤ Do you like or need to have a lot of control?

➤ How important was the object of loss to you?

Here are some examples of how the ego experiences sad either consciously or subconsciously : "Things won't ever go my way." "I never get what I want." "I've lost power." "I've lost control." "Why do things always have to change?"

Bad

We experience the feeling of guilt when we think, either consciously or subconsciously, that we are in conflict with our own moral code. The general kind of thinking that produces guilt is, "I've done something wrong." We all have a moral code. It consists of a set of rules or standards that we use to guide our own behavior. It also serves as the foundation from which we judge people and ideas as being right, wrong, good or bad. We acquire a moral code from a variety of sources. In our youth, we get messages from our parents, primary caretakers and family about what is good and bad, and which behavior will yield positive reinforcements versus punishments. Throughout our teen years and into adulthood, we continue to develop ideas about right and wrong and modify our own version of morality.

Guilt is related to the idea of consequences from either internal or external sources. These consequences could be perceived as punishment, disapproval or abandonment, and could be either potential or pending. That is, the consequence is only a possibility that you know could happen but is uncertain at the moment, or you may know a consequence will happen and is only a matter of time.

Experiencing a sense of guilt is most likely accompanied by a reduction of feeling proud, a reduction of self-respect, and negatively impacts self-image. When you sense yourself feeling the pain of guilt, you will want to do something about it. That is, you will want to rid yourself of the feeling through some means. You may do this consciously or subconsciously. But you will not want to maintain this feeling for long.

Healthy methods of guilt resolution will be discussed in subsequent chapters, and specifically in Chapter 15, Managing Bad. Following the ego's agenda for managing guilt can lead to bad choices. Here are some examples of ego-based guilt responses toward another person or to yourself:

➢ Become passive and pleasing.

➢ Get angry and behave in a passive-aggressive way.

➢ Get angry and aggressive.

➢ Experience a sense of helplessness.

➢ Flee.

➢ Prove to them they are wrong.

➢ Prove to them that they are bad.

➢ Hurt them.

➢ Engage in conscious self-mutilation.

➢ Throw guilt back at them.

➢ Be a martyr.

➢ Engage in denial.

➢ Manipulate them.

➢ Worry or fret.

➢ Engage in subconscious self-harming behaviors (pick, pull, bite, chew, scratch, cut, burn).

➢ Develop or increase an addictive behavior or obsession.

➢ Develop a stress-related or somatic physical ailment.

Here are some examples of how the ego experiences bad or guilt either consciously or subconsciously : "I didn't do anything wrong." "This is all your fault." "Now I'm in trouble, how can I get out of this mess?" "Maybe she won't find out what I've done." "I gave up too much power." "I gave up too much control." "I should have been able to prevent that." "I hate myself." "Maybe I'd be better off dead."

Fear

Tom Anderson works as an insurance broker. He has been with the same firm for fourteen years and has always gotten a great deal of pleasure in helping other people plan for their future, and their retirement years. "Now I'm not so sure that's even realistic. Look what happened with my father, he worked his whole life, and now his so called 'golden years' are a mess. There he is, living with his own son, who is barely able to be in the same room with him. Is that what I'm going to do; is that what I have to look forward to? I really loved doing stuff with my family, now it's all I can do to just walk in the front door at the end of my day. My oldest son is going to be eighteen at the end of the month. I'd planned on doing some kind of father-son outing, like maybe go camping. And now I keep having this strange idea that he and I are going to have some kind of falling out."

Tom continued, "I keep asking myself, *was it really that bad?* I thought I'd put all this behind me. I thought I'd come to terms with it, him, whatever you want to call it. Now I'm having these sort of flashbacks of when I was growing up. I can see him so vividly. He had this splotchy red face and shrunken lips, and I see him screaming at me. After all this time I can still smell the whiskey and cigarettes on his breath. I keep remembering more lately, about the past, the things he did to me. I can remember back when I was maybe eight years old, he'd grab me by my neck and say stuff like, 'Yer good for nothing, you will never amount to anything boy, yer just like yer lazy no good for nothing mother.' When he'd say stuff like that, my body felt like it just ached, and I knew that one day I could see that man squeezing my head right off my body. He could get so angry that I swear I could see blood vessels popping in his eyes during one of his ranting lectures."

We experience the feeling of fear when, either consciously or subconsciously, we perceive, think about, or anticipate what we believe are eventual negative consequences. Fear originates from an old part of our brain, which is responsible for our survival in the face of uncertainty or of known danger. We need to be able to experience fear. Like the other emotions, it has a place in our lives. It lets us know that we need to pay attention to what we are perceiving and possibly take some action.

Fear is arguably the basis for the three other basic emotions—guilt, sad, and mad. In other words, it is possible that all negative emotions are a form of fear. Underneath the feeling of anger could be the fear of not getting what you want, or the fear of attack. Then with your anger energy, you could attempt to control or eliminate the feared outcome. Sadness could result from your fear of loss of a valued object or idea, or of being alone. Guilt might be a fear of punishment, or fear of disapproval or abandonment. If mad, bad, and sad are fear-based emotions, then they are a type of emotional reactivity. This may be an interesting theory for mental health professionals or philosophers to ponder or debate. However, I believe that working with five basic emotions is much more helpful in determining course of resolution when engaging in a problem solving process. Notwithstanding, in Chapter 16, Managing Fear, there are specific resolutions for dealing with guilt, sadness, and anger as forms of fear.

So then, why do we fear? In some respect, we fear in order to survive. Because we fear, we are on the lookout for problems, concerns, dangers, and things that might be generally harmful to us. Not only do our physical brains stay on alert, but also the ego maintains a type of alert system, creating a redundancy of protection. On some level, we know that even if we could stop fearing, we would be vulnerable to potential harm.

Following the ego's agenda for managing fear can lead to bad choices. The human ego operates to control, or even better, eliminate the potentially painful experience of fear. That task however, is undoubtedly beyond its grasp. That is, total elimination of fear or total control of objects is not possible. There is no complete controlling of objective reality and all of its problems. There is only risk management, which can be flimsy at best. So, we will continue to experience everyday worry and anxiety. Our brains will run amok with worry and create mountains out of what are possibly just molehills. Here are some examples of how the ego experiences fear either consciously or subconsciously : "I can't lose control of him." "What if I just go crazy?" "What else can go wrong?" "I'm losing power over her." "What if I lose everything?" "Everyone will see that I'm weak."

"Minimize emotional pain," is the call of the ego. The subconscious ego perspective of feeling goes something like this, "These painful anger, sad, guilt, and fear feelings are not good and are surely dangerous unless they can produce a result consistent with the overall agenda. Get rid of them as quickly as possible, and then move on to the next agenda item, maximize my pleasure, now!"

Exercise 2-1: Think about the unhealthy ways that you attempt to minimize your physical and emotional pain. Get honest with yourself here.

What are the worst ways that you try to deal with stress, or painful feelings? How does your ego get involved? What does your ego want you to do with uncomfortable anger, sadness, guilt, and fear? What are your problem patterns of feeling management? Go to appendix F, and make these entries.

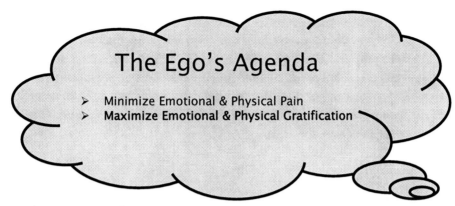

The Ego's Agenda

- ➤ Minimize Emotional & Physical Pain
- ➤ **Maximize Emotional & Physical Gratification**

Maximize Gratification

"For the past several months, I've been putting on some weight, this is no mystery to me though," Tom Anderson spoke further. "I know exactly what's going on. I've been eating a lot of junk food, and just a lot more food in general. When I'm driving home after work and I'm thinking about getting home, the only thing that seems appealing to me is planning the kind of stuff I'm going to pig out on for the rest of the night. Here's another thing. Sometimes I find myself peeking around the corner into his bedroom, in my own house I might add, and I have this weird fantasy about jumping on that bed and pounding my fists into his body. I know that's bad. Believe me, I know I could never do a thing like that, but the images in my head are so clear, and I can just feel my body oozing out anger through my hands, like I'm punishing him for all those years of slamming me up against walls, and putting my brothers and sisters through holy hell. These thoughts don't last very long. I know it sounds terrible to say, but I feel a sense of relief when I'm thinking those things."

"If something feels good, do it. Whatever feels good is good." Again, this is the subconscious voice of the ego. "That which feels good, must be good, get more, and get more now." Although these may appear to be greatly oversimplified exaggerations of thinking, keep this in mind: The ego follows simple and concrete rules that are powerful and compelling. If you have any doubt of this, look no further than your own persistent and habitual maladaptive behaviors. There you will find the ego's agenda. There is no doubt that we want to feel gratified and will seek it out in many forms.

The primary and ultimate objective of gratification is to feel emotionally good, or glad. However, based on early childhood experiences and environments, individuals will sometimes appear to seek out other seemingly negative emotional states if they can produce a secondary gain of gratification. For example, one may habitually prefer the experience of sadness or even seek out sadness in order to receive comforting attention from others. "If I appear to be sad, perhaps someone will relieve my loneliness." The same could be said for habitually maintaining guilt to gain sympathy, or fear to receive support. "I've done such terrible things, please help me." "I'm so afraid, please help me." Similarly, one may seek out the experience of anger, to the extent that in the end it serves to carry out the overall objective of the agenda. "I am going to get my way." Anger as such is clearly a tool or an opportunity for the agenda, in that the angry behavior can produce control over others and portray power. As it achieves these ends, it becomes a preferred means for some individuals, and over time can produce excitement or even an adrenaline rush.

Glad

There are four types of thinking that lead to painful feelings. There are also four types of thinking that lead to pleasurable feelings. We experience feelings of gladness as we think, either consciously or subconsciously, in the following ways:

> ➢ "This is going my way because…"

> ➢ "I am fortunate or lucky because…"

> ➢ "I am proud of myself because…"

> ➢ "I am really looking forward to…"

Perhaps you noticed that these fill in the blank thoughts are exact opposites of the thoughts that produce the four other feeling categories. There are obviously other more common words that we use to describe the glad feeling category: elated, joyful, happy, blissful, excited, proud, great, fortunate, lucky, serene, peaceful, relaxed, okay, contented, terrific, moved, and many, many more. All of these glad experiences can be traced to glad thoughts, which when combined and sustained over time, can produce global mood changes. You must, however, genuinely believe what you are thinking, as opposed to reciting positive affirmations you might read in a book, your horoscope, or a fortune cookie.

Here are some examples of how the ego experiences glad either consciously or subconsciously : "I can probably do that tomorrow. Right now, I'm going to take it easy and relax." "I'm really looking forward to the all-you-can-eat buffet tonight, because I'm going to eat all-I-can." "I know I can't really afford it, but I'm going to the mall to shop." "I finally won that argument with my wife, I knew I was right." "This car is much more than I can afford, (but it is so cool) I'll take it." "I'm the only one around here that does a good job." "I'm better than her because…" "I'm glad I'm not as miserable as that person is."

Some of your experiences in life produce enormous amounts of gratification on emotional, physical, and psychological levels. As a general rule, the greater the perceived immediacy and amount of gratification that an experience has to offer, the greater the potential for obsession or addiction. In other words, if I think something is going to feel really good right away, I could get hooked on it. If, when I win at bingo, eat pizza, consume wine, or drink a double cappuccino, I feel highly emotionally and/or physically gratified, I could potentially develop an obsession or an addiction. Obsession occurs as I begin to think about the object of my desire with increasing frequency, intensity, duration, and anticipation of the next *fix*.

Ironically, with some experiences, the less predictability and/or immediacy you have in obtaining high gratification from the experience, the more obsessive you can become. This combination of very high physical and/or psychological gratification and low predictability is most likely to produce serious obsession. For example, the gratification from gambling is high, but the predictability is low. The same goes with fishing. Both of these activities have low probability of predictable outcome, and both activities can become objects of obsession depending on the amount of gratification experienced with a positive yield. The more you value the object, such as a rare type of delicious chocolate, the more you want, and the more obsessive you can become. To be without the gratifying experience of chocolate for some period of time would create, maintain, or intensify the want of it. As soon as you find the rare chocolate, you are temporarily no longer in a state of want. You are then reminded of how much you value this chocolate and you continue along creating a vicious cycle.

Following the ego's agenda for creating gladness can lead to bad choices. We can become obsessed or addicted to nearly anything. Here are some common obsessions: specific types of food, sexual conquest, finding shopping bargains, various sports participation (the under-par round, the perfect shot, the big fish), searching out objects at flea markets or garage sales, the excitement of unknown outcomes in sports, successful shoplifting, chasing the exercise high, weekly television shows as drama unfolds, any computer/internet activity with the potential for gratifying outcomes, obtaining illicit drugs, and perusing other people who can be a source of potential gratifying outcomes. Look for the ego's agenda with any of these or other behaviors which become problematic, persistent, or maladaptive.

Tom Anderson spoke softly and shamefully, "Here's how it happened. I guess I was bored, didn't want to go home, and saw this big billboard on my drive. It was advertising the local casino. I used to play cards with my buddies several years ago, and it helped me get my mind off things. So, I started with just a few bucks here and there. As things got more stressful at home, I started going to the casino more. One day I won big…a couple of thousand dollars. I'll tell you what, at that point, I was hooked. I started to really enjoy the extra money, the powerful feeling, the attention from the people there…it was really something to look forward to. Then, gradually I started to lose. And, got into a hole. I was able to hit a few more jackpots, but never again like the big one. I found an old credit card that we never activated and started using it for cash advances. I even transferred the billing address so the bill would go to my work. There were good nights, and there were some horrible nights. I kept on going though, thinking I could eventually get back out of that hole. My body shook when I walked into that place. I also developed a taste for some high quality alcohol, and pricey cigars. I had myself convinced that I could climb back out of that hole if I just kept going back to play. Now, it all seems like a bad dream."

We may encounter negative consequences as a result of our obsessive behavior. No problem, the ego will intervene. As experiences become more gratifying over time, there tends to be an eventual need to engage in varying forms of ego-based self-deception in order to be able to deal with the negative consequences. The self-deception required is discussed in Chapter 5 as ego maintenance. I am not going to get into a lengthy discussion of addiction theory here. Suffice it to say that the more we like junk food—and continue to gain weight— the more we will need to talk ourselves into believing it's okay to continue to eat the junk food—and ignore the consequences to our body. I think that an interesting way of looking at obsession and addiction is that you are essentially being fooled by your body/ego into believing that what it wants is what you need!

There are no Fishing Anonymous meetings that I am aware of. There may be some spouses out there however who would like to see such an organization. Also, I don't believe there are casinos with big lines of people waiting to play penny slot machines that pay off a big five-dollar grand prize. We want and like big gratification! We get hooked on things that are highly and immediately gratifying such as: food, sex, alcohol, drugs (street and prescription), gambling, pornography, computer/internet, and people. There are recovery meetings for all of those problems. Theoretically, an addiction involves an out-of-control, increasing progression of behavior, with a significant and/or substantial amount of negative consequences combined with a potentially high payoff. In other words, there has to be a great amount of physical and/or psychological gratification. The addictive process then occurs over time as we experience the gratifying *fix*.

To overcome obsession or addiction, you will have to rid yourself of ego-based self-deception such as, "I don't have a problem," "This isn't so bad," or "It could be worse." This kind of deception interferes with the perception of consequences and/or with making different choices. That means you have to make reality the guiding force in conscious decision-making and problem solving.

Predictability was critical in maintaining the obsession or addiction in the first place, "I know that bag of potato chips is gonna taste/feel good." In making new choices, you must be able to predict a different and highly valued outcome, "I know it will feel good to make a healthier food choice." That is, you have to want something else more than what you have been experiencing. So instead of eating out of control and becoming increasingly unhealthy, you make different choices resulting in a healthy you that you highly value. The new healthy you becomes more important than unhealthy eating habits. Easier said than done. However, this is conceptually sound. For some problem behaviors, it is necessary to seek out medical treatment in a program of supervised recovery. In the final analysis however, problematic obsession or addiction comes to an end as the following points are well established and maintained:

> First, you are very certain about the negative outcomes that result from the problematic behavior.

> Second, you clearly decide that you do not want the negative consequence(s) anymore.

> Third, you identify a very specific different positive outcome; you decide to value something different, which requires a different choice.

> Fourth, you seek out and establish an effective plan to produce the positive outcome. The plan becomes the right thing to do.

> Fifth, you consistently make the different choice. You come to expect yourself to make the choice.

> Sixth, you experience the positive outcomes of the new choice/behavior. In essence, you become the choice, "I am this different choice."

Still, there is ego.

Exercise 2-2: Think about the unhealthy ways that you attempt to maximize physical and emotional gratification. Remember to get honest with yourself. What are the unhealthy ways that you try to create immediate physical pleasure? What are your problem patterns of seeking out immediate emotional gratification? How does your ego get involved in this pursuit? Go to appendix F, and make these entries.

3 The Instinctual Management of Life

The Ego's Agenda

➢ Minimize Emotional & Physical Pain
➢ Maximize Emotional & Physical Gratification
➢ **Establish and Maintain Power & Control**

Power and Control

"When something feels good, try to get control of it so you can maintain the gratification predictably." Once again, this is the subconscious voice of the ego. Who taught you that pain should be minimized or avoided? Who taught you that what feels good should be maximized, sought out, and created? You didn't need instruction in these matters of life. However, you did need limits placed on how you sought out these agenda outcomes. The same can be said of the third agenda objective. Who taught you to seek out control or power in your environment? All you know is that when things go your way, when you can have what you want, when things are in your control, and when you can predict an ideal future outcome—these things feel good, and you experience a sense of power. You were not taught these things, they are known to you naturally, or instinctually. Not only are they known on a feeling level, to some degree, on a much deeper level of subconscious awareness, these ideas even seemed *right*.

Tom Anderson attended the next session right on time as usual. "The other night I woke up from this dream. In the dream I guess I was about nine or ten years old, and there he was, into his usual tirade after coming home from his job. He had just walked in and slammed the front door shut behind him. Just like in real life back then, everyone had already found a hiding place in various places in the house. That day I guess I forgot to hide, and he found me. He snatched me up by the arms and was right in my face. As he was yelling at me, I could see myself grabbing some kind of rope and trying to strangle him with it. This was my own father, but I almost felt like there was no other choice, it was either him or me. Actually, I think this was more than just a dream, I remember having those fantasies all the time once I got into my teen years. Sometimes those fantasies and images came up as he was hurting me. And sometimes I would think those thoughts at night when I was lying there in my bed and couldn't sleep. You know, at the time it seemed like those fantasies were the only thing that gave me some sense that I could have some control if I ever really wanted it."

In infancy, we get a basic sense of what is painful and what is gratifying. In fact, for the first two or three years of life, we are for all intents and purposes obsessed with these matters. In the second and third years of life, we develop more effective physical mobility, more effective verbal communication, and we become much more aware of environmental dynamics. We are then equipped to seek out our desires, and we do so with the intent of developing predictability. According to the ego's agenda, predictability requires attempting to control the environment and the people in the environment. A safe and secure environment combined with a steady supply of the good stuff would be ideal. We begin to then ask for, demand, manipulate, or negotiate for what we want. Essentially, we make attempts to establish controlled predictability.

The ability to create predictable control is essential for survival. In and of itself, this is not a bad thing. We can survive the harsh elements of the outdoors by building shelter and wearing clothing. In this we attempt to control the weather, the environment, and whatever danger lurks in the darkness. The ability to control effectively makes survival easier. At any moment, there is evidence of this truth all around you.

According to the ego, "Those who control, collect power. Those who are born into power, use it to create control." Power is experienced in a subjective and abstract sense, while control is more objective and concrete in nature. You may feel a sense of a person's power, but you can describe the means by which someone maintains control. Power can assume control, and control can assume power. If you are given power, you then have the means to establish controls. If you are able to establish controls on your own, you can create a sense of power. From an ego perspective, power and control go hand in hand; which one comes first is not important as long as the entire agenda can be maintained.

In the grade school years, we begin to experience and learn much about social relationships. We learn how to manipulate and negotiate for what we want and we learn the finer points of how control and power are involved or used in relationships. At the heart of most unresolved relationship conflicts, you will find a basic desire to have your way, or to have control of relational outcomes. As a means of establishing predictability in everyday life and with everyday things, control is sought out and can be positive. To the extent that you try to gain control over people, it can become abusive. To the extent that you attempt to over-control your life, you increase your risk of developing an anxiety disorder.

A major concern or focus of the ego is that of establishing and maintaining power and control over environments and people. One outcome of this pursuit is that of being valued by others, if not genuinely, then certainly out of fear or need. In other words, if you are the king or the queen, and have power and control over others, others will value what you have to say, or what you do, out of a fear of punishment, or a need to survive. They may not like you, but they do value you because of their own ego need to survive. According to the ego, "When you are valued by others, you have a better chance of survival, and of getting your own agenda to be the agenda of others."

Not everyone can be royalty. On an instinctual level, we know that there is safety in numbers. We stand a better overall chance of survival in a group. However, to experience the benefit of the group, or community, and to function effectively within it, we need to follow the rules. When I don't follow the rules of the group, I risk disapproval, maybe punishment, and possible banishment. This leaves me vulnerable. So it seems that for survival and therefore ego based reasons we highly value being approved of—we value being valued.

Tom and Laura attended another session together. Laura was clearly frustrated as she walked into the office and sat in the chair opposite her husband. "This is very hard for me," she reached for the tissue box. "I don't understand what's going on here, and I'm scared."

I looked at Tom, hoping that he would do the right thing here and respond from genuine concern, without my verbal prompt. Thank goodness he spoke up, "I am so sorry, this is all my fault, Laura. It's just that for the past several months, I've been feeling so bad, so afraid that I'm wrecking our lives. After my father moved in with us, sometimes it seemed like you were taking sides with him. I know we were both stressed, I also thought you blamed me. I started to think that maybe you didn't love me anymore. For a while, there was a part of me that really started to think I didn't need anyone, and I could just do what I wanted to as long as I didn't get caught. I wasn't considering what I was putting you through. I guess I didn't care at the time, it was like I didn't need you to approve of me. I knew I didn't want our marriage to end, and I still know that. I was just hurting so bad, and was feeling a lot of stress. I really do need you though Laura, and I don't want you to be scared. Now, I'm afraid I might lose you. I guess it's about time that I tell you what's been going on for the past several months."

We do seem compelled to seek out the company of others. We would also like to have the experience of being valued, accepted, and loved by them. Perhaps on some deep level of awareness we equate this experience with survival. From the perspective of the ego, when we don't have this experience, we may feel great amounts of anxiety. We may even think that if we are not *unconditionally* valued, accepted, or loved by someone, then there is something to fear. The ego's answer to this fear is, "Apply the agenda."

"You don't value/accept/love me," thinks ego. When in fear, the ego will subconsciously or consciously attempt to apply its agenda. In relationships, this will undoubtedly mean bad choices. For some, this will amount to either demonstrations of power or attempts to establish and maintain control. For others, this will mean be compliant, please others, and do as you're told to avoid greater fears and/or further problems. In either case the objective is the same, "I will get you to value/accept/love me." Obviously, this will not work in the long run.

The experience of unconditional love in adult relationships may be rare. Some may even say it is a myth, or a silly romantic notion. If you experience it, then be of good cheer. If not, there is nothing to fear. You will survive. Realistically however, keep these things in mind:

1. There is safety, and efficiency, in numbers.

2. How others regard or value us is absolutely conditional.

3. As adults we will not die without unconditional love.

1. There is safety, and efficiency, in numbers. Angry ego says, "I don't need anybody." In order to benefit from a group, we need to follow the rules, or conditions that exist in the relationships with those people. Thus, we have group mentality; we behave well in the group because we know that there is increased safety there. While we know that there is safety in numbers, we also know that there are two ways to be able to benefit from the group; a) practice acceptable group behavior, or, b) lead the group. How does one get to be in a position to lead the group? Power and control over the group is one answer. Another answer is to have self-control, demonstrate inner-power, and to lead with integrity by example. Having self-control means consciously choosing behavior when things do not go as expected. We must be able to deal with frustration and angry feelings. Experience with the group as member, or leader, will have its frustrations, although there will be certain benefits.

It would seem that we all want to feel valued on some level of awareness. This sense of value can come from two sources: it can come from others, and it can come from ourselves. With one of these sources we have no control, (although your ego would think otherwise), and with the other source, we can have complete control. For adults, I am suggesting that value, acceptance, and love by others are strongly desired wants, and not needs. On the other hand, I suggest that value of self, acceptance of self, and love of self are needs. The day may come when the group and your integrity are no longer compatible. The final analysis will require a choice—ask the group to change, find another group, create a new group, or go solo.

2. How others regard or value us is absolutely conditional; relationships are conditional. Bad ego says, "I can do whatever I want in this relationship." As infants, we should expect to experience unconditional caring by our caretakers as they continually take care of our basic needs, no matter what. Children do require positive or loving regard from others in order to develop a healthy self-image. When they don't get it at a young age, the eventual consequences are immeasurable. Communicate to a child that they are valued so that they know it on a subconscious level of awareness; this is one of the most important goals of parenting. There is a point at which children make a transition from total dependence on the adults around them, to independence and self-reliance. The transition can be very trying for everyone involved and is generally referred to as rebellion. Rebellion is an absolutely necessary mechanism for transition into adulthood and prevents children from remaining dependent. Through this transition of rebellion, parents learn that what started out as being an unconditional parent-child relationship, gradually becomes a relationship with conditions. So, instead of tolerating many unpleasant behaviors unconditionally as you would for an infant, you may wind up full of anger and in some cases ultimately reject the teenager as they seem to push every emotional button you have. Unconditional caring may not last forever. Eventually, rebellion will test the parent-child relationship, sometimes resulting in disaster.

For adults, it is simply not reasonable to think that we can behave any way we want to and be valued. We have to follow the rules of relationships and communities. When we don't follow the rules, society has a way of dealing with us. Some may try to catch a free ride in life and not deal with rules or responsibilities. There is no free ride. If one looks closely enough, there is a cost to any free ride. When we don't follow the rules of human relationships, we will eventually find ourselves to be alone; isolated by our own doing, or forced into it. Relationships are conditional. Do not expect them to be otherwise. Conceptually speaking, love is unconditional—some relationships are love-based, some are not. Even love-based relationships have rules.

3. As adults, we will not die without unconditional value, acceptance, or love. The ego in us will seek this out nonetheless. Fearful ego says, "I need your approval, acceptance, admiration." Your ego will likely urge you in many ways to seek out people and situations to create and/or increase a sense of your own importance. Knowing this ego tendency will assist in making sense out of mysterious feelings and behavior. In other words, the ego's strong desire to feel valued explains much of why we behave in ways that don't seem to make sense, ways that appear to be self-defeating. It explains much of why people remain in unhealthy relationships or continue to seek out approval from those who won't give it. We seek out this sense of value, though we don't really need it. Your ego would have you believe if you don't "get unconditionally loved, idealized or valued" from others that your very survival may be in jeopardy. The fact is, as an adult, you have nothing to fear.

We have a natural ego-based inclination toward establishing control and power over external reality. When our attempts to manipulate external reality fail, we manipulate our own internal reality. These internal manipulations occur on all levels of awareness. The primary purpose of internal manipulation is to maintain the agenda of the ego. Thus we have again, what I call ego maintenance, which will soon be fully explored, to include how you may cooperate with your ego to establish and maintain an idealized image of you, or an ego-ideal.

Exercise 3-1: Think about the unhealthy ways that you attempt to establish and maintain power and control over people, situations, and environments. Are there people or situations that you are habitually in conflict with? How do you try to "get your way" with them? How does your ego get involved in the process? Go to appendix F, and make these entries.

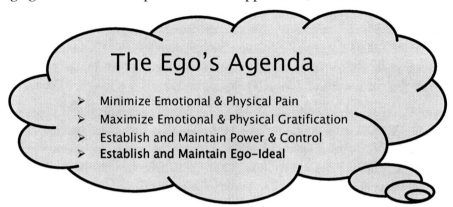

The Ego's Agenda

- ➤ Minimize Emotional & Physical Pain
- ➤ Maximize Emotional & Physical Gratification
- ➤ Establish and Maintain Power & Control
- ➤ Establish and Maintain Ego-Ideal

Ego-Ideal

Tom began his next session recalling a significant turning point in life. "I need to tell you what happened a long time ago. You see, things really changed on the night of my eighteenth birthday. I had gone out with some of my friends to celebrate, had way too many beers, and got home pretty late. He met me at the front door and slammed his fist into the side of my head. I was pretty well caught off guard and wound up on my back in the front yard. I'll never forget the feeling that came over me…something like pure rage. For the first time, I had no fear at all in his presence. I somehow managed to stumble onto my feet, and my friends said that I ran into him like I was some kind of mad man. It still seems like a blur that was over in a couple of seconds. They said that I had him on the ground and was just hitting him all over like I was in a frenzy. They had to pull me off of him. When I realized what I had just done, there was a bloody mess of a man on the ground in front of me. He was just sitting there with a weird kind of blank look on his face. My friends grabbed me and got me out of there. He and I didn't speak again for a very long time. Actually, it was when my mother passed away about ten years ago that we saw each other again. It was just before her funeral. That was a pretty rough time for me. She put up with a lot from that man. Right after that my father and I gradually began to talk again and we managed to form sort of an awkward relationship, but we never spoke about that night on my eighteenth birthday. Still haven't."

In Chapter 7, I will introduce the concept of the belief system that includes having beliefs about who you are, or a self-image. In many ways, self-image and ego-ideal are opposites. The most significant difference between these two concepts is a matter of perspective:

> ➢ Ego-ideal describes how the ego would like to be seen by others (an other perspective), and this ideal is consistent with its agenda.

> ➢ Self-image describes the person you know yourself to be (an inner perspective), which is consistent with you living out a consciously developed set of values and morals.

Your ego is very busy attempting to establish and maintain what it believes is an ideal situation. This is what your ego would very much like to believe:

> "I am valuable, powerful, in control, and superior to others. I know what is most important and what is ultimately right. I am needed and wanted by others. I am perfect, and everyone else is aware of these facts."

Okay, obviously this is a highly exaggerated example of the ego's ultimate fulfillment; it is the ideal situation à la ego. Unless you are a narcissistic personality disordered individual, you will not relate to it (at least on a conscious level). It is, nonetheless, ideal. In order for the ego to fully accomplish this situation, there can be no doubts or deficits recognizable to itself or others. That would be tantamount to sure death, or so it would have you believe. According to your ego, when these instinctually based characteristics, or images of you, are well established, your survival chances will be greatly increased.

The ego is very much interested in external idealization. The ego-ideal could also be called other-image, as it refers to the way you want others to see or regard you. Being instinctually desired characteristics, they are in some part determined according to gender. Examples of gender-neutral ego-ideal characteristics would include the following:

Primarily:

> ➢ I am supremely valuable.

> ➢ I am powerful.

> ➢ I am in control.

Secondarily:

> ➢ My belief system is superior.

> ➢ I know what is universally important.

> ➢ I know what is universally right.

> ➢ I am important-needed-wanted.

The feminine specific instinctual version of ego-ideal includes (but is not limited to):

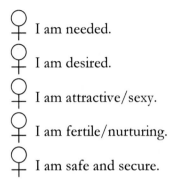

I am needed.

I am desired.

I am attractive/sexy.

I am fertile/nurturing.

I am safe and secure.

The masculine specific instinctual version of ego-ideal includes (but is not limited to):

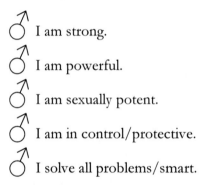

I am strong.

I am powerful.

I am sexually potent.

I am in control/protective.

I solve all problems/smart.

Now it's probably obvious that there isn't an actual location in your brain or body that a surgeon could point to and say, "There's your ego." As an intangible concept, however, clearly the ego is the body's representative. Again, its primary objectives are: 1) the reduction of the body's pain, 2) the gratification of the body, 3) power and control over environments and people, and 4) the establishment and maintenance of an idealized situation—the ego-ideal. Your ego may pursue these objectives in spite of your better judgment. There are countless addictions and unwanted behaviors that would bear out this truth. Moreover, there are many avoidances (physical exercise, various phobias, doctors, dentists) that bear out the same truth. Perhaps it is hard to believe that such an agenda may exist within you. You may have considerable doubt about the influence of the ego's agenda in your life. In that case, examine any thinking, feeling or behavior that you wish you could stop, or start, but are unable to. Then, look for ego-based influence—look for the agenda.

The ego voice can be a pretty powerful entity to contend with. It will attempt to persuade you to take care of its needs in very effective ways, oftentimes involving deception. How does the ego attempt to deceive you? As your body's representative, your ego simply knows what feels good to you and will attempt to convince you to seek it out. The ego is very accurate because it has physical reality on its side. It knows what you like factually, and it knows in a very clear and direct way what feels good in the present moment.

Exercise 3-2: What is your ego's version of ideal? Think about the ways that you attempt create an ego-based ideal (e.g. I'm right, I'm richer, I'm tougher, I'm smarter, I'm better, I'm better looking, etc.). Remember to get honest with yourself. Are there people or situations that you are habitually in conflict with; what are you trying to prove to them about "who you are?" Go to appendix F, and make these entries.

4 Behind the Scenes of Choice

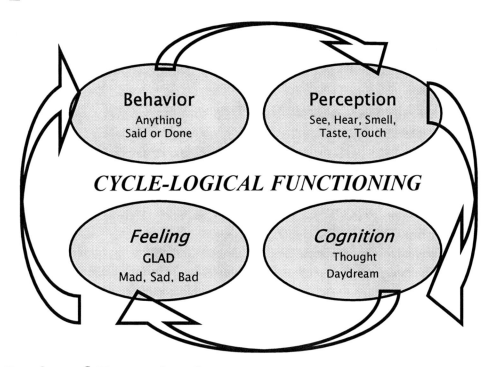

CYCLE-LOGICAL FUNCTIONING

Behavior
Anything
Said or Done

Perception
See, Hear, Smell,
Taste, Touch

Feeling
GLAD
Mad, Sad, Bad

Cognition
Thought
Daydream

A Cycle of Functioning

People generally don't wake up and think, "Okay, how can I maximize my gratification today?" The ego's agenda operates largely beneath the level of your conscious awareness. This means that you may behave in ways that seem *mysterious* to you. Fortunately, your personal functioning can be broken down into components of a predictable cycle involving perception, cognition, feeling and behavior, in relation to a system of beliefs. This is what I call cycle-logical functioning (also see illustration above and Appendix A).

The first component of cycle-logical functioning is perception. A great amount of what we experience in our daily lives is a result of sight and sound. You can't attend to every single thing in your visual or auditory fields at all times. So, you attend to, or perceive, what is important to you. Much of the rest of your surroundings fade to what might be called perceptual white noise. Whether in quiet meditation, or on a roller coaster ride, your brain is always on the move, processing both internally and externally perceived data.

You think about whatever captures your attention. Cognition is a fancy word for thinking. Cognition is the next component in the cycle, and basically refers to your brain's processing of information. You perceive, and then you think. You can attend to only one thought at a time, and therefore experience only one feeling at a time. While this single-track design may appear to be a limitation, there is a benefit that will be explored in later chapters in terms of problem solving. Your thinking produces your feeling; this basic sequence establishes an important foundation for being able to build an understanding of your personal psychological functioning. You experience a stream of conscious thought, and as a result, a stream of feeling awareness.

Feeling is the next component along the cycle. In order to make optimal use of the problem solving strategies in the later chapters of this book, it will be helpful to simplify your feeling experiences. That is, conceptualize your feelings as having roots in one of five physiological points of origin: anger, sadness, guilt, fear, or gladness.

We experience feelings with varying degrees of intensity and therefore have many different ways of describing them. For example, when you are very mad, you may say you are hostile, in a rage, livid, or hot. On the other hand, you may be only irritated, miffed, or annoyed. Similarly, we have an abundant vocabulary for describing the different intensity levels of the other four feelings categories giving us a means of effectively communicating our experiences to others. However, keep in mind that no matter if we have two, or two hundred ways of describing the experience of being mad, its still basically mad from a problem solving perspective.

The last component in the sequence of cycle-logical functioning is behavior. I define behavior as what is said or done. Even when you sit in silence, the behavior is definable; the doing or saying of nothing is behavior. It seems that all behavior is purposeful; we want a certain outcome to occur as a result of our behavior. Know that everything we say or do has a purpose, a meaning, a goal, and an outcome that can be determined as the driving force behind that behavior. In this chapter, I will discuss different levels of awareness. Understanding these levels will help to make sense of mystery behaviors. These are the things that we say or do that don't seem purposeful. We behave, and then we perceive the response to our behavior, which brings us full circle, and ready to go another round of cycle-logical functioning. You experience this cycle on a continual basis in your waking hours. This cycle is greatly influenced by a person's ego and belief system. I will present a closer look at the concept of the belief system in Chapters 7 and 8.

With a good understanding of cycle-logical functioning, solving the mysterious problems of life becomes a matter of detective work. You start with an investigation of the feeling clue and work through the thoughts that creates the feeling in the first place. Then you identify the problematic thinking. Now, apply some tried and tested creative problem solving skills, and you're on your way to solving that case. This book is about being your own detective. It is a guide for identifying the feelings, thoughts, and potential solutions to the challenges that are inherent in living. This approach requires facing all feelings rather than avoiding them.

Still, your ego will not like this approach.

Mystery Behaviors

"I have no idea why I did that." Did you ever do something or say something that you later thought was not like you? Maybe the behavior seemed like a mystery that you could not figure out. "Maybe I was having a bad day," or "sometimes I just do these things for no reason," or "I guess I must just be crazy, stupid, or a glutton for punishment." You may engage in repetitive unhealthy behavior that is clearly not in your best interest, and wonder, "Why am I stuck in this pattern?" All behavior is purposeful; this is a well-known and respected concept in the world of psychology. It means that everything that we do happens for some reason of our own. No behavior is produced randomly, and no feeling is produced randomly. We cannot legitimately say that we are not responsible for our behavior. There is an exception in the legal system relating to crimes that are pardoned when committed by reason of insanity. These are unfortunate and rare situations. For purpose of this discussion, we could still say that the person acted for their own reasons, although they could not appreciate the illegal nature of the behavior due to their psychotic condition at the time. For most of us however, we have no excuses for the unfortunate outcomes of some of our behavior. We must take responsibility for what we do. Moreover, we must take responsibility for what we feel, and what we choose to think about.

Even when there is no clear explanation for your mystery behaviors or feelings, there is always a reason, though at times it is difficult to determine. Such behaviors and feelings may seem mysterious when they are produced from a subconscious level of awareness. Regardless of their origin, it is possible to determine how they are produced, and how to go about changing them. I'd like to now give some practical meaning to levels of awareness.

Levels of Awareness

The terms "conscious" and "subconscious" are commonly used as ways of describing different functions of the brain, or the mind. These terms also describe different levels of awareness. As we experience life through our perceptual abilities (*senses*) we process the information on different levels of awareness. Here are my definitions for them:

> **Conscious Awareness:** A level of ongoing awareness that is experienced and represented by your stream of thought at any given moment of time. There is an awareness of perceptual information being processed and interpreted.

➤ **Subconscious Awareness:** This is a level of awareness that may not be readily knowable or available to you. However, some of the content might be accessed and determined as you give consideration to what is behind the scenes of your cycle-logical functioning. This cognitive content includes instinctual directives, basic memories, and behavioral routines. On this level of awareness, information is processed according to instinctual instructions for survival—the ego's agenda starts here. Moreover, your belief system is operating, or is organized, on this level of awareness.

Here's an example to illustrate these levels. You are driving a car, you see a stop sign up ahead, and you are aware that you must soon come to a stop. You saw data (stop sign) and processed the data. On what level of awareness did you process the information? That would depend on the circumstances. Are you a new driver? If so, you may process that information with full awareness. That is, you clearly say to yourself, "Oh, there's a stop sign, I need to stop the car." The behavior is produced consciously. If you have been driving a car for years and you have driven the route for years, you may not have any real conscious awareness of seeing the sign, or making a determination to stop. Then behavior would be produced subconsciously according to years of behavioral practice. While making this stop, you could even do some other complex task, like debating the laws of physics with the person in the passenger seat. Let's say that you are driving your regular route and you come to point where there is a new intersection with a new stop sign. You perceive the new sign, "Oh, there's a new intersection here, and a stop sign," and then tell yourself to stop. This behavior is produced consciously because it is new data. Over time, and with experience, you will think less about it, and the stopping behavior will become processed subconsciously once again.

There is a point at which stopping may become conscious behavior again. This could happen if you begin to have ideas about stopping partially, or not stopping at all because, "This is such a deserted road, I usually never see any cars out here, and rarely see any police cars." Now you would engage in a conscious cognitive process of weighing out the pros and cons of such behavior according to your belief system, which operates at a subconscious level. If you decided to attempt the partial stop, you would be producing that behavior at least initially in a conscious manner. Over time, with no external interference, it may fade again into subconscious cycle-logical functioning. *Now, let's all drive safely please.*

We experience one conscious stream of thought and therefore, one feeling at a time. Cycle-logical functioning describes a uni-directional process consisting of your perceiving, thinking, feeling, and behaving. This functioning occurs on both levels of awareness. You may be completely aware of the entire process on a conscious level, or there may be components that occur subconsciously without full awareness.

Your belief system is operating subconsciously, behind the scenes of conscious awareness. However, the specific content (your values, morals, expectations, and self-image) is accessible by conscious examination of the cycle-logical functioning. For example, you decide that you will continue to stop at the new stop sign even though you have not seen a soul, law enforcement officer or otherwise, on that route in months. In that case, why would you stop? A conscious examination of your subconscious belief system content would provide us with a reasonable answer:

1. You value your money and your safety and would not risk either for a few moments of saved time. In other words, money and safety are more important than moments of time to you.

2. You have a moral code standard that tells you that it is wrong to break any law of the land under any circumstances.

3. You have an expectation that there is always some chance of being caught and that the consequences would not be worth the risk for the potential gain (moments of time).

4. Your view of self as a patient, responsible, law-abiding citizen person.

Subconscious awareness, as a concept, is a bit of a mystery. I believe it is a phenomenon of: 1) instinct, 2) memory, and 3) ego agenda maintenance. Let's take a closer look at these concepts.

Much of the behavior, mystery or otherwise, engaged in by people can be explained as an outcome of pure **instinct** on a subconscious level. Our primary instinctual goal is to survive. This includes, but is not limited to, being able to avoid danger, seek out sustenance, maintain shelter, establish controls, and predict outcomes. Oftentimes, we seem to follow these preprogrammed directions beyond our own best judgment to a point of pure frustration. Due to our own normal physical responses (various hormonal and neurotransmitter activities), we are subconsciously urged and later rewarded when we attempt to reduce the bodily stress of hunger, fatigue, sexual tension, loneliness, and perceived danger. Subconsciously we believe, "I am this body, and I must do what it urges me to do. When I do so, I feel good. Keep doing it." These are instinctually established dynamics that we did not develop by experience of trial and error. These very basic instinctual directives are at the root of much obsessive and addictive behavior. Again, one way of looking at obsession and addiction is that you are essentially being fooled by your body/ego into believing that what it wants is what you need. Without a doubt, it can do this very effectively and convincingly. The ego is clearly operating in accordance with physiological dynamics on this level of subconscious awareness.

Another way of looking at subconscious awareness is that it is a type of **memory** storehouse. This type of memory is subconscious because it is not part of our present and ongoing stream of conscious thought, nor is it represented specifically in your belief system. These subconscious memories are stored in different forms as a result of input from all of the elements of cycle-logical functioning over the course of your lifetime. I believe that it is possible to categorize subconscious memory storage resulting from input along all components of cycle-logical functioning. In other words, you store perceptual memory, thought memory, feeling memory, and behavioral memory. Perceptual memory is evident when we have a flash mental picture of a physical object. This may be a building, or a person's face. A song or scent can trigger powerful memories from the past. You can probably imagine the taste of your favorite food right now if you clearly think about it.

We store behavioral memories and act on them without specific conscious thought. Examples of this would be, driving a car while looking for a radio station, playing a drum set or other musical instruments, juggling, tying shoelaces, tying a necktie, typing, etc. Essentially, behaviors that we practice for hours, days and years are later expressed as behavioral memories. They are behavioral memories in that we have established them well through repetition. They have become subconscious, inasmuch that we are no longer aware of the individual smaller behaviors or thoughts that established them in the first place. Although they may be routine and automatic now, the individual thoughts and behaviors may have been connected with fear, worry, anxiety, anger, or frustration. Over time as automatic behavior is established, the individual thoughts and feelings fade away. However, the now complex automatic behavior itself could have thought and feeling connected to it (such as performance anxiety).

Thought memories are evident when we are asked to recite a line from a poem, give our phone number, or any number data. And finally, feeling memories are evident when we remember how good or bad something feels. This type of memory is recognized when we say, "I remember how that felt, and it was so scary." Feeling memories are very powerful and are most likely at the root of most obsessive and addictive behavior. The attachment of feeling to any memory will make it powerful. Your brain is an amazing data storehouse filled with all of these kinds of memories, from all of the years of your life.

When I'm seeing a client for a first time evaluation, they may explain that they are either engaging in a behavior they cannot stop, experiencing depression or anxiety, or don't feel good about themselves. We then search for an explanation of the problem in the realm of their belief system. In other words, I am looking for a logical and conscious explanation. When we can find no obvious explanation, I invoke my own rule of thumb: "There must be a subconscious process going on." To illustrate, let's return to the previous stop sign example: One day you are driving down the road, encounter the new stop sign, and with full perception, drive right through the intersection without stopping. On recollection, you cannot figure out why you did it, having made a conscious choice previously to stop, and you have done so many times by now. You have searched your belief system and found that this behavior is essentially against your morals and values. Moreover, it is inconsistent with your self-image, and you certainly expect others to stop at such signs for your own safety. There does not appear to be any rational or reasonable explanation for your behavior and so you are left wondering why you did it.

The fact of the matter is that you did run it. All behavior is purposeful, no matter what level of awareness is producing it. Therefore, we are left to believe that there is a subconscious purpose to running the stop sign. Exactly what this purpose is can only be guessed at from the cycle-logical functioning involved. A good guess would begin with determining the feeling surrounding the behavior. Based on the feeling, we can assume the purpose of the behavior, even if it doesn't make logical sense. If, for example, you felt a sense of anger as you sped through the stop sign, we might deduce that you have some subconscious anger at something, someone, some entity which could be then explored further. We might speculate that you have some anger at the State for what you consider to be excessive taxes and you have expressed that anger in your behavior at the intersection. On the other hand maybe you just had a fight with your controlling mother who always demands that you follow all rules without question, and you have an image of her as you speed through. Although the exact meaning and purpose behind the behavior may remain unknown, having identified the specific feeling you might be able to determine a direction for problem solving. At any rate, in then end you would still need to make a conscious effort to follow the law.

Your feelings can tell you about the motivation behind mystery behaviors, and can help to explain the content of your fantasies, dreams, wishes, and daydreams. Any feeling you experience is an invaluable source of feedback about your subconscious cycle-logical functioning. Moreover, your peace of mind is dependent on understanding that feedback.

We have now looked at the subconscious conceptually as instinct and memory. The last concept, **ego agenda maintenance**, will be explored next.

5   Ego Maintenance

The Ego's Agenda
- Minimize Emotional & Physical Pain
- Maximize Emotional & Physical Gratification
- Establish & Maintain Power & Control
- Establish & Maintain Ego-Ideal

Subconscious Ego Maintenance

Conscious Ego Maintenance

Support for Bad Choices

Your ego believes in its instinctual agenda. It believes in this perspective of what to do about the challenges of life. It is trying hard to maintain your attention to its agenda.

Your ego is on guard against any threat to achieving its goals. That is, anything that might stand in the way of emotional/physical gratification, power and control, or ego-idealization will stimulate your ego's attention. When stimulated as such, like a red flag signifying danger, internal strategies will be employed in an effort to maintain the agenda on one or both levels of awareness. When there is a gap, barrier, or an incompatibility between what your ego wants and reality, maintenance strategies become established as a perceptual fix—to *bridge* the gap. For example, Jeff has a difficult time in maintaining friendships. Though he would like to have friends, he has none at present, and feels very sad when he is alone. In reality, let's say his behavior is boring, arrogant, unreliable, and obnoxious. Essentially then, his ego might attempt to reduce or eliminate the pain of sadness, rejection, or thoughts of inferiority. Additionally, a façade of control is created by maintaining anger, and the hope of future gratification. His ego will attempt to deal with his situation by concluding: 1) I don't have time for them anyway, 2) They are jealous of me and therefore don't like me, 3) I need to take on more projects at work, 4) I am going to read as many books as I can on being a powerful influence over people. 5) Soon, people will think I'm cool and will be begging to hang out with me."

I will address levels of ego maintenance in the next section with more examples. For the moment however, here are some definitions of these levels:

Conscious Ego Maintenance: This is a conscious level of ego functioning. At this level you make conscious attempts to minimize painful feelings, thoughts and experiences while increasing gratifying feelings, thoughts and experiences. You identify with the ego's urge to establish and maintain external power and control and create ways of doing so. This includes dealing with any threat that would be potentially damaging, unacceptable, or intolerable to the ego-ideal. The strategies that you consciously create may eventually operate subconsciously to the extent that they are effective in maintaining the ego's agenda,

Subconscious Ego Maintenance: On this level of awareness, effective consciously developed strategies have become routine so that they function automatically. This level of maintenance can be characterized as highly automated patterns of perceiving and processing information. These patterns occur subconsciously for the purpose of protection against painful feelings and/or thoughts that would be potentially damaging, unacceptable, or intolerable according to the ego. At this level, the ego automatically and systematically attempts to maintain its instinctual agenda. These patterns begin as instinct, are further developed in childhood, and become neurologically entrenched.

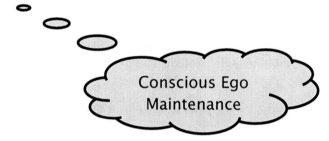

Conscious Ego Maintenance

Can we really fool ourselves into ego-based behavior? "I won't get fat." "It's okay for me to smoke…I wont get cancer…that happens to other people." "She won't find out." "Other people do this all the time." "I turned out okay didn't I?" "My drinking is not so bad." "That's not my problem…if I did have a problem wouldn't I know about it." "It could be worse." "This is really their fault." "I can handle this." Sound familiar? This private inner dialogue that we engage in is essentially a form of internal self-manipulation. Conscious ego maintenance is perception, cognition, feeling, and behavior that you consciously develop in compliance with your ego's agenda. Although this cycle-logical functioning may not ultimately be in *Your Own Best Interest*, you engage in it nonetheless. In other words, you talk yourself into doing things that minimize your pain, maximize gratification, establish and maintain power and control, and idealize your sense of self. Again, when conscious ego maintenance is effective, it becomes subconscious ego maintenance over time; we tend to repeat what works.

Perhaps you begin to have a candy bar at the end of each day on the drive home. At first you tell yourself that you "had a hard day" and that you "deserve this little bit of joy, it's not hurting anyone" and you "keep the chocolate makers in jobs." To the extent that these consciously developed ego maintenance thoughts are effective, over time they can become established as highly automated patterns of perceiving and processing information. In other words, on this level of awareness, consciously developed and successful ego maintenance patterns have become so routine that they function automatically behind the scenes. Over time, your ego's way of looking at eating the candy bar will fade into subconscious processing and become a way of maintaining your ego's agenda, perhaps even generalizing into other unhealthy patterns of eating. The ego's agenda says, "You had a hard day, and you deserve a little bit of joy." Certainly this makes sense from its perspective. Remember, the ego's perspective is, "Feel good now." As you begin to put on extra pounds, your ego may employ other conscious maintenance strategies to continue its agenda such as, "Its only a few pounds, I'll start a diet next month…I'll just skip a few calories at the next meal…if people don't like the way I look, tough luck for them."

Ego maintenance may be gender specific. That is, whether or not you are biologically a man or a woman, you may have an instinctual ego preference to be viewed as a masculine or a feminine being. A masculine gendered ego establishes maintenance patterns to help one feel strong, powerful, sexually potent, in control, and effective at problem solving. A feminine gendered ego would be likely to establish maintenance patterns to help one feel nurturing, attractive, desired, needed, and secure. For some, this gender preference can be a powerful and important cause of behavior, generated from any level of awareness.

Janie is a thirty-six year old woman, in her twelfth year of marriage. Over the course of her marriage she has struggled with what she believes to be a lack of satisfactory intimacy with her husband. From her perspective, it appears that he has lost interest in her and doesn't seem to find her sexually attractive any more. On a subconscious level of awareness, she has developed considerable doubt about her attractiveness and sexual desirability. On a deeper (subconscious) level, she doesn't feel important or needed. Janie begins to have a flirtatious relationship with Doug, the new sales executive in her office. As time goes on, she feels desired, and understood by him. She consciously decides (with ego based thinking) that, "Everyone engages in infidelity at some time in a relationship." By coming to this conclusion, she will be more likely to do the same, without guilt, and feel like she fits in with the rest of the world. At the same time, she starts to notice everyone else who might be doing the same, and this further solidifies her belief that it is acceptable behavior. Finally she consciously gives herself permission to do the same when the opportunity arises. At this point, it is only a matter of time before Janie finds an opportunity and acts on her now well established belief.

To Janie's ego, the affair is an object of desire and is consistent with her ego's agenda: it reduces the pain of loneliness and rejection, it feels good emotionally and physically, it creates a sense of control in her life, and she feels powerful. Any guilt sensed by her ego will be denied, reduced or quickly addressed with maintenance such as, "What my husband doesn't know won't hurt him." As time goes on, her sense of gratification will further justify her behavior, and her ego's maintenance strategies will become subconsciously established and maintained.

In order to convince yourself to engage in ego-based-behavior, your ego would generally need to manage the feelings: reduce the fear (of consequences), reduce guilt, maintain a determined or angry motivation of what you want, deny the potential loss, and focus on feeling glad or being gratified with the outcome. In Janie's case, in order for her to pursue the affair, her ego needs to attend to the following maintenance tasks: 1) Reduce her fear about getting caught, "I'll be very careful." 2) Convince her that she really isn't doing anything wrong, "Everyone does this." 3) Maintain frustration toward her husband, "I hate my marriage." 4) Ignore the potential loss of her marriage, "He would never leave me, but I don't care if he does." and, 5) Focus on how good it will feel, "I can hardly wait to talk to Doug and feel him against me." Your ego can be pretty effective at getting its agenda attended to.

When you think about ego-based-behavior from a non-ego perspective, you can see the folly of the ego. I have heard some pretty good ego maintenance statements in my time. I have also concluded that people can justify almost anything to themselves when they are highly motivated. With persistent ego pressure, we consciously attempt to fool ourselves into ego-based behavior. Such behavior may then go on for many years. Ask any recovering smoker, gambler, alcoholic, sex-addict, food-addict, or person-addict about the convincing power of the ego. We can perhaps fool ourselves for now. However in the end, the reality of the consequences of such behavior may prove us to be fools. There is apparently some truth to the old adage that, "You can pay now, or pay later."

Here are some examples of how conscious ego maintenance works based on Janie:

Minimize emotional pain: At times, Janie experiences some feelings of guilt as she daydreams about her co-worker. She consciously says to herself, "I can't believe I'm having these thoughts. Oh well, I have nothing to feel bad about, my husband doesn't seem to want me, but I know who does. I'm tired of feeling so alone, so I'm going to start flirting with Doug. I'm going to be very careful. I won't get caught. I don't think my husband would ever leave me, but I don't care any more if he does."

Later, this subconsciously becomes: This is all my husband's fault. I don't care. I'm okay.

Maximize gratification: "I think everyone eventually has an affair, I see it and read about it all the time, so why not me, I deserve some happiness too. I hate my marriage, so I'm going to do things my way whether he likes it or not. He'll never know anyway. I can hardly wait to talk to Doug and feel him against me. I feel so connected to Doug." Janie has begun to notice that the people in her office flirt with each other on a regular basis. She sees a man and woman leave at lunch together and makes an assumption, "I'll bet they're having an affair...I like them, they aren't bad people."

Later, this subconsciously becomes: I'm ok; my choices are normal.

Establish and maintain power and control: Janie is very frustrated with the way her marriage is going. She thinks, "Maybe I should talk this out with my husband," but doesn't say anything to him. Instead, she consciously looks for, and finds even more fault in his behavior, which creates more conflict, and more emotional distance, "He'll never change, and I'm so tired of this marriage. I've tried and he just does the same old thing... all that car and sports stuff. I'm going to do what I want for a change. He's a grown adult, if he finds out, I'm sure he'll be just fine. In these modern times, we know that monogamy isn't natural, I've seen the research that proves it... relationships aren't meant to last forever."

Later, this subconsciously becomes: Everything my husband does is wrong. Monogamy is unnatural, he should know that.

Idealization: "Doug understands who I am and likes me. I can tell by how he looks at me and pays attention to what I am interested in. I feel attractive and alive for the first time in years... like I'm someone who matters." Janie spends increasing amounts of time in the office, working late hours, and hoping that she can develop some close and meaningful relationships with some of the men in the office. She feels "understood" by them. "My job is very important to me. I work harder than most, and need to network with my coworkers. The subsequent and eventual close working relationships are critical for my career advancement. I'm working hard, and that's good.

Later, this subconsciously becomes: Doug knows me, my husband doesn't. It's right and good for me to work more. What my husband wants doesn't matter.

These are consciously developed ego-based strategies that with time and experience, can become subconsciously maintained. In other words, according to the ego, "They get the job done so well that they get hired on a full time basis." They work hard so you don't have to.

Subconscious Ego Maintenance

Subconscious ego maintenance can happen in relatively insignificant ways on a regular everyday basis. For example, William loves to play board games and is very competitive. As he is playing a well-known crossword game with his family, he makes a suggestion to add a new rule. If a timer were used to limit the amount of time a person can take on their turn, more stress would be added, a new dimension of competition would be created, and the game might go faster. If the next game is played with a timer, and William wins, he will feel good, continue to regard himself to be a superior player, and more than likely he will want to continue this new rule. For anyone who lost and suggested that this was not a good rule, he would argue against and defend the new rule. He would subconsciously generate support of, or value in, the new rule and come to greatly appreciate the rule.

This is a subconscious level of ego maintenance. At this level, the ego attempts to establish and maintain ego-idealization. It is as if on a subconscious level William's ego thinks, "Hmmm, when the game is played like this, I am gratified, sooner, and more intensely, I feel superior and powerful, have more control of maintaining this ongoing feeling through winning, and these people think I'm really great and smart. Anyone who denies me this experience is a threat to me and I will find good reasons to keep this rule." William's subconscious commentary would more than likely take place in a micro-second, which means that he would not have any conscious awareness of it, unless for some reason he stopped to think about why his ego was interested in the new rule. In that micro-second, he has experienced the effects of ego maintenance.

Subconscious ego maintenance can also occur in substantial ways over the course of a lifetime. Tammy is a 35-year-old female who was verbally and physically abused throughout her childhood. Her father was domineering and violent with her when he determined that she was not following his rules of the home.

While growing up in this environment, Tammy's self-image was at risk as her father called her names, hit her, and criticized her ideas and appearance. Her internal protection from this abuse was taken care of by her ego. At an early age, her ego instinctually began to formulate ideas about her father's behavior and perception of him to assist in her emotional and physical survival. The more severe the abuse was, the more her ego needed to rely on extreme measures (distortions) to assure Tammy's survival.

Over time, her emotional and physical survival was based on her ego's perception that, "He is only doing what's best for me." In the interest of her own survival, she subconsciously became very compliant and never rebelled against her father's wishes due to the potential for great harm. Her ego automatically developed this survival strategy according to environmental factors, and she engaged in compliance with most people in her life, even when it did not seem to be in her best interest.

As an adult, she began to question her compliance and unfounded fearful perception of others. However, she could not get herself to change, and could not figure out why she was so afraid. She continued to see men as generally as a threat to her, and had a very difficult time in trusting people. She was also stuck with an old and concretely formed idea, "Father always knows what's best for me." On some level, these patterns of perceiving and processing information may be with her for the remainder of her life.

Subconscious ego maintenance can be characterized as highly automated patterns of perceiving and processing information around you. As a young child, you have very little control over your physical environment, or the people who are regular parts of it. When reality becomes too emotionally or physically painful, the ego instinctually steps in to lend a hand. In other words, your ego strives to spin things in such a way to leave you feeling painless, gratified, in control, and powerful (with others hopefully coming to the same conclusion). These early patterns of perceiving and processing information are instinctually based, further established in childhood, and neurologically entrenched. That is, when you are very young (0 to 6 years old) and your brain is still literally growing, these patterns become deeply neurologically established in response to the environmental conditions of that time. Your ego wants and needs to know that you will survive; that you are powerful and in control, and that you are valued. Your ego thinks that emotional, physical, or psychological pain could be a hindrance to meeting its objectives and engages maintenance subconsciously and instinctually.

Subconscious ego maintenance describes a process of managing painful feelings and thoughts that would be potentially damaging, unacceptable, or intolerable to the ego-ideal. When you are young, your ego naturally attempts to establish and maintain an idealized self-image. This might involve trying to change external factors like people and situations around you more to your liking. When efforts to manipulate physical reality have been exhausted, the ego attempts to transform the perception of reality into an idealized outcome.

Because of her father's severe abuse of her, Tammy's ego needed to address priority number one; establish her survival. Her ego automatically continued to follow its agenda; value and pursue physical survival, and spin/perceive an idealized situation, or sense of self. Her ego ideally wanted to perceive, "I am valued, safe, and loved by my caretakers." As her "loving" caretaker was abusing her, her ego needed to make sense of this apparent mismatch, or assemble the information into an acceptable reality, thus, the "spin". The idea that your own parent seems to hate you, and causes you ongoing pain, would create too much fear for a child to be able to tolerate. Therefore, rather than perceiving his behavior as abusive, controlling, and harmful she concluded, "This must be what a parent does when they love you, and it's for your own good." And in the end, her perception becomes, "He can't be wrong about me, I must be bad…other people's perceptions of me and reality are more accurate than my own." Subconsciously, she then began to notice and look for information to support this concluded belief in her everyday experiences with her father and other people in other environments. When we go looking for evidence to support our strongly held beliefs, we tend to find it!

For the remainder of her childhood, Tammy's ego had a significant dilemma to resolve, "How could someone who claims to love me and do what's best for me, cause me so much physical and emotional pain?" The ego's answer to this developed subconsciously over time and the conclusion resembled something like this: "You are bad…your father is right about you, there is something wrong with you, and you need to change or figure it out so you can be more acceptable to him, yourself and others…whenever conflict occurs in relationships, they are probably right and you are wrong, do what they say to do…this is how you survive."

Strategies, or patterns of maintenance, developed early in childhood can last well into adulthood. To the extent that they work to effectively maintain the agenda of the ego, they can be stubbornly generalized into other environments as well—thus, mystery behaviors.

To illustrate, let's return to Tammy's experience and see how her adult cycle-logical functioning is subconsciously effected by ego maintenance due to her past. Tammy doesn't recall much of her childhood. She periodically experiences overwhelming feelings that seem to come out of nowhere. She has frequent bouts of depression, and curiously wonders why other people want to live in such a "bad world." Tammy has a poor self-image. She clearly has a perception of herself as being basically "bad" although she doesn't know why. "I am bad…wrong…stupid"; therefore, she believes that most people "know" this about her, and don't like her.

She experiences a lot of mystery fear of men who are in a position of authority, and feels compelled to do as she is told—to please others without question. When men become angry with her, she assumes that she has done something wrong and that she needs to changer her behavior to meet their needs. "It's understandable when my boss yells at me, he has these 'stressful' days and I often don't do the job like he wants me to. He is just trying to help me. It could be worse, he could fire me, then what would I do."

Tammy has a very difficult time in expressing anger with people that she is in regular contact with. Instead of expressing her anger with them, she either engages in self-destructive behavior, or takes her anger out on things. She uses food or alcohol as predictable ways of feeling good. She is drawn to volunteering her time at the local women's abuse shelter during the holidays.

Based on her adult cycle-logical functioning we can deduce that the following specific ideas or beliefs have been established by her ego and are expressed as subconscious maintenance:

Minimize emotional pain: Forget the past, and you will feel no pain about it. Father is right. If you do what you are told, you won't have guilt. If you expect people to be mean, you can protect yourself. Do things as perfect as you can, then you won't have to worry about criticism. Do what father says, and you won't have pain. If you do things for others, you forget about your own problems. Other peoples' anger makes you feel bad, reduce their anger to make your bad feeling go away.

Maximize gratification: If you start to feel bad, you can eat and drink whatever you want, as much as you want, and don't worry about the consequences because tomorrow may never come and this feels good now. If you start to feel bad, you can do whatever you want to yourself to feel better as long as you don't hurt other people. Making an assumption that other people are right will be less of a struggle for you. People like you when you please them, that feels good to you. It feels good to ignore bad feelings or to find ways of making them go away.

Establish and maintain power and control: To be safe, do whatever authority figures tell you to do, never question them, submit to their authority, they know what's best and right. You must do the best (perfect) job that you can do at all times in order to maintain approval from authority. Other people will want to control you, therefore, isolate yourself from others as much as possible. Only trust people who have clearly demonstrated over time that they are not going to cause you pain. Power is gained when others are afraid of you. If you're going to have emotional pain, its better that you be the cause of it, and be in control of it, rather than giving others the opportunity. The world is a dangerous place, so protect yourself at all times. You can maintain some control if you don't allow very many people in your life, then, you have power over your world.

Idealization: If you don't remember the past, it must have been good. You are only ideal when your father tells you so. You had a good father, and you know because you see other fathers who are worse. Except for your father, men are not trustworthy. You can take a lot of pain and get through it. You are stronger than most people in many ways. If you do good things for other people you deserve to gain their acceptance and appreciation.

As can be appreciated from Tammy's experience, the ego acted in her best interest by compensating for her lack of problem solving abilities as a helpless child. These internal manipulations were instinctual and effective in dealing with the pain of the environment. At first glace, it may seem that her ego's eventual response to her environment, "I'm bad...I'm wrong," is contrary to the ego's agenda. We cannot forget priority number one—survive. As survival becomes more predictable, the ego will move on to other agenda items such as feeling good and establishing idealization.

"Maintain the agenda," this is the subconscious voice of the ego.

Exercise 5-1: In what ways do you engage in conscious ego maintenance to support bad choices? In what ways do you engage in subconscious ego maintenance to support bad choices? Go to appendix F, and make these entries where appropriate

6   Anger

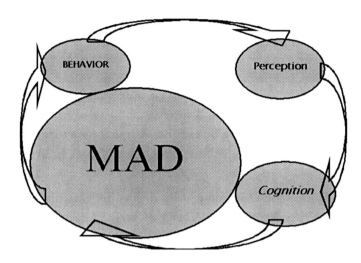

The Trick

Perhaps we are born into this world feeling mad. The entry to an air-based environment from a liquid-based environment is the first major change we encounter as human beings. Shortly after that, we have most all of our important needs taken care of for approximately the next 24 months. The first two years of our neurological development is based on the notion that we are magically taken care of by someone else when we simply cry, utter primitive grunts, manufacture rudimentary words, or use other forms of body language. We experience and then expect enormous amounts of attention and care for the first two years, and may spend the rest of our lives trying to reverse that expectation. Ultimately, we are responsible for ourselves and must meet our own needs. Some of us truly take a lifetime to figure this out, some of us never figure it out, and some are fortunate who *get it* prior to reaching adulthood.

The trick is that we start out in life thinking we "have it made" and then we are asked to be patient, do things for ourselves, and clean up after ourselves. They pull the old *switcheroo* on us, "Now you have to do it yourself." This notion is met with a two-year-old sense of contempt, frustration, disillusionment, outrage, and basic anger. The corresponding behavior consists of *temper tantruming*. We would say that the child is then going through the *terrible twos*. The manner in which caretakers handle this switcheroo transition is very important with respect to how the child deals with anger from then on. The switcheroo environment will now be further explored.

The Environment

The environments that you experience in the first decade of your life have a critical impact on your personality development. Basic personality characteristics that are formed during this decade tend to be very stubborn and resistant to change. Fundamental patterns of thinking and behavior such as introversion, compulsiveness, aggression, and stubbornness will probably be with you for a lifetime. Any change that you make after those early years is generally not a deep-base personality change but is rather a situational/behavioral adaptation of you to the environment that you find yourself in. You may be shy and passive by nature but need to act assertive at work in order to keep your job or avoid being overtaken by the sharks that swim there.

You were trained from a young age on how to deal with being mad. You learned what to do, and not to do, when things weren't going your way. The learning did occur, and the teaching was provided by the environments and significant people that you were exposed to. Over the course of your life, you are exposed to, and are involved in, a variety of environments. Some of them are only temporary, and some are for extended periods of time. These environments would include the family you grew up in, classrooms, jobs, grocery stores, the shopping mall, theaters, etc. Each of these environments had its own level of tolerance for negative behaviors; its own environmental tolerance. There are four factors to consider with the idea of environmental tolerance:

1. The expectations, or rules, of the environment.

2. The consequences imposed on behavior.

3. The consistency, timing, and delivery of the consequences.

4. The clarity of communication about the other three factors.

Far more could be written about this subject but for now here are some best and worst case scenarios. The best-case scenario is having realistic, reasonable, and fair rules, that are communicated clearly at age level, with a balance of both positive and negative consequences occurring as soon as reasonably possible. For an example you could imagine most any typical warm and loving television family. The worst-case scenario would be an environment with combinations of the following conditions. The rules are unknown, unfair, or unrealistic. The consequences are harsh, cruel, abusive, or ineffective. The consequences are random, inconsistent, stated—but not followed up, started—but not finished, or are delayed beyond what is reasonable. The rules and consequences are communicated as needed, not at all, in too much quantity, in bits and pieces, and are associated with anger or excessive guilt.

Consider Jennifer, who was 32 years old, a mother of two, and had been single for four years after a pretty vicious divorce. While growing up she was not allowed to express anger in a safe way. Any expression of dissatisfaction by her was met with a harsh consequence by her mother and stepfather. Jennifer learned early in life that if she was not happy with some aspect of her home life she would be better off if she just accepted it. She met Mike about six months ago. "I should've never let this guy in my life, or my house. I want to tell him that it's just not working with us, but I have a hard time doing that. He doesn't have a job, and sleeps all day after he drinks all night. I should have paid attention to the danger signals, the red flags, all the warning signs of a mess just waiting to happen. I can't seem to stand up for myself. Why do I do these things? I met Mike through a friend. At the time I was feeling pretty sad and lonely…pretty miserable. To be honest, I think he gave me the attention I needed. Before I knew it I was so much caught up in what we had that I couldn't seem to turn back. I know it sounds crazy, but a month later he was living in my house. I knew at the time that he got drunk once in a while. Well, maybe more than once in a while. I knew that he had a whole lot of debt. I also knew that he had just gotten fired from his job, and a couple of other jobs before that. But there was just something about him that I liked. The sex was great, and we did have some fun. At first I felt like someone actually cared about me. I think that I made a mistake. I just wanted to feel better. Why am I always making choices that I wind up regretting?"

These factors related to *the trick* and *the environment*, lead us to an important conclusion in how we experience and express anger as adults. The environmental training and tolerance you were given in your first decade is most likely responsible for how you deal with anger today. The way you deal with anger is like a personality characteristic or style. As such, you may find that it is very difficult to change fundamentally how you deal with anger. However, it is entirely possible for you to make adaptive changes. It is also entirely possible for you to choose how to deal with anger as an adult. If you choose to live according to a consciously determined belief system, you cannot allow your ego or the environment to determine how you manage anger. You must choose how you deal with anger.

The Past

The subconscious refers to a realm of awareness that may not be readily knowable or available to you. Its content can be assumed by your cycle-logical functioning. Oftentimes, what you experience with your subconscious mind will occur on a feeling level, "I just feel mad, I don't know why." When you have a feeling that: 1) you cannot explain, 2) seems to happen without any thought, and 3) is difficult to "put words to," you could assume that you are dealing with the past. The origin of subconsciously produced feeling is often rooted in the environments of your early childhood experience. Specifically, subconscious anger might result from a history in which some aspect of your needs and/or wants were not valued or fulfilled over a significant amount of time. In other words, things did not go your way for quite a long time, and this happened at a time when you could not efficiently put the experience into words. This is old anger based on a child perspective of history.

In therapy, I frequently suggest to a client, "You may not want to act (behave) on the basis of intensely felt anger." An experience of high intensity of anger suggests that the present situation may be triggering old emotion based on history that may or may not be relevant to the present situation. It may be more appropriate to first take some time to reflect on the emotion and the relevant history. Then you can decide on a course of action that is in your best interest for the present situation. In your reflection of any intense emotion, you may be able to guess at what the subconscious issue is by looking at the circumstances related to the feeling and then identify any related thoughts. For example, if you are feeling sad for what seems to be no good reason, you could assume, "The situation I'm in now, seems to be triggering some loss in my past…what could that be?" If angry for some unknown reason, you could assume, "This situation seems to be triggering some chronic unmet expectation from my past…what could that be?" The mystery anger that you feel in the present is related to the past. It is as if you are saying, "I didn't get what I wanted then, and I'm not getting it now." The critical question is, "What was it that I didn't get then?" After you come up with a probable answer to that question, you can begin to grapple with if and how you can get that in a healthy way now. Look for explanations of your mysterious cycle-logical functioning as though it makes sense in the context of a previous time and place.

Whatever you didn't get enough of when you were young is then typically subconsciously longed for as an adult. If you weren't accepted as a child, you would want for it as an adult, and therefore tend to want it from your partner. If no one understood you in your youth, you would want that from others including your mate. It is quite common in relationships that these and other subconscious expectations can go unmet and become experienced as anger. You might not have specific conscious connection from your current unmet relationship expectations to your youth. However, if you look at the patterns of anger that are currently present, you may find something that resembles the experience of your early years. You might come to subconsciously expect that your partner will: tolerate your behavior unconditionally, make you feel good about yourself, take care of your responsibilities, make you feel safe, make you feel valued, or take care of countless other unmet childhood needs and/or wants. When you don't have those corrective experiences with your partner you get angry, because you perceive that you are not being valued in a way that you want to be valued. For various reasons, it is not realistic for you as an adult to expect that your partner (or anyone else for that matter) can make you feel any of those things mentioned above.

In order to create a healthy functioning relationship, I encourage partners to specifically describe their needs and wants in a realistic, reasonable, and fair way for each other. That brings those expectations out of the realm of the subconscious and into what becomes a consciously developed relationship. It is generally reasonable in the context of an adult relationship that you would expect to feel valued or important to them. You probably want to have experiences with your partner that leave you feeling appreciated, cared about, understood, respected, and accepted. In the end, there is a very big difference between you wanting to feel valued, and needing your partner to *make* you feel that way.

I think that due to the nature of the ego's agenda, most people would always want more if they could get it. Wouldn't you always want more admiration, more money, more free time, more food gratification, more sexual gratification…more, more, more, if available? Be that as it may, you learned long ago that some things were not immediately attainable. Acquiring money and possessions takes time and effort, and there are only so many hours in a day. As a result, you learned to have patience or you decided that you simply could not have certain things. You also learned that certain behaviors, although highly gratifying, have certain painful and unavoidable consequences. You found out that eating too much produced a stomach ache, or produced extra pounds on you. You found out that when you lie, cheat, or take something that is not yours, you could get caught and become very embarrassed or feel guilty. You came to know those consequences as real and highly predictable. As a result, you discontinued those behaviors and accepted the reality of your situation. Essentially then, over the course of your life, on a subconscious level of awareness, you have managed a lot of unmet expectations, and accepted a lot of loss. There are some things you would want, but have realistically decided you can never have. Apparently, you are already an expert at anger management. Not convinced?

Imagine that you encountered a magical genie, and that genie was willing to grant you unlimited wishes. What wish would you start with, and how far would you go? Like most people with whom I do this exercise, you might start off with wanting some superficial things. Most common wishes have to do with changing how you look, eating food without consequences, and sexual gratification. Later on people will usually desire the kind of gratification that comes from control or power, travel, getting approval or recognition from others, and sometimes various altruistic pursuits. Toward the end of this exercise when you have developed a magical genie level of control over life, something is realized. There are countless things and situations that we would like to be different in our lives. There has been much disappointment we have come to terms with long ago, and we simply accept that much of life will not go our way. Additionally, in this exercise there is a realization of what is truly important to us after we experience all the physical and emotional gratification that we can imagine, have seen everything, and experienced all experiences. Generally we reach the following conclusions:

> ➤ The most important things in our lives are the relationships we have with people.

> ➤ The most important thing we do is to create and experience the joy of the relationships.

> ➤ We want integrity; we want to experience peace of mind.

So, it seems that in reality, much of life does not go your way. You've made a tremendous amount of adjustment to change along the way. You might even go a step further and ask, "Is there anything at all that has completely gone my way in my life," when you look at it from the perspective of a genie level of control? We have, on a subconscious level, decided to accept certain unalterable aspects of our lives and seem to deal with that just fine. We have on some level of consciousness, and at some point in our past, chosen to use skills of anger management very effectively with certain desires or wants. In other words, we have chosen acceptance of what is not realistic to expect, and made a subsequent decision to then move on. This is a very healthy skill to possess. We could certainly learn from that process of turning unrealistic wants into realistic acceptance (after appropriate conscious consideration of course).

There is still this mystery anger, "I'm mad, but I don't know why." This is the anger that persists, and rears its ugly head from time to time. This is the kind of anger that we cannot seem to rid ourselves of, that won't go away, and that doesn't seem to make sense to us. With this anger, we apparently continue to hold on to a subconscious and presumably questionable expectation that has gone unfulfilled since childhood, "You should love me unconditionally, you should understand me without explanation, you should do whatever I ask of you without exception, I deserve to be taken care of by you." For some, it seems that subconscious feelings surface in a way that is virtually uncontrollable. Once they start, it's like a floodgate of feeling energy has been opened. Predictable thoughts seem to follow, ego maintenance is aroused, and the whole process seems to take on a life of its own. Although this may seem like a hopeless and helpless experience, with time and effort, the mystery can be unraveled. Chapter 13, Managing Mad, provides a method of resolution for anger produced from any level of awareness. While the specific angry thought may remain mysteriously fuzzy, the resulting behavior is always a choice.

Exercise 6-1: Do the "magical genie" exercise and then make notes on how you would pursue ego-based pain reduction, immediate gratification, control and/or power, and ego-ideal. Also, make notes on any values that emerge. Go to appendix F, and make these entries where appropriate.

The Future

> "Why can't you for once, just trust me, you make me so mad when you do this."
>
> "It's the same thing day after day, I get home after that one-hour commute and I'm angry with anyone who crosses my path."
>
> "When will I ever learn that I can't live up to the expectations of my father?"
>
> "Women just seem to reject me without ever really giving me a chance, I hate them."

Subconscious anger is a type of patterned and repetitious anger, which you might recognize as a regular or predictable frustration. This type of anger is generated from subconsciously maintained expectations of self, others, or the world. Subconscious anger may be generated from a perspective of your history, in which things did not go your way as stated above. Conversely, subconscious anger can be generated from a past where certain aspects did go your way—and you still want those ways. How do you recognize this anger? With this anger, you hold on tight to your expectations even though they routinely are not fulfilled, and find yourself regularly frustrated. For all intents and purposes, you hold out for:

➢ What you think you want.

➢ What you think you can control.

➢ What you think you can change.

➢ What you think will eventually change.

You want for something more, something that more fully meets your expectations, and maybe something that gratifies your ego. You might recognize this kind of anger in relationships, at work, or when driving. "My father just won't approve of what I have chosen to do for a living. For once I would just like to be accepted for what is important to me." "My boss drives me crazy. She is always belittling me and I can't stand it." "These idiot people need to learn how to drive. Every day it's the same thing. I just hate it." With this type of anger, at some point you may want to clearly identify and honestly evaluate the expectation against these soon to be familiar four standards: 1) Reality, 2) Reasonability, 3) Relational fairness, and 4) Relative importance. I call this, the **expectation test**. Ask yourself the following four questions about your expectation: 1) Is what I'm expecting **realistic** (possible) considering the entire set of circumstances (the big picture context)? 2) Is what I'm expecting **reasonable** (probable) considering the context? 3) Is what I'm expecting **relationally fair** considering the context? 4) How important (**relative importance**) is this expectation considering the context? When you are finished with this evaluation, you can decide whether or not you should hold on to your expectation, consider changing it, or let it go. With pattern anger, you will likely determine that your expectation fails against one of the first three standards, which would explain why you continue to be angry. This means that it is time to establish a different expectation. For example, it is realistic to think that a father could approve of the chosen occupation of his adult child. It would be a fair thing to ask for. But it very well may not be reasonable when considering the big picture context. Perhaps this particular father has a history of not being able to accept much about any of his children's choices. The pattern of the father's personality in this and other related situations would also suggest that he would not likely change his mind. So it may be time to adjust the expectation for this father, "From now on I will expect my father to disapprove of what I do for a living. Oh well, that's just the way he is."

So let's say that your expectation fails the test, you then make an attempt to change the expectation, but you still find yourself angry. For example, on some level you recognize that "drivers will not change in their driving practices, there will always be crazy drivers." Having readjusted your expectation, you still find yourself angry. The most likely reason for continued anger would be that some part of you has not come to a 100% conclusion of certainty about your new expectation. You must ask yourself, "What about this belief do I continue to maintain, or, is there a part of me that still believes this, wants to believe this, or needs to believe this." To the extent that there is doubt, uncertainty, or desire about the expectation, there will be a resulting equal and opposite physiological reaction of anger the next time the expectation is not met.

You may have made a decision to maintain your original expectation. In that case, you must have concluded that your expectation was realistic, reasonable, relationally fair, and relatively important. Your expectation passed the test and now you may need to take some action, "I would like for my boss to treat me with respect, and this is very important to me, so I will need to formulate an assertive plan and discuss this with her." In Chapter 13 you can read about how to take positive steps toward the resolution of justified anger. For now I can say that you will want to take some kind of action that demonstrates consistency with your belief system. Over time, such consistency will produce a sense of having integrity.

"He really knows how to push my buttons." This is a commonly used expression to indicate that an emotionally sensitive spot has been touched upon. A button is your own perceptual point of emotional vulnerability from which you can experience intense feelings very quickly. Among other feelings, a button can represent anger maintained on a subconscious level. It can represent a particular old expectation that you have. The beginning development of such buttons, or repetitive anger is most likely, though not always, rooted in childhood. A button could be a manifestation of an old psychological wound, or a pet peeve. With anger buttons, again, you hold out for what you want, think you can control, think you can change, or think will change on its own. To be clear, the button belongs to you, and you are responsible for its maintenance. If the button continues to cause pain, or anger, an *expectation test* might help you to disconnect the button.

Some of our expectations can be persistent. They are stubbornly maintained in our minds, and they beg to be validated by our experiences. We want to be right about what we believe, and we won't settle for anything less. We want others to see things from our own point of view. Having this kind of stubborn conviction about our expectations can work out in the end to our advantage. We could take a look back in history and find plenty of examples of individuals who persistently believed in something that not many others (if any) believed in. Nicolas Copernicus, Christopher Columbus, Abraham Lincoln, Mahatma Gandhi, Albert Einstein, and Martin Luther King, Jr. just to name a few of these individuals. If these individuals had given up on what they believed in, we may be living in a very different world today. How long should I hold out? Maintaining stubborn conviction is not always in your best interest. It seems that with some expectations we are able to quickly realize that they will not be met. In those cases we adjust and we move along. With other deeply held expectations, we may need to have many disappointing experiences to come to a conclusion that what we want simply will not happen in a way that we want it to.

Sometimes you have to work out acceptance of reality, in reality, not just in your head. Perhaps I want to think that I can eat anything I want and have no consequences for doing so. I want to believe it very badly because food is highly gratifying to me. I want to think I can break the rules of good nutrition and get away with it. I want my experiences to bear out these subconscious expectations, "I want my way with eating." At times I overeat and experience horrendous indigestion. Over time I notice that I cannot fit into my favorite clothes anymore. Excess weight is beginning to drag me down. I continue my eating habits in spite of the frustration, the physical pain, the eventual loss of mobility, and increased self-loathing. I continue to focus on the gratification and engage in conscious ego maintenance strategies to maintain what I like and what I want, "I can eat anything I want and have no consequences." I will need the painful outcome of not getting what I want to free me of the expectation. "I just can't do this anymore. I guess I can't just eat whatever I want to, it's too painful." I had to work out acceptance *of* reality, *in* reality. This concept applies to relationships as well. Perhaps in a relationship, you ask someone to change, wish that someone will change, or try to get someone to change. If they resist (and they usually do), you may eventually reach a point of acceptance after you come to a certain conclusion, "He is not behaving like I want him to, I cannot change him no matter how hard I try, I need to accept that and move on."

Unfortunately, we sometimes only reach these conclusions very gradually over time when combined with many painful experiences; reality prevails.

There is a big difference between a Gandhi type frustration and an "I can't change him" frustration. In the former case, a man had an expectation that people might see the world from his point of view, "Use passive-resistance to achieve freedom." He believed in his idea and was willing to face ridicule and punishment to make it a reality. I'm sure his ego was not happy about that. Here then is a final suggestion to consider when dealing with subconscious anger. As you take a look at the thinking behind this anger, you may find the ego's agenda. Oftentimes, ego desire will only diminish when the pain is too much to bear and the consequences interfere with the maintenance of the overall agenda. In other words, from an ego perspective, when there is more pain than overall gain, you will consider change. In that case, when you recognize subconscious ego expectation, do not hold out, and do not waste your time; change the expectation.

Conscious Anger

By this point, you probably know what anger is, where it comes from, and who is responsible for it. Also, you probably know when you are mad. You would have just perceived something in your environment, or in your daydreaming that prompted you to think that something was not going your way. Then you noticed that certain feeling in your chest or stomach that occurs along with the acceleration of your heart rate or breathing. You might even be able to specifically identify the expectation that was not met. The effective management of anger will be thoroughly discussed in Chapter 13.

Sandy walked into my office early on a Monday morning looking as if she had just stepped off of a long roller coaster ride. Almost immediately, as she took a seat across from me, the tears began to flow. "I think my husband is going to leave me, or maybe I'm going to leave him, it's confusing. I've never been so depressed. I always thought that at 45 years old I would have my life pretty much together. But something has gone wrong." This was Sandy's second marriage. She and Dan met on the golf course, and after a whirlwind romance, married within a year's time. The first few years had gone well for them, "Dan and I have always been real active. I loved to work out at the gym, run, play golf, and I have usually been able to stay in pretty good shape. It all changed about two years ago. At work I was given a special project which required me to work about two extra hours a day. For the next few months, I wasn't able to do any of my usual activities. During that time, I gained some weight, about twenty-five pounds, and I had to hear about how Dan kept our regular active routine without me. Over time, I became pretty angry about the whole thing with my weight gain and Dan's disinterest in me." Sandy started to drink a few more glasses of wine with dinner, and in a matter of a year, it would not be uncommon for her to finish the bottle before bedtime. "I just don't know how to deal with this. I am so angry about how I look, so to feel better I don't know what else to do but comfort myself with my glass of wine. We started to fight more. Usually it was over the stupidest things. And now he won't talk to me. It's like I've lost all control in my life." Sandy continued to discuss how she has begun to hide money in a bank account that Dan is unaware of, "After my first divorce, I got taken to the financial cleaners, I won't let that happen again. I do have a right to protect myself don't I? The problem is that I really feel guilty about it. I just don't know if it's right for me to do that to him. After all, it's our marriage and our money but I am just so scared and angry. Here's the strange thing, I now have more time to resume the active life that I used to love, but I'm so angry that I don't want to now. I hate to admit it, but I seem to get something out of the idea that I don't have to, and fight against it especially if Dan really wants me to. I think I'm a good person, but I just don't understand these choices I'm making."

There are four well-known and established basic styles of dealing with anger that I believe deserve a reference at this point. Because there is already much written about these styles, I'm only going to give my own brief definitions, for the purpose of referring to them as needed, for the duration of this book. These styles are helpful in understanding some basic human behavior. You may determine that you routinely act in one of the four styles, although your style might differ from one environment to another, and from one person to another. The four styles are: passive, aggressive, passive-aggressive, and assertive. Each of these styles describe the manner in which an individual would relate to self, others, and the world.

The **passive individual** has fears about how to relate to self, others, and the world. They fear rejection from others and have a poor self-image. When other people do not behave in a manner in which the want, they discount any idea about asking for change. When things do not go the way they want them to, they accept the situation even if they want things to be different. They avoid conflict with others, and quickly succumb to the wishes of others. They view their rights as secondary to the rights of others. They generally attempt to communicate with others in a very pleasing way so as to win them over, subconsciously attempting to gain approval and acceptance. They relate primarily to the feelings of sadness, guilt, and fear. They regularly utilize ego maintenance strategies to reduce or eliminate anger.

The **aggressive individual** relates to self, others, and the world in a demanding and sometimes harsh manner. They may experience a subconscious anger of the world in general, including a lack of trust in people or things. When others do not behave in a manner in which they want, aggressive individuals rely on methods of power, control, and coercion to cause change. When things do not go the way they want them to, aggressive individuals attempt to force their way upon the thing or situation. They approach conflict with others eagerly as they see the conflict as an opportunity to gain power and control. The rights of self will generally take precedence over others. They attempt to communicate to others in an intimidating and forceful style that lets others know that they will not be taken advantage of and that they are ultimately right about most issues. Subconsciously, they fearfully perceive anyone else's differing viewpoint as a potential threat to their own belief system. They relate primarily to the feelings of mad and fear. They regularly utilize ego maintenance strategies to reduce or eliminate sadness and guilt.

The **passive-aggressive individual** relates to self, others, and the world in a dual anger/fear-based manner. When others do not behave as they wish, passive-aggressive individuals respond with an initial façade of cooperation, and then later do as they choose. When things do not go the way they want them to, they engage in developing a strategy to covertly leverage for what they want. They take action with or without the other person's participation. They approach conflict with caution, distrust, and with the objective of appearing sincere enough so that that they will eventually have things go their way. The question of rights is a not an issue; the only thing that matters is if the manipulation works or not. Subconsciously, passive-aggressive individuals perceive the world with a great deal of suspicion, where survival is based on the ability to effectively manipulate their way to the top. They relate primarily to the feelings of mad and fear. They regularly utilize ego maintenance strategies to reduce or eliminate sadness and guilt.

The **assertive individual** has a positive relationship to self, others, and the world. They respond to people in a realistic, reasonable, and relationally fair manner, and adjust their expectations as needed. When things are not going the way they want them to, assertive individuals assess the situation and apply the *expectation test*. Assertive individuals approach conflict with an expectation that it is a part of life and relationships. The desired outcome to conflict would respect the needs, wants, rights, and responsibilities of all involved. They attempt to communicate their thoughts and feelings with others in a respectful manner. To the best of their ability, they relate to, and process feelings on all levels of consciousness with the intent to create and maintain their own integrity (peace of mind). They avoid use of ego maintenance strategies to reduce or eliminate feelings. The assertive individual might consciously establish the following beliefs in relation to anger:

- ➢ Things (self, others, world) will not always go my way.
- ➢ Maintain a functional anger style (see Chapter 8).
- ➢ Expect that loss will be a part of life.
- ➢ Compromise can feel good.
- ➢ Practice patience to learn its value.
- ➢ There is value in assertiveness.
- ➢ Expect assertiveness from myself, and request it from others.

➢ With time and practice, "I am assertive."

➢ I can't get what I want unless I ask for it.

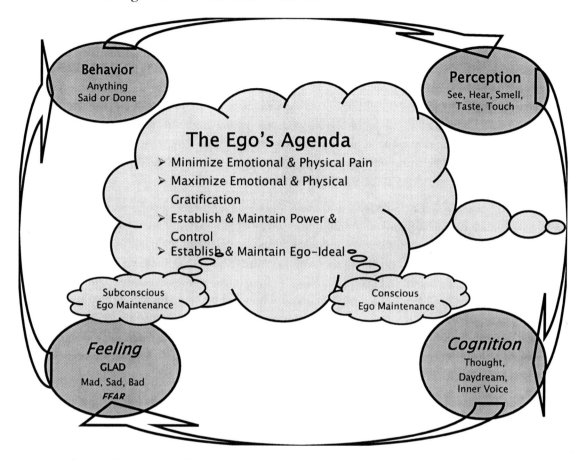

So why do we do it?

Why *do* good people make bad choices, not just once, but perhaps habitually? It would appear that we can engage in self-deception with expert precision when it comes to matters of overeating, under-exercising, smoking, excessive drinking of alcohol, use of illicit drugs, gambling, and sexual excesses. Are we really fooling ourselves? Why do we seem to voluntarily participate in the agenda of the ego?

1. It begins with a desire to get rid of pain as soon as possible, and feel good as soon as possible. There is a tendency to maintain a perceptual focus on what feels good in the here and the now. We experience an ongoing awareness of the physical and emotional sensations that occur in our bodies. As stated earlier, the ego is very accurate in knowing what feels good to

you because it has the advantage of knowing your physical reality. It knows what you like factually; it knows on a very clear and direct level what feels good and what feels bad in the present moment and urges you accordingly.

2. We like to have things go our way. When we manage to effectively get our way, we become gratified by it, tend to repeat it, and attempt to establish a control of the outcome. We like predictability. There is no doubt at all in my mind that if I start eating a bag of chips that I will enjoy the taste. There is no doubt about the good taste of some foods. There is no doubt that the first puff of a cigarette will feel good to a smoker. There is no doubt that the orgasm will feel good. These are highly predictable, and very gratifying experiences that the ego has accurate and specific knowledge of. We know these things to be immediately gratifying, readily available, and with some things to some extent even socially acceptable. We identify with what feels good, and then we tend to repeat it.

3. Once you discover ego-based gratification, and fool yourself into repeating it, you may further entrench the behavior by building it into your belief system. You will come to value the behavior, establish rules to support it, expect yourself to behave in that way, and eventually identify with the behavior. Over time, and with continued ego-maintenance, you will look for others and the world to support your behavior. "I love coffee, at least I don't drink it after six o'clock, it's what I have done, currently do, and will most likely continue doing, and, I am a coffee drinker, can you please make me a pot of coffee darling?" "I love chocolate, it's ok to eat once in a while, it doesn't hurt anyone, it's what I love to eat, and, I am a chocolate eater, can you pick me up so chocolate while you're at the store darling?" A positive response to these requests would be music to the ego's ear.

4. We like to have people do things our way. With certain feel-good behaviors or experiences, you may depend on another person to be able to experience the gratification. To the extent that there is other involvement in your ego-based behavior, it appears to be further justified. Other involvement may include people such as the drug dealer, the pornography dealer, the gratuitous sex partner, the casino, the approving parental figure, or the person you live with. When we find a way to effectively get them to do things our way, we become gratified by the shared experiences, tend to repeat involving them, and attempt to establish a control over their participation. Essentially, when something feels good, we look for support in repeating it, and hope to maintain it.

5. We like external power. It's good to be the king or the queen. External power can bring many pleasures. Money is often equated with power. Money can bring many pleasures. Without a doubt, there will be competition for power. Being at the top of the hill often means however that there will be attempts to knock you off. Still, we keep on climbing. Power is a key component in maintaining the agenda of the ego. However fleeting it may be, once on the top, we remember the experience, and want to get back there.

6. We like idealization. Ask the rock star, the movie star, the sports star, the business tycoon, or the lotto winner, "Is life good?" On the other hand, how many of those individuals are unable to maintain that lifestyle and run into eventual significant legal, financial, health, or marital problems? If you follow its agenda, the ego makes you a promise to create an idealized you, in an idealized situation. The question is, can it really come through on that promise?

7. We get drawn into ego maintenance. With ego maintenance, we deny the potentially painful outcomes of bad choices. We make questionable choices appear magically acceptable through creative thinking or rationalizations. We blame the negative consequences of our choices on others. Essentially, it would seem that the more physically and emotionally gratifying something is for you, the more likely you will engage in fooling yourself, or participate in ego maintenance, in order to pursue it.

8. We lack an alternative to the agenda. The ego's agenda is the default program selected for survival, problem solving and living. You will tend to participate in the agenda to the extent that you have not consciously developed a set of guidelines for running your life. You will tend to go with ego maintenance if you don't have a method of dealing with painful feelings associated with the pressures and stresses of life.

Indeed, we do make some bad choices. We like feeling good in the here and now and tend to focus on *that*. We attempt to establish control or predictability with *that*. We get others to help us feel good, get control over *that*, and continue to seek out *that*. So, maybe now it's easy to see why we actually seem to fool ourselves when it comes to voluntarily participating in the agenda of the ego. That's right, we do volunteer! Make no mistake about it, your ego is a powerful voice with an agenda that will be heard, and you will be compelled to listen as this expert motivator speaks to you with a promise of what will be good. No matter how convincing that voice may be however, volunteering to participate still remains a choice.

Your ego knows your *body* well. In order to compete with that kind of knowledge, you will need to establish your own *body* of knowledge. This other *body* becomes part of the solution to the ego. This other *body* is one that you create consciously. This other *body* is your belief system. It is in *Your Own Best Interest* to live your life according to its agenda.

Exercise 6-2: Describe your common patterns of anger and make the appropriate entries in appendix F.

> Where the ego is the problem,
> the belief system is the solution.

Part 2. THE SOLUTION

7 Going Beyond Ego

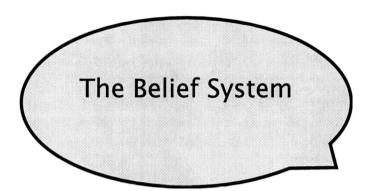

The Belief System

Creating the *Good* Choice

Surely you recall from the first chapter that Mr. Dross did not like the spitball incident. The board of education lying on his desk made that abundantly clear to me. On that day, the board was not the motivator of change, Mr. Dross was.

"There won't be any paddle used in this office today," Mr. Dross remarked calmly and took a seat at his desk. "Instead, I'm going to tell you a story. When I was about your age, I was having some problems in making good choices. My father said to me, 'Son, you have got to start doing what's right for yourself. You need to start making different choices, or life's gonna get hard for you.' So I asked him, 'Pop, how do I do that?' 'It's like this son, let's say you keep all your favorite tools in the bottom drawer of your tool chest. One day, you have a problem that needs fixed, so you go to your tools. When you get there, you find out they got exposed to water, got all rusted out, and they don't work well anymore. If you use them now, they might make the problem worse. Those rusted tools are like your old bad choices.'"

"'If you decide to throw them out, you're going to need some new tools. And, you're going to need to put the new tools in a different drawer, let's say the top drawer. Those new tools are like your new good choices. The problem will be, for a while, whenever you have a problem and need a tool, you're most likely going to look to that bottom drawer out of habit. That may be a hard habit to break.'"

"'Here's how you can help yourself. Make sure that the top drawer has some new tools. Be sure that those new tools will get the job done right. And then, make sure that you throw those old ones out. Because if you think those old tools might still work, when you have a problem to fix, you'll go looking for them. If you do, you need to find that bottom drawer empty. After you find that drawer empty several times, you won't go looking there anymore, you'll start going to the top drawer, and that will be your new habit. With time and good experiences, you'll trust that new habit.'"

Mr. Dross then fixed his gaze toward my friend, and then looked at me right in the eyes like he was drilling a path right into my head, "Boys, it's time to put those old tools away, get some new tools, and make some different choices. Now let's get you guys off to your classroom."

Maybe Mr. Dross wasn't so bad after all. Perhaps what I had seen as tough, strict, and unforgiving were actually characteristics of confidence, fairness, and consistency. It wasn't too long after that day that I developed an interest in reading about sports heroes in the library and my spitball days were over.

YOBI

"Do the right thing." Many years ago, in my beginning years as a therapist, I borrowed this mantra from popular culture as a way of establishing a direction for clients who were stuck in a moral dilemma. When they were facing a difficult decision and contemplating a course of action, the conclusion we came to would often be, "Of course, I just need to do the right thing." But that conclusion sometimes, if not always, produced another dilemma, "Hmm…well, what is the right thing?" Nowadays, (the seasoned professional that I am) I know that when you consciously establish a belief system, these moral dilemmas are much easier to resolve. In other words, when you have consciously established your values and morals, difficult decisions become less difficult! Moreover, you will then have established what you know to be in *Your Own Best Interest*.

> *Your Own Best Interest* refers to thinking and behaving in ways that represent your own consciously established belief system. Integrity and peace of mind are outcomes of this *YOBI* based behavior.

So, what is *Your Own Best Interest* or *YOBI*? In order for you to answer that question, you must already have made a conscious determination of what is important to you. In other words, you would have already determined your values, and established a priority to them. Then, you'll have a better sense of your moral code. Your moral code would reflect your values. You would know it is better to go run rather than to lie on the couch, eat chips, slam-down diet soda, and watch an episode of some sitcom from the 80's. You run because good health is more important to you than instant gratification. The "right thing to do" has been established by you, but that doesn't always make it an easy thing to do.

There are different levels of magnitude with regard to your beliefs about yourself, others, and the world. These beliefs range in magnitude from trivial matters to those that deal with "the big picture." Big picture beliefs are given to us, and/or they are established after we ask and then answer some big questions about life. Big picture life questions include: "How and/or why are we here [on this planet]?" "What is the purpose of life and/or my ultimate purpose?" "Why do 'good' things or 'bad' things happen to people?" Once these questions are asked, and then answers are sought out or concluded, we begin to form expectations of ourselves, other people, and the world. Therefore, how we answer these questions is critical. The answers form the basis for how we eventually deal with emotional pain, and obviously can have a huge impact on all components of your belief system. Determining what is in *YOBI* at any time will depend on your answers to these big picture questions.

As you consciously establish a belief system, you will likely have an overall objective, outcome, goal, or achievement in mind—an "ultimate purpose" if you will. Many people have presumed to identify for us what this overall objective should be, or, what we should be striving for ultimately. Here are some examples of the "ultimate purpose": enlightenment, Christ Consciousness, self-realization, nirvana, individuation, self-actualization, going to heaven, peace of mind. The "ultimate purpose" has also been defined as: rich, famous, king, queen, ultimate fighting machine, diva, whoever-has-the-most-toys-at-the-end-wins, Oscar winner, thin, salesperson of the year, Superbowl champions, most-notches-on-the-bedpost, retirement at fifty. Just go to the self-help or business section of any bookstore to find other examples of the "ultimate purpose."

What do you want? What is important to you? What do you seek? Obviously, each person will have their own variety of responses. No matter what you wish to call your "ultimate purpose," it conceptually describes the ultimate of what you want for yourself, and functions as a compass for your life direction. If you have one, it gives a clear, or clear*er* understanding of *Your Own Best Interest*.

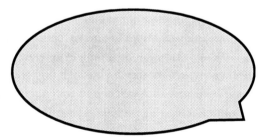

The Belief System

Ultimately, the goal of the brain is to maintain the body. It does this instinctually. One of its jobs is to help you make sense of your experiences, and create meaningful connections between what you already know, what is happening, and what may happen. It naturally organizes this information in such a way to bring meaning to what is going on around you. Just imagine the work that your brain does in your infancy to organize and conceptualize all the new things you experience. Another of its jobs is to monitor the needs and wants of your body and then signal you to maintain them at a satisfactory level. Your ego develops as you follow an instinctual agenda for taking care of those needs and wants. As time goes on, you may come to a conscious conclusion that the ego's agenda no longer works for you. Gradually, you make conscious choices about how to live life. You develop more effective and perhaps creative ways of getting your needs and wants met. In other words, you are born into this world with an instinctual brain, your ego follows, and then your belief system develops by way of your experiences.

Transition from ego agenda to belief system living is gradual. How and at what age this development begins can vary from one person to the next depending in biological and environmental factors. A belief system can appear to be unchanging for some individuals. For others, there is a dynamic quality to it that undergoes constant adjustment and realignment in response to an ever-changing external reality.

Everyone has a unique belief system. It is like a psychological fingerprint, given that no one else has one just exactly like yours. Like the ego, the belief system is obviously conceptual. It would not be possible to do brain surgery and physically locate your belief system. However, rest assured that conceptually, we all have one, and it is the driving force behind a large part of our behavior. An examination of a person's unique belief system gives us important clues in understanding their cycle-logical functioning. It tells us why some people like to go to scary movies, and some avoid them. It also tells us why some people lie, and others are truthful and honest.

Your belief system operates on a subconscious level of awareness. That is, you are probably not consciously thinking about the values of earning a living and maintaining employment when you are getting ready to go to work. You are just getting ready, and maybe worried about how to deal with your new boss or rush hour traffic. You are probably not fully aware of why you are angry with your spouse for not folding the laundry "like they should"; you just know you are angry. Although often the reasons (and solutions) for your worry and anger are beneath the level of conscious awareness, this information is accessible to you with the right approach.

We naturally establish a memory for what we experience perceptually. The memories of our experiences are necessary to help us to survive by allowing us to predict the future and attempt to establish control over our environment. As we perceive, and memories are established, our brain stores these memories in categories, which eventually become belief categories. This categorization is a very efficient method of maintenance. This tendency to store memories in categories is also why we engage in prejudice, or pre-judging. We have pre-established beliefs about things, people or situations that we then apply to new experiences on the basis of certain perceptual factors. For example, let's say I'm a caveman living near a jungle many thousands of years ago. I determine that berries are good to eat. I eat some green berries and I get sick. My memory now tells me that green berries are not good for me. The next time I encounter green berries, I avoid eating them (or give them to my enemy to eat). One reason that our feelings are so important is because of the role they play in "marking" or "tagging" certain memories on the basis of their importance to our survival. While walking in the jungle one day I encounter a tiger. It chases me, I manage to climb up a tree, but it bites off my toe. I am going to establish a strong aversion to the tiger. The memories will be emotionally tagged with fear (and physical pain) to assist me in remembering. My tiger experience illustrates the sequence and connection of the elements of cycle-logical functioning, from perception through behavior, and their relevance to survival. Moreover, there is an equal and opposite reaction quality to this feature of the brain; the more important the brain perceives the memory to be for our potential to survive, the more intensely it "tags" the memory. Thus, when I perceive a different animal that looks like a tiger, I think, "An animal that looks very much like that bit off my toe last time." A feeling of fear is produced, and I yell and run in the other direction as fast as I can, or grab a spear. Perhaps the ego's agenda isn't so bad after all. Indeed not, until taken to extremes.

Once we begin to establish certain beliefs, we engage in an ongoing process of determining the validity, or truth, of the belief. "That tiger bite off my toe, I wonder if all tigers bite?" In other words, we automatically begin to notice, on all levels of awareness, any pertinent information that will help us to substantiate our beliefs or discredit them. We are biologically predisposed toward finding evidence to support our belief systems. We cannot turn off this mechanism, nor would we generally want to. As time goes on, the more aggressive tigers I encounter, the more I am convinced that they are all dangerous. I can then establish controls to maintain my own safety, and the safety of others. Our survival is based on this ability to perceive, "tag," categorize, and remember. Perhaps the ego's agenda really isn't so bad after all. Indeed not, until controls are taken to extremes.

As we solidly establish beliefs, we begin to perceive the world in our own unique way. To some degree, our perception of the outside world is simply a model of our inner world. If I believe that the world is a dangerous place, I will see danger lurking around every corner. I will cognitively "tag" every six o'clock news story of violence as proving my theory. I will think, "Another carjacking, I knew it, there is a world full of danger out there." Out of fearful feelings, my behavior will be to stay at home more often, and buy a weapon to protect me. If my inner world (belief system) becomes my outer world, it would be to my advantage to have a belief system that is closely aligned with basic reality. It would be a bonus to have a joyful inner world.

Your belief system should help you to produce a life that you want. If you are not producing the life you want, then something is wrong with your belief system, not the world you live in. If every time you go on a date with someone, the date turns out to be awful, maybe it's not the date's fault. Maybe it's the way that you choose dates. To continue dating as usual will most likely not produce a different result. Choosing future dates by a different standard might. The physical world is operating within a set of predictable rules. These rules of physical reality do not change. When things aren't going right, and when we have made all of the changes we can in the outer world, inner world change (or resolution) may be required. In other words, to experience integrity, peace of mind, or whatever it is that we seek in this life, we need to consciously establish and/or adjust our inner belief system and then make any related cycle-logical functioning changes.

I have identified four key components that make up a belief system that we will now examine in order of their relative usefulness for problem solving. These components are: values, morals, expectations, and self-image. An understanding of your belief system is an essential step in developing the peace of mind that goes with integrity.

Exercise 7-1: What are your "big picture beliefs?" Although it is not necessary to have clearly established them for yourself, if you have a sense of them, your YOBI Profile would honor them. Write down your "big picture beliefs" in Appendix F where appropriate.

8 Belief System Components

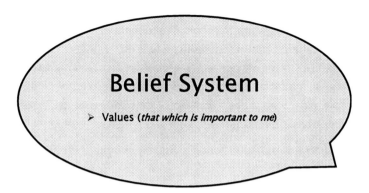

Belief System

➤ Values (*that which is important to me*)

Values

Make a list of everything that's important to you. Also write down what you regularly spend your time doing. Those items on your list—those are your values.

Your belief system includes a values component, which is representative of your beliefs about what is important to you. Your values include things, ideas, and concepts; both tangibles and intangibles. Some common values are: family, job, a hobby, spouse, money, honesty, boat, freedom, house, health, appearance, food, sex, security, fun, reading, children, sports, television, service, charity, etc. This list of potential values could go on for many pages. Values are unique to each person and are developed over the course of a lifetime based on unique experiences. Each item on your own values list has a relative position of importance. That is, some things or ideas are more important to you than others. When something is high up on your list, you will likely spend your time and energy engaged in that valued behavior.

At any given moment, we perceive with our senses what is going on around us. While there may be a massive amount of information available in some environments, we can only attend to and process a small part of it. Therefore, we focus on a small part of what we see. Most likely the points of our attention are a reflection of what we value, and therefore, what we think we want and need. Because of the ego's agenda, we attend to what we believe will bring us the most pleasure and least pain. So we tend to fixate on those things that are pleasurable or gratifying. As some men stroll along inside their local shopping mall, they are gratified as they watch all of the attractive women that enter into their perceptual field. For other men, mall strolling gratification is obtained by visiting every fast food establishment and sporting goods shop available. Then again, other men value not going to the mall at all.

A good indication of your values is seen in your daily behavior. How do you spend your time? What you do is apparently important to you. Indeed, you may be doing things that you aren't necessarily proud of. You may be engaging an addiction such as sex, gambling, or food. You might just spend lots of time on the couch eating cookies and drinking wine. Ego maintenance might say that relaxing and eating are both important to you, and are included in your values. Fortunately, your values are not etched in stone. You have the capacity to make changes in your values, which would have an important impact on your behavior. Like most people, you probably engage in an assortment of activities that are both in your best interest and not in your best interest.

There are some common basic values among people. Some are clearly vital to your physical and psychological survival, like eating food. While the origins of some of your values are instinctual, they can be pursued excessively for the purpose of pure enjoyment. For example, producing offspring is collectively required for the continuation of the human race; recreational sex has no survival value. Eating food with basic nutritional content is necessary for living; consuming eight plates of food at the all-you-can-eat-buffet is gratuitous.

An individual's values are influenced in some part by what society deems important. Advertising on television, radio, Internet, billboards, and magazines gives us powerful messages about what should be important. We can see an indication of societal values in what most people spend their money on: cars, houses, cell phones, clothes, fast food, etc. We also see the values of the masses in the content of what we seek out for entertainment: music, competition, reality TV, sporting events with violence, sex as power, movie star lifestyle, fashion model appearance, news, drama, action, etc. In the event that you have bought into societal values, you will likely see yourself spending your time, energy, and money in pursuit of those objects of importance. Is that what you really want to spend your time, energy and money on? Have you thought it through lately? Maybe as members of society, we have been brainwashed into believing that these objects are the only things worthy of pursuit. Is that really so? Is it time to consciously reconsider what is important to you as an individual? If you want to change your life in some way, you will very likely need to change what is important to you.

Here is a useful rule that will be brought out in later parts of this book; you cannot value something until you find value in it! This is a simple, yet essential concept to consider when attempting to make belief system changes. It is no accident that values come first in order of the belief system components. You are much less likely to engage in any change unless you have first found some kind value for yourself in the change. Moreover, no one else can truly tell you what should be important to you.

There are questions you need to answer with regard to creating or changing your values. For example, I'm thinking about reducing the amount of television I watch, and starting an exercise program. "Why is this important to me?" "What's in it for me?" "What's my motivation?" You must consciously identify specific value in the change you want to make in order to have a successful outcome. You can learn more about developing values in the next chapter.

Oftentimes, decisions are difficult to make because of a values conflict. That is, your values compete with each other for attention and/or gratification, which can create an inner conflict. After a tough day at the office, I want to go for a run because I really like running for stress reduction. However, I also love to relax on the couch with a snack and a beer. Those are both important to me; I like them, or value them, both. Given the opportunity to engage in both simultaneously, I would. However, they are mutually exclusive activities. So I must choose. Clearly I have a conflict of values. Thank goodness the run almost always wins out or I would be shopping at a different type of men's clothing store. Obviously, many values conflicts are not this clearly distinguished and perhaps involve more than two values in debate. As they remain unresolved, such conflicts can produce vast amounts of anxiety, guilt, and frustration. In the end, one must prioritize and choose, or creatively combine. Resolving inner conflicts in this manner will help you to consciously establish standards of behavior—the result is your moral code.

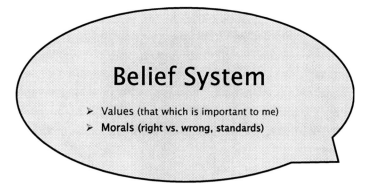

The Moral Code

The morals component of your belief system is representative of your beliefs about right and wrong, good and bad, fair and unfair. Essentially, morals refer to an individual's rules about the right and wrong way to live. These rules are sometimes referred to as a person's standards, ethics, code of conduct, or their conscience. Cartoons have depicted the moral code as Jiminy Cricket, or an angel sitting on your shoulder debating with the devil. Sigmund Freud referred to it as an element of the superego. These moral ideas represent your conclusions about concepts such as: honesty, behavior in relationships, abortion, capital punishment, etc. The sum total of your moral beliefs will be referred to as your moral mode. As with values, morals are unique to each individual and are developed over the course of a lifetime based upon unique experiences.

Although a moral code is initially established in childhood, there may be major transformations in adolescence or adulthood as we encounter and are influenced by a variety of people and situations. The most likely major code contributors would include: parents, grandparents and other extended family, teachers, schools, religions, organized sports, military experiences, employers, mentors, and religious persons or icons. The morals component of a belief system is not necessarily religiously or politically based. In fact, an individual's moral code may have nothing to do with organized religion or politics. On the other hand, it may be based exclusively on an organized religion or other external organization. The moral code is simply your set of rules, your established standards for living.

As with values, each item on our own moral code list has a relative position of importance. That is, some moral issues are more important to us than others. Also, as with values, we can experience a **morals conflict**. This occurs when you are facing a situation where you must make a decision, yet your moral code is telling you two different directions to take for two good, but conflicting reasons. The conflict continues as long as the moral principles are equally or closely valued. For example, you are up for a job promotion that would require you to move two hundred miles to a different state. This would be a great opportunity for you and your family. However, your parents are getting older, and you are the only child. They will undoubtedly need your assistance in the next few years. That is a moral conflict. A good friend that you also work with begins having a couple of glasses of wine during the lunch hour on a regular basis. You have discussed your concerns with him about drinking, but he only responds that he will eventually stop. Later, the boss asks you about your friend, sensing that there may be trouble, and asks you what you know. That is a moral conflict.

A clear indication of an individual's moral code can be noted when a they make statements that include words such as "right, wrong, good, bad, fair, unfair." For example, "Its not right to enable someone to keep drinking." "Its not fair to us that she comes to work late every day like she does." "It's not right to abandon your family when they are going to need you." Or, "You're right, I should have called you when I knew I was going to be an hour late." Here are some examples of common moral beliefs:

> ➤ Tell the truth, do not lie.

> ➤ Do not steal.

> ➤ Do not cause another person intentional physical or emotional harm.

> ➤ Treat others like you want to be treated.

> ➢ Work hard.

> ➢ Be nice to others.

> ➢ Follow the rules.

> ➢ Exercise.

> ➢ Give to the less fortunate.

> ➢ Do not cheat.

There is a direct connection from the feeling of guilt to the morals component of your belief system. That is, when your behavior or thinking is in conflict with an aspect of your own moral code, you will expect to feel guilt on some level of awareness. If not, you are probably experiencing the effects of ego maintenance, which enables you to behave in a way that you know is not right or good for you. This tendency toward ego maintenance is part of the human condition; to override our own moral beliefs and overdo what is gratifying to us.

It has been my experience that there are two major types of thinking or processing styles. First there are concrete thinkers who see and process information according to categories. In contrast, abstract thinkers see things in shades of gray and analyze information. Concrete thinkers tend to rely greatly on a firmly established moral code to assist them in making decisions. Abstract thinkers tend to struggle and analyze issues to arrive at a conclusion and use their moral code as a set of flexible guidelines to think within. There is not necessarily a right or wrong way to process information to arrive at a conclusion. Indeed, there is perhaps a time and place for each style. For example, when deciding on a career path or a car to purchase, one would want to carefully analyze the information and maybe struggle a bit with their morals and values. One would not however want to struggle with a decision on whether to purchase the 39 cent can of tomato sauce versus the 43 cent can for very long, or with very much moral deliberation.

Belief System

> ➢ Values (that which is important to me)
> ➢ Morals (right vs. wrong, standards)
> ➢ **Expectations of Self, Others, World**

Expectations

The expectations component of your belief system is representative of your beliefs about what you expect from yourself, other people, and the world around you. We expect ourselves to behave in certain ways. We expect others to behave in certain ways. We expect the world around us to operate in a certain way. We all have expectations of how things should be. Again, having expectations is unavoidable and is a vital aspect of our natural inclination to attempt to predict the future and to attempt to exert control over our environment.

There is a clear and direct connection from the feeling of anger to expectation. Essentially then, when you are angry you can trace the feeling back to the some unmet ego-based expectation, or to a consciously established expectation of your belief system. If you become angry with your neighbor because they are playing loud music at midnight, the origin of your anger can be found in your belief system expectations, "People shouldn't play music so loud at this time of day," or ego-based thoughts such as, "That jerk should respect me more than that, who does he think he is, I'll teach him a lesson that will fix him."

A good indication of an individual's expectations can be noted when they make statements including words such as "should, have to, must, expect, and could." For example, "I should have studied harder for that test." "I can't believe that my wife did that, she should really know better." "You should not have yelled at me because of such a minor thing." "Do you suppose you could leave the cap on the toothpaste next time?" "This weather is not cooperating with our plans like I hoped it would." "The damn flooding ruined our basement, I should have better luck than this."

As previously mentioned, we naturally establish memories related to what we perceive to be important. Those past memories become part of our expectations for the future. They are necessary to help us to survive by allowing us to predict and maintain control. If through my experiences I come to expect that green berries will make me sick, and that a tiger can bite me, I can avoid these dangers and will have a better change of making it to the next day. It is when expectations are not consistent with your experience of reality, but stubbornly maintained anyway, that they can become problematic. Let's say that my expectation is, "I should be able to drive to work every day without any complication arising from my fellow motorists." *Reality says* that I will probably encounter some inexperienced or uncaring drivers at least on some days. Consequently, I will more than likely experience anger on a regular basis as I drive to work. In that case, my choices would include: change the expectation to something real, maintain the expectation and continue to be angry, or creatively change the situation perhaps by changing my route, or working at home.

Belief System

> ➢ Values (*that which is important to me*)
> ➢ Morals (*right vs. wrong, standards*)
> ➢ Expectations of Self, Others, World
> ➢ Self–Image (*I am...*)

Self–Image

The self-image component of your belief system is representative of your beliefs about who you are. Self-image is revealed in "I am…" statements. Some example self-image statements are:

➢ I am smart.

➢ I am a loser.

➢ I am attractive.

➢ I am boring.

➢ I am a good friend.

➢ I am weak.

➢ I am resourceful.

➢ I am inferior.

Obviously, these statements can be self-esteem boosters when positive, or self-esteem busters when negative. In order to have high self-esteem, you must identify or develop positives in your "I am…" statements. Moreover, you would want to experience a sense of being generally proud of yourself. Being proud is different than experiencing pride. Pride is related to ego: protecting it, expanding it, growing it, and maintaining it. Being proud on the other hand, is very different and may even be related to selflessness, or the opposite of ego enhancements. To be proud is a form of self-recognition that you are behaving in accordance with your moral code. For example, if your moral code tells you that it is good to give of yourself, you will be proud when you do so. Suffice it to say that having a positive self-image will greatly contribute to the maintenance of a high self-esteem.

Over the course of your life, you are continually monitoring your own thoughts, feelings, and behaviors on all levels of awareness. Self-image is formed by way of these observations of yourself. It is also influenced by the feedback that you receive from others. Ultimately however, (as an adult) self-image is for you to establish and maintain. This can be accomplished by the following method of transformation which I will now summarize and expand on with greater detail in subsequent chapters. The steps are as follows:

1. Clearly establish your own values.

2. Clearly establish guiding rules (morals) about how to behave in accordance with those values.

3. Have reasonable expectations that you will behave in accordance with your values and morals, but that others may or may not.

4. Begin to observe yourself behaving in accordance with your values and morals, resulting in a transformed sense of who you are.

If you believe that you are already behaving according to your own values and morals but still don't feel good about yourself, you may want to do some self-image troubleshooting. In other words, re-examine the following:

1. Clearly examine your values to be sure they are your own and/or truly important to you. In other words, are you living according to someone else's values that do not work for you?

2. Determine if you are generally following a reasonable moral code developed by you.

3. Make sure that your expectations for following your morals are not too high or too low. In other words, are your expectations realistic, reasonable, and fair?

4. Give yourself credit for the positive elements of your behavior. Expect that you cannot be perfect.

5. Develop values that would result in a self-image of your choice.

6. More carefully evaluate the feedback from other people and your environment, making sure that you are attending to not only the negative, but the positive as well.

7. Consider the source of the above feedback. In other words, are you involved in struggles over power and control? If so, there may be high amounts of unwarranted negative feedback toward you.

The next three chapters will provide you with a method for establishing a belief system, including self-image, based in conscious choice. Chapters 12 through 17 will provide further support by giving you specific tools for the management of feelings that may interfere with living according to your belief system. Together, these chapters become *The Method* by which you begin to overcome the powerful influence of the ego's agenda, and begin to experience peace of mind, and the joy of integrity. Living your life according to a consciously established belief system is the solution to many emotional, behavioral, and relational problems.

Still, there is ego. Perhaps the most challenging obstacle standing in the way of your integrity is ego-generated emotion. If you choose to maintain a perspective of YOBI, then you will want to choose a functional method of dealing with emotion, especially anger.

A Choice of Perspective

As compared to the other basic emotions, mad or anger is clearly an emotion of change. "Things aren't going in a way that I want them to—I want this to change." Although anger oftentimes gets a bad rap, there is nothing inherently bad about it. The purpose of any anger related feeling is simply to alert you that something is not happening in a way consistent with your expectations. This alert is very practical. You are naturally equipped with a built-in device to prepare you for the possibility that you may need to take some kind of action.

"I can't believe I just ate that entire half-gallon of ice cream, I must be an idiot."

"My boss is always picking on me, this has got to stop."

"My mother can't seem to mind her own business, now I'm going to confront her on this."

"This traffic is making me crazy, I can't go through this every day."

"My husband won't ever help me around the house, who does he think I am."

"I can't seem to keep to a regular exercise program, something's got to change."

"He never wants to have sex when I want to, this is so wrong."

There is no doubt that for many of us, anger is an uncomfortable feeling. However, unless you can rid yourself of all expectation, you will continue to experience periodic anger. So for those of us who are not practicing monks, we might as well get used to it, and deal with it efficiently. Correcting the popular notion that anger is bad would be a good starting point. I prefer to describe a person's response to anger as either functional, or *dys*functional. When I perceive, think, and then feel anger, "What an idiot, I can't believe that guy just pulled out in front of me like that," there may be resulting behavior. How I respond to this external situation (driver) will depend on my perspective. To the extent that I function from my belief system, the behavior will be produced functionally, "Oh well, I can't expect that everyone will drive like saints, I guess I'll move to a different lane." To the extent that I function from my ego, I am more likely generate a dysfunctional response, "I'm going to chase that idiot down and teach him a lesson about driving with respect." A *dys*functional response to anger would generally involve one or more of the following choices:

1.   Attempt to force what you want on the situation or person—aggressive.

2.   Fearfully ignore or deny your anger—passive.

3.   Pretend you are not angry, and later on, covertly force what you want on the situation or person; engage in manipulation—passive-aggressive.

Simply put, a functional response to anger involves a process of conscious problem solving. It involves the following conscious steps:

1.   Identifying the internal feeling of anger when it happens.

2.   Identify further that, "Things are not apparently going in a way that I want them to."

3.   Specifically identify, "What was not going my way?"

4.   Specifically identify a preferred outcome, "What is it that I would want or need instead?"

5.   Evaluate the outcome with the *expectation test*: "Is what I want…"

    a.   Realistic, given the circumstances of this situation?

    b.   Reasonable, given the circumstances of this situation?

    c.   Relationally fair, given the circumstances of this situation?

    d.   Relatively important enough to pursue with respect to my belief system?

6.   Taking action, as necessary, that shows consistency with your belief system.

The functional response to anger fits very well with the choice to perceive life from a *YOBI* perspective and to live out a consciously developed belief system resulting in integrity. It also decreases ego maintenance, and de-values a behavioral quick-fix to "things not going my way." Not only were those last two sentences a mouthful, but it if you understood them, you have a good sense of what you have read thus far. They include most of the major concepts we have covered. As you attempt to manage your anger on all levels of awareness, you will find that it is a full time job. You are actively monitoring how you relate to self, other(s) and the world (situations). A functional response style involves taking the time and energy to determine a course of action that maintains your integrity. The dysfunctional style seems much easier and can obtain results much quicker. This is why it's so tempting. There is however a higher potential for unwanted consequences that come along later. If my children are misbehaving in some way, it is easy to yell at them to "knock it off" while relying on my body language, volume and tone to scare them into different behavior. However, in obtaining quick-fix results, I do damage to the relationship and instill fear of me. If I functionally deal with my anger, I'll take the time to explain to them how their behavior affects them ultimately and help them to develop a fear of those consequences instead of me.

So far I have identified the agenda of the ego to include establishing and maintaining control and power over environments and people. There is another *object* it desires to control. I can only clumsily refer to this *object* as higher consciousness, a non-ego perspective, your belief system, or simply—your power of choice. In other words, your ego also wants to control your perspective. Your ego wants to be able to direct your behavior in a way to maintain its objective. How will you respond to your ego? For now, you should know that your relationship to your ego is critical; how you choose to treat your ego-self may be how you eventually treat all other relationships.

The only thing that you ever really have complete control over in life is your choice of how to respond to it. You can control: 1) how you choose to think about things (your beliefs), and 2) your choice of behavior (what to do or say). With time and a good plan, you can greatly influence your perception, feelings, and deeper levels of cognitive processing. You can even influence life around you. You cannot however, completely control people, things, events, or environments. Your ego will not like this information. It is no wonder then that your choice is a virtual battleground.

Monitoring your thinking, maintaining a functional response to anger, and behaving assertively, are important and perhaps necessary features of an ambition to *go beyond ego*. To go beyond may require much of your energy, attention, and effort—at least initially. To expend this effort, you want to know if it's worth it. The question is, "What's in it for me if I choose to not follow my ego's agenda…if I choose to go beyond it?" The answer could be this:

> ➤ Peace Of Mind: This is a state of consciousness in which peacefulness exists between your ego and what you have determined to be Your Own Best Interest. You have essentially made friends with your ego; the inner battle is minimized, and/or compassionately understood.

➢ Self-Control: This is valued and sought out, instead of external control of others or environments. A sense of decreased worry and/or fear is experienced as you give up trying to control the uncontrollable.

➢ Self-Image Clarification: You develop a better sense of who you are and who you want to be—instead of pursuing an ego desired or idealized appearance for others and the rest of the world, as in the ego-ideal.

➢ Integrity: An increased sense of knowing that you are living your life with a purpose. You proudly experience a joyful satisfaction, instead of a focus on immediate gratification. You experience more satisfying relationships with others based on trust and mutual respect.

Still, there is ego.

Part 3. THE METHOD

9   Conscious Values

> ## The Consciously Established Belief System

The Development of a Belief System

Are two heads better than one? When engaging in problem solving, they say two heads are better than one. Two different perspectives and twice the idea power would seem to be better. It really depends on whether or not the two heads can cooperate, and if they can appreciate that different is not necessarily right or wrong. With very different agendas, two heads can mean a lot of trouble. For confirmation of that, just ask any marital therapist.

When making decisions as individuals, we frequently struggle between what the heart wants and what the head wants. Ancient and modern cartoonists frequently depict us the position of a mediator determining a course of action while a devil and an angel are perched on our shoulders engaged in debate. Moreover, a study of mythology, religion, and culture clearly shows this battle between good and evil, in a theme that has dominated our interest consistently through the ages. As a species, it would appear that we are drawn to these dual contrasts of right and wrong, good and bad, fair and unfair. We like to observe this drama as it is played out in modern cinema, and in the behavior of people around us. Its one thing to observe drama, and quite another to experience it first hand. In the depths of our own decision-making inner-drama can be quite stressful and perplexing; whether to go with your heart or with your head?

Many different words are used to describe these two subjective perspectives involving the heart and the head. On the heart side you find your feelings, your gut, your intuition, or your instinct. The head side is where you find the reasoning, thinking, intellectual, moral, or logical perspective. Whether or not you should go with your heart or your head is dependent on you answering one critical question: are you living your life according to your ego's agenda, or according to a consciously developed belief system? If you have not developed a belief system of you own conscious choosing, you will most likely make choices to follow your ego's agenda;

reduce pain, feel gratified, increase control and power, pursue ego-ideal. Making choices according to what feels good is a relatively easy way to go. There's not a lot of thought involved. Unfortunately feeling choices may lead to disastrous results such as obesity and infidelity. After you have consciously established a belief system based on determining *YOBI*, then inner (and outer) debates occur less frequently, less intensely, and take less time to resolve.

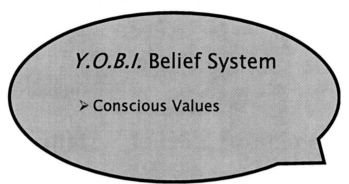

The Development of Values

If you don't consciously establish your values, you will be much more likely to live according to your ego's agenda or someone else's belief system by default. What will you value? Here are some examples of typical values:

Education	Money
Cars	Sex
A good book	The World Wide Web
Career success	Looking good/attractiveness
Spending time with my children	Exercise
Playing golf	Health
Watching television	Youth
Spending time with friends	Integrity
Honesty	Fishing
Political activism	Religion
Serving God	Gardening
Meditation	Pleasing others
Running	Relaxation
Good food	Traveling
Clothing	Music
Spending time with family	Use of mood/mind altering substances

This list could go on for many pages. I have associated no good or bad judgments with these values. The "goodness" or "badness" is up to the individual to decide. There are tangible values (such as clothing, money, and cars) and non-tangible values (such as honesty, hard work, devotion, commitment, and competition). Ultimately, no one else can tell you what is important to you. You have to decide for yourself. As a word of caution, if you attempt to live primarily according to someone else's values, there is a significant chance that over time, you will suffer emotionally and/or psychologically. This is because the other person may or may not have your best interest in mind. Moreover, you would not be living your life—you would be living theirs.

For some of my therapy clients, there is a great deal of frustration with this concept of establishing your own values. They have generally learned to look outside of themselves for a sense of direction. This is perhaps an old pattern, resulting from a need to survive a demanding, critical, or abusive childhood environment. In other words, in their crucial developmental years, there was an important parental figure dominating or interfering with their own decision making process, telling them what should be important to them. For others, they were criticized or judged about what they did or said, to the extent that they gave up on what was important to them in favor of what was necessary to survive emotionally. For still others, they were physically or sexually abused to the extent that they spent so much of their time in survival mode, that they were unable to determine any other positive direction for their life.

Those who suffer from years of childhood criticism, judgment, or abuse often continue as adults to value day-to-day survival-based functioning, and are not accustomed to seeking out joy or value in life. For years, they learned to value just making it from day-to-day, and to look no farther down the road than just that. They learned how to tolerate and avoid pain, and value that. In establishing your values, you will want to consider not only today, but also tomorrow, and perhaps well into your future.

Even if you grew up in a relatively healthy and happy environment, you may find yourself from time to time struggling with unwanted behaviors, decisions, dilemmas, or questions regarding the direction of your life. You may seek out clarity for what your life is about, or will be about. You may seek purpose. Here are seven ideas on how to consciously develop values:

1: Develop a value of your choice. There is a tendency for all of us (no matter what the childhood environment was like) to come to a point in life and ask, "Is there anything else…what is worth living for…surely there has go to be more to life than this…I don't know what's important any more?" When my clients come to this point, I generally ask them, "What would you like to be important?" Use a creative approach in answering this question. If you could live life in any way you choose, what would that be like? Write these ideas down, and develop realistic values from those ideas.

Consider big picture questions such as suggested in Chapter 7, "How and/or why are we here [on this planet]?" "What is the purpose of life and/or my ultimate purpose?" "Why do 'good' things or 'bad' things happen to people?" Values may emerge from answering these questions.

A well-constructed belief system begins with a well-constructed set of values. Even if you are not absolutely sure, or you are not used to deciding what is important to you, you can figure out what you would like to be important. You can start out with some general/broad categories, such as the ones mentioned at the beginning of this chapter. You could decide that you would like to start to value health, friendships, and your career. Even if you have not previously valued those things, for whatever reason, maybe you would like to now.

If you want to value health, you may need to solidify your conviction about it. Consider my value rule: You cannot value something, until you find value in it. In other words, you would need to spend some time in evaluating why being healthy is in your best interest. Why is healthiness good for me? What are the short-range and the long-range benefits? When you can answer these questions genuinely for yourself, you will have developed value in the outcome, and the new value will become important to you. You will have found value in it. The critical word choice I have made here is—you. *YOBI* values are developed from your non-ego perspective, not from someone else's. Nor are they developed to gain someone else's approval, affection, acceptance, or love. If your values are for someone else, watch out. When their approval, affection, acceptance, or love is taken back, your values go out the door with yesterday's trash. On the other hand, you would want to develop your values to gain your own approval, affection, acceptance, and love. To assist in the task of solidifying values, I have developed a useful tool called, Establishing A New Value. This is a worksheet you can find in Appendix B. It will assist you to find the value in what you are trying to do, clarify the value change for you on multiple levels of awareness, and link the value to all aspects of your belief system.

2: Use other people as a guide. If you are unsure about what you want, take a look at the people around you who appear to experience peace of mind and find out what they are doing. Do you have a hero? What do they appear to value in life, is that something that you could do, or value as well? Is there someone that you admire, or someone who inspires you? How do they behave? What appears to be important to them? Their behavior would be a representation of their values and morals. There may be a specific thing they do or say that you believe is very admirable. Whenever you see it, you get a sense of "wow!" Whatever that is, you might want identify it as a value to cultivate in yourself.

3: Use your ego in a limited way. Getting yourself to value something in the here and now is difficult to do when the gain or benefit of the proposed value is not immediate, or when there is some amount of pain involved. Your ego may not like that. Let's say you want to value exercise. For many individuals, most forms of exercise are unpleasant physically and/or emotionally. Regarding it as painful, their ego will not like the unpleasant experience. As a result, your ego will naturally try to maintain its non-exercise life and defend its agenda. "You don't have enough time for that today…you can skip today, there's always tomorrow…I'm just not in the mood today, its been a rough day…I can't find my favorite workout outfit…if they don't like me for how I look, then tough luck…my father never exercised, if he didn't and lived, why can't I…I'm tired…I just don't feel like it…." Your ego may be quite accurate about exercise not feeling good in the moment. It knows the body directly though experience. From that perspective you may likely not find any value in it unless it is immediate. However, some individuals experience a stress relief from exercise that happens soon after it is begun. For those individuals, exercise will be much more agreeable to their ego. At times, for difficult changes, you may want to involve your ego in the decision to make a values change. In other words you ask, "What's in it for my ego?" For example, weightlifting can be a painful workout. When I work out with weights, soon after my muscles engorge with blood, I look muscled up. As I look in the mirror, my ego likes the result, is glad, and wants more. As I'm running my first mile, the tension from my day melts away, emotional pain is relieved, my ego is glad, and wants more.

The agenda of the ego is a force to be reckoned with and to the extent that you can involve it in your decision-making, you may find that you are more likely to maintain new behaviors. To be clear however, I am not suggesting that you allow your ego to run the show. Establish the overall value from a non-ego perspective, but see if you can also find some ego value, "Along with the value of health and exercise will come the pumped up look, the reduction of stress, and the looks of admiration or envy from others." The ego will be glad with that. Involving the ego is helpful for developing some values, some of the time, and for some of the overall value. It is not good for developing all of your values, all of the time, or for all of the value.

You may recall that all work and no play made Jack a dull boy. Jack may have completely disregarded his ego's agenda. On the other hand, all play and no work made Jack a narcissistic bum. As with most things in life, achieving a balance is the key.

4: Use your feelings. You might use your feelings as a way of determining your values. Let's say that you experience subconsciously produced anger. That is, you frequently find yourself angry with the same person, situation, or thing. You could take a closer look at this dysfunctional anger and determine what the ideal and functional value would be. For example, Jerry frequently finds himself angry and frustrated with himself when he gets into arguments with his wife and yells at her. He knows that that these yelling arguments are causing problems in his marriage and wants to change. Through some observation of himself over time, he determines that his ego "gets in the way" and he feels like she is trying to control him. Jerry decides to value something different than "winning" these arguments. He makes a conscious decision that something other than winning will be more important. The valued behavior from now on will be: Having a calm and reasonable discussion about conflicts, and establishing a compromise outcome when needed. Essentially, he will value the opposite of the usual win-lose scenario which his ego values. He will behave as his new value no matter how his wife behaves because this is his value, not necessarily hers. He needs to hold true to his values and expect that others may not do the same. There is a possibility however, that as he behaves consistently in accordance with his new value, she will begin to do the same. However, he should not count on her to change as this would follow his ego's agenda, "I know what's right for her." He will now expect this valued behavior of himself, and he will experience a sense of being proud of himself when he is able to behave consistently with this new valued behavior.

When do you feel proud about yourself? Is there a behavior that is related to that feeling? See if you can determine the non-ego nature of that feeling. In other words, what is the non-ego thinking and/or behavior that produces the sense of being proud? Then, make sure you include that thinking or behavior in your values list. For example, George came to therapy because of stress in his life. In our discussion, he relates that he has generally tended to engage in procrastination. He "puts things off and lets things pile up." He has been begun to notice a pattern of increasing stress lately and is worried about maybe losing his job. We discussed a method of list making in which he would write down and then prioritize what he needs to get done at work. After a couple of weeks of this method, he notices less worry, and as he checks off his accomplishments, he experiences a proud sense of self-respect. This behavior of list making and prioritization will become a value of his from now on. It serves him well in terms of reducing worried thinking, fearful feelings, guilty feelings, and produces a positive feeling outcome. In consciously establishing this value, he increases his overall peace of mind. The work of organization is not totally acceptable to his ego while he is engaged in it. However, the eventual and overall outcome is acceptable because of the tension reduction. In this sense, he has involved his ego in the overall value.

You can follow the same process with other feelings to establish new values. If you experience a persistent fear, such as losing your boyfriend or girlfriend, you could value (among other things) developing independence in your life. If you experience guilt about the large amount of money you make, you could develop a new valued behavior such as doing volunteer work on a regular basis. Instead of eating in unhealthy ways and continually worrying about your weight and health, develop a value in healthy eating and then integrate it with your belief system. Again, you may want to use the Establishing A New Value worksheet in Appendix B.

5: The 24 Hour method. Here is another way to look at the idea of values. Suppose you were given the unfortunate news that you had one day to live. What would you do in those last twenty-four hours? If you really take some time to struggle with this question, you will have a different perspective of what your values are, or what you would like them to be. The next question might be, are you living your life in some way that resembles those values. This life is not forever. Now is the time to be living your life in a meaningful way. You might determine that you are not living your life in such a manner reflective of those 24 hour values. In that case, remember the value rule and the Establishing A New Value worksheet.

6: The Genie in a Bottle. In Chapter 6, I described an exercise that I give my clients at times. In the exercise, you imagine that there is a genie in a bottle who grants you unlimited wishes. What would you start to wish for, and how far would you go in making wishes? This exercise is helpful in determining values. This is especially useful for those who have grown up in environments where their needs and wants were not valued by others. If you are not used to paying attention to your own needs or wants, this exercise may be difficult or slow going at first. Be patient with yourself and try to extend out your wishes as far as you can. At the end, you will find out what is really important to you.

Unwanted Behavior	Becomes	Wanted & Valued Behavior
Overeating	⇨⇨⇨⇨	Healthy Eating
Procrastination	⇨⇨⇨⇨	Planning Ahead
Worry	⇨⇨⇨⇨	Serenity
Anger	⇨⇨⇨⇨	Patience
Disorganization	⇨⇨⇨⇨	Organization
Passivity	⇨⇨⇨⇨	Assertiveness
Substance abuse	⇨⇨⇨⇨	Appropriate Use
Out of shape	⇨⇨⇨⇨	Staying in Shape
Obsessions	⇨⇨⇨⇨	Appropriate Focus
Aggression	⇨⇨⇨⇨	Assertiveness
Boredom	⇨⇨⇨⇨	Activity
Avoidance	⇨⇨⇨⇨	Direct Action Plan
Sexual	⇨⇨⇨⇨	Appropriate Friendship
Loneliness	⇨⇨⇨⇨	Social Contact

Transforming non-YOBI behaviors

7: Transformation of non-*YOBI* behavior. How do you spend your time? A good representation of your current values is seen in your daily behavior. You probably engage in a mix of activities that are both in your best interest, and not in your best interest. Your non-*YOBI* activities may have become habitual, or subconsciously maintained. Or perhaps, you are quite aware of the behavior, but have been thus far unable to change. In either case, identifying the unwanted behavior is the first step. The next step is to identify the alternative wanted behavior. You can transform any unwanted behavior into a new value. The Establishing A New Value worksheet can help you to make these changes. Here are some rather generic examples of unwanted behaviors that can be transformed into new values. You will want to be much more specific in describing the both the wanted and unwanted behaviors (see table on p. 101)

"First things first—what's first?"

After you have developed a values list, you will want to establish a sense of priority to the listed items. In other words, you believe you know what's important to you, now its time to determine what's most important, and next most, and next. When you establish this priority, you will see your belief system begin to take shape in a way that is meaningful to you.

Stephen is a 33 year old, single man who came to see me for extreme depression. He was suicidal at times, and had been depressed and anxious for several years. After a few weeks of traditional therapy, and seeing little difference in his mood, we began to evaluate his belief system values. Here is what he originally wrote down, and the priority that he gave them:

1. The guidance of my parents.

2. Working, doing a good job so that people like me.

3. A good friend who makes me happy.

4. Eating and drinking alcohol after a hard day.

5. The few friends that I can trust, and try to make me happy.

6. Movies (that distract me from my life).

7. Books (that distract me from my life).

8. My dog, "She doesn't take sides and loves me unconditionally."

9. Music, it makes me feel happy.

10. Doing work in my backyard.

There are some obvious problems with the values we identified, and the priority that we identified. He depends on others to tell him what to do and to feel happy. He prioritizes other people's happiness over his own. He is very involved in avoiding his feelings and his life. We did some work to determine what he would like his life to be about, what would ultimately bring him peace of mind. Here is what we came up with:

1. My peace of mind.

2. Being assertive.

3. Spending time with my friends.

4. Developing other healthy friendships.

5. Healthy solitude while working in my backyard.

6. Going to movies with other people.

7. My dog.

8. Reading a variety of books.

9. Listening to good music.

10. Working well (not perfectly).

11. A healthy relationship with my parents.

12. Walking, and developing a lifestyle exercise program.

In the end, we literally turned his life (values) upside down. His depression was a result of living his life in a way that was the opposite of how he really wanted to. The values he held on to for years were based on avoiding anger, sadness, guilt and fear. He had been approaching life primarily from an ego-based perspective lacking in conscious direction. After re-establishing his values and prioritizing them, there was no longer any confusion about the right way to solve his problems. When you develop a sense of priority to your values, making difficult decisions is less difficult. You know what is important to you, and you know in what order to live. However, there is no guarantee that knowing the right thing to do will make it easy to do.

Oftentimes with my clients, there is a need to clearly define their values because they lack a direction for their lives, or they have a depression that is mysterious. I have them list their current values. In order to obtain accurate results, they must write down how they spend their time, from day to day, in any average week. Again, the way that you spend your time is an accurate reflection of your values; people do what is important to them. Sometimes, there is a big difference between what a person says is important, and how they spend their time. Jane can say all day long that she values a healthy diet, but then engage in junk food eating binges as she pleases. When it comes to values, we can either talk the talk, or walk the talk. I might say that I love to run, and that running is very important to me. The fact of the matter is, if I only run once every two months, it is not that important no matter how much I say that it is. It would be much more accurate to say: 1) I would like it to be important, 2) I want other people to think that it is, or 3) it is somewhat important to me, but other things are much more important, at least right now. The truth is in my walk (or run), not my talk.

As you begin to live some of your new values, remember that you may need to try on new behaviors to see if they fit you. Give yourself plenty of time to behave in new ways to determine that the new values fit, don't fit, or need some form of modification. With some things in life, only experience will tell you if you like them or not. You cannot know if you like broccoli by someone else telling you about the taste, or by looking at it. You need the experience of taste to tell if you like it, don't like it, or that it may need some cheese poured on top of it. The same goes with new jobs, new people, new hobbies, or new television shows. You will essentially find that there are tastes acquired over time, and sometimes there are immediately recognized enjoyments.

Here are some suggestions for your consideration in developing values. These are contrary to the ego's agenda:

➢ Value a tolerance, and/or, acceptance of, appropriate painful feelings as a necessary part of problem solving.

➢ Value a delay of immediate gratification when appropriate, thus, the development of patience.

➢ Value inner-power—not power over others.

➢ Value self-control—not control over others.

➢ Value self-acceptance, in favor of acceptance from others.

➢ Value consciously developed values, morals, and expectations.

➢ Value acceptance of a realistic, reasonable, and relationally fair amount of influence over life, combined with the ability to adapt—as opposed to perfected control over life.

➢ Value a functional anger style—assertiveness.

➢ Value peace of mind instead of "feeling good."

So, what is it that you seek for your life? This is the question that sets the stage for your belief system. What will be important to you? Remember, you cannot value something, until you find value in it. By using the Establishing A New Value worksheet, you can look for the advantages in the object of your desire, and then build them up in all levels of awareness and feeling realms. You develop healthy gratifying feelings for the object of potential value. You then determine its priority. You then establish an associated moral code line. You predict a proud or self-respecting feeling associated with corresponding behavior.

Exercise 9-1: Use the "seven ideas on how to consciously develop values" to make a list of desired values for yourself. Don't be concerned initially with the order of your list. When you feel good about your list, order the items from most to least important. Go to appendix F to make the appropriate entries.

> **First you value.**
> **Then you establish a rule around _that_ value.**
> **Then you expect yourself to behave _that_ way.**
> **When you do so consistently,**
> **you produce _that_ self-image,**
> **and—a sense of integrity!**

10 Conscious Morals

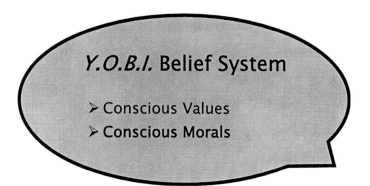

Y.O.B.I. Belief System

➤ Conscious Values
➤ Conscious Morals

The Development of a Moral Code

After having established your values, your moral code can begin to take shape. Think of your moral code as your consciously established standards for living. Ideally, your moral code is the guide that you use to judge your own behavior. The priority of your values will have an extremely important impact on your moral code. Let's take another look at Stephen's revised values list to illustrate.

1. My peace of mind.

2. Being assertive.

3. Spending time with my friends.

4. Developing other healthy friendships.

5. Healthy solitude while working in my backyard.

6. Going to movies with other people.

7. My dog.

8. Reading a variety of books.

9. Listening to good music.

10. Working well, not perfectly.

11. A healthy relationship with my parents.

12. Walking, and developing an exercise program.

Stephen's prioritized values list creates this moral code for him:

➤ Be assertive whenever possible.

➤ My integrity—peace of mind comes first.

➤ Make time for friends.

➤ Develop quality friendships.

➤ Work on my backyard as time permits.

➤ Take good care of my dog.

➤ Read a variety of books.

➤ Listen to good music.

➤ Work well, not perfectly.

➤ Develop a healthy relationship with my parents.

➤ Make time for walking and maintain an exercise program.

Stephen received an offer from his boss to be promoted, but it included having to increase his weekly hours from 40 to 65. He should have no difficulty in making a decision to turn down the offer. This difficult decision has essentially already been made, by him. He doesn't need to do what his parents want him to do like he did in that past. They may not even agree with his choice. He knows the right thing to do for him. He knows what is in his own best interest.

Obviously, a person may have additional moral code entries that do not relate specifically back to their values list; they are implied by societal norms. These are time honored or traditional rules such as those mentioned in Chapter 8: don't steal, tell the truth, don't kill, do not cause someone else intentional physical or emotional harm, treat others like you want to be treated, work hard, be nice to others, follow the rules, give to the less fortunate, and do not cheat. Now you might say that these norms or rules are related a desire for group security and we follow them so that we might remain part of the group, because we value being part of the group, and we want to survive. Nevertheless, these are the basic rules that most societies are built on. Some individuals do not want to be an active part of a group or society. Some individuals break these rules. Some individuals therefore do not benefit from the group, or society.

There are **pre-established moral codes** that are associated with **pre-established belief systems**. A pre-established belief system can provide a specific type of structure to the lives of those who want it. There are many reasons why an individual would seek out a ready-made belief system. These reasons include, but are not limited to: 1) the individual had been exposed to very little healthy structure in their family of origin, 2) the individual had experienced some form of ongoing abuse and was stuck in survival mode for many youthful years, 3) the individual was exposed to a mal-adaptive parental belief system, and/or 4) the individual is looking for a specific desired result that the pre-established belief system is promising. For any of these, or other reasons, it might make sense that an individual would eventually seek out a different way of living because what they were doing wasn't working. Pre-established belief systems are offered by:

Cultures	Cults	Authors
Religions	Gangs	Therapists/ coaches
Military organizations	12 Step Programs	Corporations

These belief systems aren't necessarily good or bad, and they are chosen consciously by the individual. If they are fully developed belief systems, they attempt to answer big picture questions and will have some features in common. For example, the above systems tell you:

➤ **The goal, or, end result** (the ultimate purpose): a proud family, eternal life, a disciplined life, family bonds, brotherhood, sobriety, peace of mind, life improvement, a successful career and future.

➤ **What's important:** tradition, being with God in heaven, honor, giving to your leader, staying tough, staying sober, integrity, being assertive, making money.

➤ **How to live right:** do what your parents tell you to do, follow God's ten commandments, obey your superior officers, do what your leader tells you to do, hurt before being hurt, change people-places-things, follow your values, confront your fears, follow the policy and procedure manual when in doubt.

➤ **How to live wrong:** don't sell out to mainstream cultures, do not ignore *the word*, don't think of only yourself, don't let other people tell you what to do, you can't have a drink once in a while, don't act out your anger on others, don't stuff your feelings, do not give away trade secrets.

➤ **What to expect:** people will try to change you, the devil is hiding where you least expect, expect the best of your self at all times, people won't understand you like we do, people will try you, you may try to do things your way and relapse, change takes time and a good plan, you will make some mistakes and get right back in the saddle, other people will want that money if you don't.

➤ **Who you are:** you are your history, a child of God, a soldier, God's child though me, a brother or sister, an addict in recovery, the center of your universe, a capable person, a money making member of this corporate family.

Pre-established belief systems can, and do, work for some individuals very well. If the system can convince you of a specific outcome (a proud family, eternal life, a disciplined life, family bonds, brotherhood, sobriety, peace of mind, life improvement, a successful career and future), and there are other people who have experienced that outcome, then you will be more likely to try it. Testimonials are known to be very effective in sales for this reason, especially when given by people you already know, trust, or admire. To the extent that you have found a pre-established belief system that produces a desired result or outcome for you, consider yourself lucky.

The pre-established system doesn't work for everyone. This book will be useful for those individuals wanting to develop their own. Your moral code is an outcome of having consciously developed your values. If you have determined that honesty is important to you, then your rule might be that you are honest with everyone, or those that you care about. If your health is important you, then you will establish guidelines about the eating and exercise habits that you follow. If a loving relationship with your partner is important to you, then you will have standards about how you behave in relating to them. In a *you-established* belief system, your moral code contains your rules for living, consciously developed by you, reflecting your values.

It has been said that, "You cannot serve two masters." When one of my clients experiences anxiety, oftentimes we are able to trace the anxiety to a conflict of two or more morals. That is, their own rules are incompatible for resolving a particular problem. Knowing that morals are a reflection of values, we may determine that there are conflicting values as well. For example, let's say that I value regular relaxation, regular writing, and regular exercise. Whenever I have spare time, I experience some anxiety as I am forced to choose one valued behavior over the others. Oftentimes anxiety is caused by the struggle of choosing; when the struggle is done, the anxiety is done. Generally the anxiety resolves when: 1) I clearly determine the priority of the values in question (exercise is more important than relaxation, or writing) and, 2) create a specific moral code rule that would easily guide my decision making, in a pre-determined manner. As I encounter spare time in the future, the decision is made about what to do, and I feel good about it because I know that the pre-determined choice of behavior is in my best interest. Again, knowing the right thing to do, does not always make it the easiest thing to do. Chapters 12 through 17 will address this emotional problem more specifically.

Exercise 10-1: Use your values list to establish your moral code. This is your code to guide your behavior (not the behavior of others). If it is helpful, think of your moral code as a list of "dos and don'ts" for your behavior. Your moral code should honor your values. Also, your moral code should address and resolve any values conflicts that you experience on a regular basis. Don't be concerned with the order of your list. Go to appendix F to make the appropriate entries.

11 Conscious Expectations and Self-Image

> **Y.O.B.I. Belief System**
>
> ➢ Conscious Values
> ➢ Conscious Morals
> ➢ Conscious Expectations

The Development of Expectations

If you are a living breathing person, you have expectations. You have expectations of yourself, other people, and the worldly environments you find yourself in. Oftentimes we use our own standards or moral code as a measure of judging other people's behavior. We expect other people to value what we value, and behave according to our own highly held standards. This can occur on any level of awareness. This blending of morals and expectations is what I call having moralistic expectations. The tendency to expect others to behave according to your own moral code will likely lead to much anger. You may feel very strongly about your morals, however, others may not. While this may seem obvious, when you experience intense anger towards others, check your thoughts for this tendency. An important quality of a healthy belief system is not expecting other people to live their lives exactly according to your values or morals. It is simply not reasonable to expect someone else to live a carbon copy of your belief system. Well then, what can you expect of others? Realistically—some people, will share some of your morals, some of the time, under some circumstances.

Consider Todd, a thirty-six year old divorced male, who began to experience depression four months ago. The depression began soon after he was laid off from a job he had with a major marketing company. He was fortunate enough to have gotten a six-month severance package, which would help him in transitioning into another job. He had worked for the marketing company for eleven years and was planning on retirement with this company. The lay-off was a complete surprise to him. We decided that Todd would begin a journal to keep track of any intensified feelings experienced, along with the associated thoughts. Through an examination of his journal, we determined that the origin of his depression was in his expectations. He had expected to have this job for a long time, now it was gone. He was expecting to have no changes, but this was a huge change. He wanted his career to go his way, and now it wasn't. Now he expected that more bad things were sure to happen. Over the next few sessions we closely examined these depression-producing expectations, and developed different expectations. As you have no doubt guessed, the new expectations were more realistic, reasonable, and fair for him. The transformation in his thinking made a big difference in his mood over the next few weeks.

Obviously, your expectations are unique and personal, resulting from a lifetime of your own experiences. They have probably changed over time, as your life circumstances have changed. On a rather global level, here are some suggestions of what you might want to consider expecting of self, other, and world:

➤ Expect that your values will change over time as your life changes and evolves.

➤ Expect yourself to follow your own moral code consistently, but not perfectly.

➤ Expect that in life you will make mistakes, or fall short of your own standards along the way.

➤ Expect to experience loss in your life.

➤ Expect that you cannot anticipate every possible change that life has to offer.

➤ Expect that everyone out there has an ego with an agenda. Some are more aware of this than others. Some attempt to transcend or go beyond it, and some do not.

➤ Expect that other people are going to make mistakes just like you.

➤ Expect that building any kind of trust will require time and experience. The amount of time and the amount of experience will vary from circumstance to circumstance.

➤ Expect that things will not always go your way.

➤ Expect that change is part of life—you change, other people change, and that will never change.

➤ In general, have your expectations be realistic, reasonable, and relationally fair when it comes to self, others, and the circumstances you find yourself in.

Exercise 11-1: Refer back to your common patterns of anger. Use the expectation test to transform the anger into healthy expectations. Make a list of expectations you would like to guide your thinking and behavior toward yourself, others, and the world. Don't be concerned with the order of your list. These expectations should be consistent with your values and morals. Go to appendix F to make the appropriate entries.

Y.O.B.I. Belief System
- Conscious Values
- Conscious Morals
- Conscious Expectations
- Conscious Self-Image

The Development of Self-Image

Self-image describes the person you know yourself to be. Ideally, it is a perspective of yourself that has been established by you living out a consciously developed set of values and morals. When you experience a self-image that you can be proud of, you will be sustained through the difficulties and challenges of life. When people criticize you, judge you, or try to impose illegitimate authority over you, knowing who you are and what you believe in will help you to maintain integrity. A simple method of self-image modification was outlined in Chapter 8. Here it is again:

1. Clearly establish your own values.

2. Clearly establish guiding rules (morals) about how to behave in accordance with those values.

3. Have reasonable expectations that you will behave in accordance with those values, and that others may or may not.

4. Begin to observe yourself behaving in accordance with your values and morals, resulting in a transformed sense of who you are.

Self-image is developed as you observe yourself behaving. It is therefore very different from other-image or ego-ideal. You may have been exposed, for many years, to other people telling you who they think you are, "You're no good, you're just like your father, you're dumb, you're the best, etc." At present, do you currently think of yourself as who you were told you were, or who you know yourself to be now? I realize this is a tricky question, but there is an important distinction here to consider. Are you [limited to] your history? If you have difficulty answering this question, consider looking at my Self-Image Inventory exercise in Appendix D. I sometimes have my clients fill out this inventory when they are struggling with an old and troublesome self-image. I developed this inventory to identify specific self-image deficits that result from conclusions you made about yourself in childhood. As a child you may have concluded, "I'm weird...I'm stupid...I'm ugly...I'm bad." You may or may not have overcome these conclusions as an adult. These deficits may be present on a subconscious level of awareness and may be noticed by you when you are emotionally stressed. For example, Jill is a twenty-three year old successful model. In her early childhood years, she was told over and over again by siblings and peers that she was "ugly." Over many years, she came to see this as a reality about who she was. Her conclusion was, "I am ugly," and the environment apparently supported this conclusion. When she reached her later teen years, she began to develop into an attractive young lady, and by the time she was twenty years old she was making a good living as a fashion model. When she loses a modeling job to a competitor, Jill feels emotionally stressed; a combination of sadness, anger, and fear. As she searches for reasons as to why she lost this job, she concludes, "I guess I'm ugly." This self-image deficit "ugly," is still present in her subconscious awareness and processing, even though her current reality substantially suggests otherwise. Therefore, you might say that at times, she still thinks of herself as who she was told she was, not who she knows herself to be now. Ideally, therapy will help her to reach a different conclusion about herself based on a belief system of her choice. By using the Self-Image Inventory you may be able to identify your own potential areas of modification.

Your view of yourself has origins in: your childhood history, your ego, feedback from others, and in any consciously developed values that you live out. Your history is whatever it is, and unchangeable. Your ego is what it is, and virtually inescapable. Feedback from others is out of your control. If you have a self-image problem, that leaves only one realm of origin for you to modify: how you live out consciously developed values. You have complete control in the realm of personal choice. You can fully determine what is important to you. Once you do that, and begin living that way, you will begin to see yourself as such.

Consider, Georgette, a forty-five year old woman who became involved in therapy because she was having difficulty with controlling her eating habits. Over the course of the previous eight years, she had gained over sixty-five pounds. She had tried various fad diets and generally lost and gained back the extra weight without any sustained results. As we explored her history, we discovered that she was overweight as a child, had managed to lose the weight in adolescence, and kept it off for most of her adult life. Eight years ago she experienced a major loss. Her mother died after a yearlong battle with cancer. Georgette began overeating during that time as a subconscious way of managing her stress and worry. She wanted to lose the weight she gained, and return to her previous active lifestyle. In time, we made use of my Self-Image Inventory and discovered an unresolved old self-image belief, "I'm fat." This judgmental perception had been brought to her attention by others on a regular basis. We needed to correct the belief in order for her to be able to move on. This was a matter of consciously establishing who she wanted to become, and what would be important to her now. Georgette would need to establish for herself, "I'm more than a body, I am a healthy active woman." Then we moved on to establish matching values, "Regular exercise, and healthy dietary choices." We used the Establishing A New Value worksheet to comprehensively develop the values. Then, we prioritized them within the context of her other already established healthy values. The priority helped her to establish a moral code entry, and an expectation that she would behave accordingly. From there, therapy was a matter of fine-tuning the changes, and helping Georgette to trust that the changes being made by her were clearly in her best interest.

Georgette then spent a substantial amount of time in therapy, and on her own time, fine-tuning her new values. She did some research to develop a healthy eating style that would realistically work for her. Additionally, she developed a reasonable exercise plan that she thought would be enjoyable, and that would produce positive results. This was work that her ego was not exactly thrilled about. However, she was greatly motivated by knowing that the changes were in her own best interest. As Georgette began to live out her newly valued behaviors, over time her self-image was transformed. She began to see herself as "more than a body…I am a healthy and active woman." Moreover, she began to live her life in a way that would contribute to her peace of mind.

If you decide to use my Self-Image Inventory, you may check off some characteristics from the right hand column. In that case, take one of those items and transform it into a new valued belief. For example, let's say you check off "stupid." Maybe you have been able to overcome this characteristic as an adult. In other words, "I have come to think of myself as being quite bright and capable in most areas of my life." On the other hand, let's say you continue to harbor doubt in this area, and at times find yourself feeling sad, angry, or afraid any time issues of intelligence are brought to your attention. In the latter case, you will want to establish a new valued belief. This new value will be based on a realistic and appealing belief for you, and will represent a solution to the associated painful feeling. The valued belief will guide you to come to a new and healthier conclusion, based on you finding supporting evidence. For example, instead of getting angry about being called stupid, you decide that words such as stupid, smart, intelligent or dumb are, "Labels that are not useful in describing a person's entire being." Instead, you will begin to see people, including yourself, through the following new valued belief: "Human beings develop with an endless accumulation of characteristics and talents unique to them. Some people have talents at different levels of mastery than others." You will find it important to see people as whole beings. That is the perception that you will value, it is what you will look for in people, and find to be true. You will pile up evidence in your experiences with people from now on to confirm this new valued belief, "People are whole beings." With time and experience, you will find such evidence, and your new value will be real to you. Moreover, you decide that you are one of those people who are whole beings, and you were one of those beings, as a child as well.

Maybe you have checked off "inferior," in the Inventory. Instead of having a belief that people can be inferior or superior to one another, you decide to value something different. You decide that when you strip people of their possessions, titles, and money down to just flesh and bones, there are no levels of worth from one person to the next. If I asked you to look at a dozen babies in a hospital newborn room and point out to me which ones were inferior and which ones were superior, you would probably look at me like I was crazy. We form these, and other extreme labels, or self-perceptions over the course of a lifetime of experiences. It will take still more life experiences to change these labels into realistic and healthy beliefs. Here is the key point with regard to transforming your belief system: Establish the valued belief first, and then, make it so. Remember from Chapter 1, "You are the center of your universe, and…in control of your universe." The new valued belief might go something like this, "I don't believe in people being inferior or superior to others. I believe that we are all on our own path in life, learning as we go. No person is intrinsically more or less valuable than anyone else. We all get to the finish line eventually, and cross it with what we came into this world with, pure consciousness. What really matters is that you live your life with integrity and quality." From now on, whenever you get that sad feeling of inferiority, you remember your newly established valued belief, and say it to yourself with the confidence of a loving parent. With time and many experiences, you could create a shortcut label for yourself describing the new value, "The integrity finish line." With still more time and experience, the new value may become subconsciously established. In that case, you may experience brief sadness when you see someone in a "better position" than you, only to wonder how that sadness left you so soon. After some pondering, you may conclude, "Oh yeah, the finish line."

Exercise 11-2: Go to appendix D and use the Self-Image Inventory to see if there are any self-image deficits that you want to correct. If so, create values, morals, and expectations to correct the deficit(s) and add them to your YOBI Profile. Also, think about the kind of self-image you would like to have in the future. Remember, self-image is a choice made by you. Project your thinking into the future; think, "I am _____." Now fill in the blank space. Do this several times. Go to appendix F to make the appropriate entries.

12 The Conscious Management of Feelings

Feelings Can Get in the Way

When it comes right down to it, most of us know how we would like to behave or how we would like to change. It is all too common to hear one of my clients say, "I have this problem, I know what I need to do, but I just can't get myself to do it. Sometimes I can anticipate what I'm about to do, but I can't get myself to stop, it almost seems like I'm two different people." Feelings produced through ego cognition can get in the way of change, and in the way of doing what you think you should do. Maybe you would like to eat less, exercise more, argue less, and love more. The decision to value, these or any other behavioral changes, is relatively easy. The decision is just the beginning of what can become a tremendous struggle to carry out a plan for desired change. Such a struggle can evolve into something that resembles a never-ending inner-battle.

It was easy for Henry to say, "Ok, I'm going on a diet, this weight has got to come off." With relative ease, Henry also made some belief system changes toward resolving his weight gain. He began by deciding that in his life, something else would become more important than what he called "food joy." He created moral code standards to support his new values. He established realistic, reasonable, and fair expectations for himself to follow his values and morals. With time, he anticipated that he would experience a new sense of self-image. These belief system changes were not difficult to establish, nor were they the result of rocket science. There were many good diets that Henry had previously attempted to follow. They worked for a short time. He eventually returned back to his old habits. Theoretically, his diet plans could work, and any related belief system changes could also work if they were properly formulated. Indeed, a solid and consciously well-established belief system is a good start toward the experience of integrity and peace of mind.

In the end, the struggle to make some changes will happen on a feeling level. For many of us, including Henry, the struggle is, "To get myself to do what I just don't feel like doing, but know I should do." The solution to this struggle may involve ignoring some feelings when they are no longer applicable to present life situations. The struggle might also involve manipulating some feelings, or creating feelings that haven't been there previously. Belief system changes are a necessary good start in creating changes in your life, but as you step onto the final battleground of change you may very well find yourself facing a stubborn opponent. On that battleground will be your ego's desire against *YOBI* (conscious desire) for something else. There is no doubt that your ego will wage war. However, its battle plan has been clearly exposed. The question is, how will you choose to respond? Will you fight back with equal intensity, join in its cause, surrender, or negotiate? Perhaps you will want to enter into peaceful negotiation. To do so, you will need to be able to understand and manage the feelings involved. You will want to be able to enter negotiations with a plan that involves creating *Peace in your Mind.*

It has been suggested that you can't love someone else until you are able to love yourself. Fortunately, you can choose how to respond to, and perhaps love your ego-*self.* If you can learn how to create your own peace of mind, you stand a much better chance of creating peace around you as well. As noted in Chapter 8, "Your relationship to your ego is critical; how you choose to treat your ego-self may be how you eventually treat all other relationships." Once you understand how to create and maintain your own peace of mind, all other relationships are automatically transformed!

Features of the Management Method

We experience feelings much like a light bulb experiences the energy of electricity. In our homes, we use switches to control the lighting. Some light switches have only two positions; on or off. The bulb filament receives the electric energy flowing fully or not at all. There are also dimmer switches that can be used to control energy flow. With these dimmer switches there is a range of energy flow that allows for a customized lighting display. The experience of feeling is sometimes like an off and on switch; you are either feeling, or not. At other times, feeling is experienced as it ebbs and flows with a variety of intensity. When we are not experiencing a particular feeling, the energy potential for feeling is maintained in a dormant state. It is when we focus our perceptual attention on something, either inwardly or outwardly, that we experience feeling. We have the ability to influence feeling intensity though our thinking; we can choose to either turn up the intensity, or turn it down.

Any feeling you experience will be produced from the perspective of your belief system, or from the perspective of your ego. The agenda of the ego will most likely produce much emotion. This is because the ego is in a constant state of want, and desire for control, which can lead to much disappointment and worry.

Henry's ego would like to be gratified by food as much as possible. He is finding out that a lifestyle of ego based eating is leading to many consequences, "Why can't I be like other people, they can do it without any problems." Ego based feelings are generally easy to spot; you will notice them whenever the agenda of the ego is being challenged in some way.

In order to make optimal use of the problem solving strategies in the next five chapters, it will be helpful to simplify your feeling experiences. That is, conceptualize your feelings as having roots in one of five physiological points of origin: anger, sadness, guilt, fear, or gladness. There is an advantage in rhyming the feeling categories so that you can quickly reference them. With little effort you can ask yourself, "Am I feeling glad, mad, sad, bad, or fear?" If you are used to using generic feeling words, or avoiding your feelings, it may be difficult at times to figure out a specific category. In that case you can use a process of eliminating the feeling(s) that you know you're not experiencing. Or, you may try to determine the feeling by identifying the precipitating thought. Either way, you will want to specifically identify the feeling.

When Henry came in for his regular therapy appointment, he started by saying, "I'm really having a bad day. I just don't know what's wrong with me. I can't seem to get my eating under control. I don't really know how I'm feeling." Our first task was to engage in a process of eliminating the feelings that were clearly not involved, "I know I'm not feeling glad about this, and I'm not feeling bad or sad. I guess I just want my out-of-control feeding-frenzy to stop." Because Henry did not like his own behavior, we concluded that he was angry with himself. Additionally, he was concerned with the possibility of future negative consequences, "I sometimes think I'll never get this under control," which means that he also felt fear. Once Henry and I identified his feelings, we could begin the process of problem solving.

There is, of course, a good reason for the title of this chapter, *The Conscious Management of Feelings*. The purpose of the next five chapters is to provide specific information and effective strategies for managing the intensity of feeling through conscious problem solving.

> To the extent that you engage in feeling management on a conscious level of awareness, you reduce the possibility of your ego becoming involved in an effort to maintain its agenda.

In other words, if you don't consciously *lead the way* in matters of resolving your painful feelings, your ego probably will by employing it's agenda and maintenance. Chapter 18, Integrity One Choice at a Time, will clearly illustrate that solving problems in a conscious manner will require that at a minimum you are able to identify feelings, recognize your ego's agenda, and know your own belief system. Additionally, you would want to have some effective feeling management strategies. Because your ego will not be going anywhere else any time soon, feeling elimination is not possible. This means you need to manage feelings. Each of the feeling categories will now be more fully explored to include the following features for each:

> ➤ ALTERNATIVE FEELING INTENSITY WORDS.

> ➤ THE TYPE OF THOUGHT THAT PRODUCES THE FEELING.

> ➤ EGO VS. *YOBI* PERSPECTIVES.

> ➤ THE COGNITIVE CHALLENGE.

> ➤ POTENTIAL RESOLUTIONS.

> ➤ BELIEF SYTEM FORMULA.

> ➤ THE PERCEPTUAL CHALLENGE.

> ➤ APPLICATION OF THE METHOD.

➤ ALTERNATIVE FEELING INTENSITY WORDS.

We use many words to describe our feelings. This is useful of course for being able to communicate in precise ways to each other. For the purpose of problem solving, however, it is necessary to bring your emotional experience into focus. In this first feature, common feeling words are listed to describe a variety of feeling intensities. It may be helpful to commit these primary feeling categories to memory in order to quickly and efficiently identify your feelings for problem solving management:

Mad   Sad

Bad

Fear   Glad

➤ **THE TYPE OF THOUGHT THAT PRODUCES THE FEELING.**

Not all of our thoughts produce feeling. However, when you do feel, there is a cognitive origin. The cognition will originate from either a conscious or subconscious level of awareness. The connection from cognition to feeling may be quite obvious, or quite mysterious. This connection however is without a doubt uniquely yours. There is a type of thinking specifically related to each feeling category. In this feature, examples are provided for each. It is helpful to commit the feeling-thinking connection to memory in order to access them for quick problem solving:

MAD: "Something's not going the way I want it to."

SAD: "This is about loss."

BAD: "This is a moral conflict."

FEAR: "Possible negative consequence ahead."

➤ **EXAMPLES OF EGO VS. *YOBI* PERSPECTIVES.**

Quite regularly a client will ask me, "Is this ego or *YOBI* thinking, sometimes I have a hard time figuring out the difference?" The cognitive origin of a feeling has both a level of awareness and a perspective. Ego maintains a survivalist perspective, and *YOBI* represents the perspective of your belief system. You want to know if your feeling experience is based in ego cognition or *YOBI* cognition. While it is extremely helpful to determine the origin, it is not always clear. In order to figure out the perspective, ask yourself one or all of the following questions:

1. "Is this thought and/or feeling attempting to achieve a reduction of painful emotion, increase immediate gratification, establish/maintain power and control over people and things, or increase an appearance of superiority in relation to others?"

2. "What is the intended goal or outcome for this thinking and/or feeling?"

3. "These thoughts and/or feelings are maintained to what end?"

4. "Does my feeling serve my ego, or my consciously determined best interest?"

5. "Is my self-image enhanced/honored, or, is my ego's ideal served?"

The recognition of ego based feelings and thinking is critical to developing peace of mind. Examples of each perspective are given in this feature.

➢ **THE COGNITIVE CHALLENGE.**

The experience of any feeling is a real event as it is rendered as part of your cycle-logical functioning. A persistent painful feeling will no doubt catch your attention. In order to resolve it, you will first need to identify the feeling, and then evaluate or challenge its cognitive origin and its current validity. In this feature, you are given an effective method for doing so through a set of guidelines. You will recognize these standards as *the expectation test* introduced in Chapter 6.

An important function of each of the feeling challenges is to determine the course for resolution. That is, "Will I pursue an internal change, or an external change?" The challenge steps take you in the right direction for resolution, and may save you from unnecessary pain. Then, much like a resolution menu, you choose the most appealing problem solving strategy. In order for the challenge to work, it is critical to be honest with yourself, and with regard to all of the relevant elements of the *big picture*. In other words, you need to identify all of the people, places and things affected in your appraisal of the situation and related decisions. You must be aware of the potential interference of ego maintenance.

➢ **POTENTIAL EXTERNAL AND INTERNAL RESOLUTIONS.**

Your ego will urge you get rid of painful feelings. After all, that is a fundamental aspect of its agenda. Obviously, none of us likes to be in any kind of pain. However, in order to engage in effective problem solving and experience emotional growth, it is necessary to experience painful feelings at least long enough to identify the feeling category and thought content. The alternative is to quickly rid yourself of the feeling through ego maintenance strategies and risk the possibility of ongoing problems. Ultimately, feelings are not willed away, they are transformed though your thinking.

In this feature, I have assembled a variety of conscious problem solving strategies that are presented and described for each feeling category. Some resolutions you will recognize as common, others use terminology unique to this book. The resolutions are divided into two categories, internal and external, depending on the outcome of the cognitive challenge. External resolutions involve behavioral change. Internal resolutions involve belief system modification.

➢ **BELIEF SYSTEM FORMULA.**

In this feature, each resolution is shown in terms of belief system components. These are suggestions only, and represent just one way of incorporating these resolutions into your belief system. As these examples demonstrate, when creating new beliefs, you want to establish them in a manner that brings out the best in yourself, others, the world, and transforms painful feelings into peace of mind. The emphasis here is on an outcome that brings about peace of mind and integrity instead of the maintenance of the ego's agenda. In order to make real changes in how you live your life, you have to establish and find truth in new beliefs. If your life is determined by your belief system, you may as well be at the helm.

DO YOU BECOME YOUR BELIEFS?

➢ THE PERCEPTUAL CHALLENGE.

This feature suggests that it may be possible to perceive painful emotions as opportunities for growth, learning, and transformation. "This is an emotionally painful experience, but maybe there is something good that can come from it." The challenge asks you to perceive your life experiences in a different way. A different perception brings a different understanding. A different understanding brings a different belief. With a different belief you perceive differently. Now you have a different perspective.

Peace Of Mind—It's all about perspective!

➢ APPLICATION OF THE METHOD.

In this final feature, the case example of Henry is provided to illustrate the use of the cognitive challenges, resolutions, addition of belief system components, and perceptual challenges. Here is an introduction to his story:

Henry grew up in a poor family, with an alcoholic mother, where things were scarce, but food was plentiful. By his ninth birthday he was already medically obese. His earliest childhood fears were quelled by the notion that "when there was a problem, there was always food for the solution." Through his later teen years, he made a commitment to a healthy diet and regular exercise and was able to maintain a relatively fit and healthy body.

In his early twenties, Henry's dating habits picked up significantly and he spent the next three years of his bachelorhood "in search of a wife." His eventual marriage to Theresa was "perfect" until she began to drink alcoholically, then his "weight came back on" as his healthy lifestyle slowly fell apart. The more she drank, the more he ate, "Even though I could see myself losing control, I just could not stop what I was doing, I felt compelled to eat even when I knew it was wrong for me. Sometimes I just ate because it seemed like the only thing that felt good. It makes sense I guess, when I look back on that time, I can see that I wanted to feel a predictable form of security when I felt powerless and unable to control her drinking. In my eating and weight gain, I eventually created a distance between myself and my wife that I needed in order to feel some sense of control and power. In my mind, I may have achieved that, but in the process, lost my own sense of integrity."

In our beginning session, Henry and I discussed his sense of being powerless, lack of control, and the influence of his ego in his history and his current situation. Henry decided that he wanted to make some changes, "I would like to know what it's like to live according to my own set of healthy rules. For a long time now I've been following a bad pattern and that's got to change. I guess I need to define who I want to be, and maybe I can regain my integrity." I suggested that if he were to establish a healthy relationship within himself, his marital relationship would also change. He was ready and willing to begin.

13 Managing 'Mad'

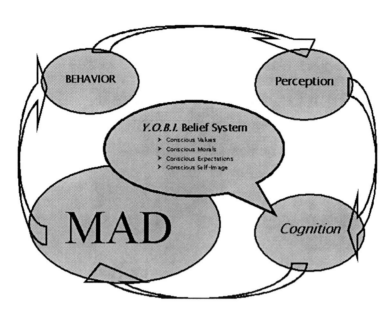

The Desire for Change

The feeling of anger (mad) results from an expectation not being met. Anger can be experienced as a build-up of unmet expectation over a course of time, as a surprise situation that catches us off guard, or anything in-between. Moreover, anger can be experienced on any level of awareness. Regardless of the duration, intensity, or level of awareness, it originates from unmet expectation. Anger can permeate any point of your cycle-logical functioning. It goes without saying that you can think or behave in angry ways. You can also perceive angrily; anyone who is pessimistic anticipates that life will not go the way that they want it to. They expect life to be negative, look for negativity, and then find it of course.

Underlying the experience of anger, you will find that you want something to change. Fundamentally, you become angry when things don't go your way. If you take that a step further, there is most likely a way that you would like things to go. That is the change, or the outcome that you want. Thus, underlying the experience of anger is a desire for change. Understanding the concept of anger in this manner may transform how you deal with it.

➢ **ALTERNATIVE MAD INTENSITY WORDS.**

Livid	Angry	Frustrated
Irate	Ticked-off	Annoyed
Furious	Outraged	Irritated

➢ **THE TYPE OF THOUGHT THAT PRODUCES MAD.**

"This is not going my way."

"This is not what I expected from myself."

"I don't like how they are behaving."

"The world should behave in a way I want."

"I want them to be different."

"I want myself to change."

➢ **MAD PERSPECTIVES.**

Ego Mad: "I want it now."

"I want to have control over this now."

"I want to have power over this now."

"I can't stand it when I don't get my way."

"You are making me mad."

"You are not doing it my way."

YOBI Mad: "This is not what I expected."

"I'm not behaving according to my values."

"I'm not behaving according to my morals."

"I may need to make a change."

"I need to pause to consider my options."

"This is not what we agreed on."

➢ **THE COGNITIVE CHALLENGE FOR MAD.**

The challenge associated with mad is to "apply the *expectation test*." The *expectation test* will only work when you have clearly identified what is not going your way, and by contrast, what you want. If you answer yes to each of the conditions in the third step, you will most likely want to look for an external resolution. If you answer no to one or more, you may want to pursue an internal resolution, or revise what you want so that you get yes answers. The steps are as follows:

1. Identify precisely what is not going my way.

2. Identify precisely what you want.

3. When I consider the big picture (all of the relevant circumstances), is what I want integrity-based and:

   a) Realistic?

   b) Reasonable?

   c) Relationally fair?

   d) Relatively important?

> **EXTERNAL RESOLUTIONS FOR MAD.**

GET ASSERTIVE. Work your way through the steps of The Cognitive Challenge. If necessary, formulate an action plan or an assertive solution that is consistent with your belief system. With this resolution, clearly identify your needs, wants, rights, responsibilities, and weigh those with the other(s). Make sure you consider the *"big picture."* Can you convert your anger into an assertive request for change? Remember, you can't get what you want unless you ask for it. Your ego may want to take a passive, aggressive, or passive-aggressive problem solving approach. This resolution is about getting assertive. Review Chapter 6 on Assertive Behavior and Chapter 8 on Functional Anger.

> **The Belief System Formula:** I value assertiveness. Assertiveness is right for me. I expect myself to challenge my anger. I am assertive.

> **The Perceptual Challenge:** I see anger as an opportunity to learn about assertiveness.

ESTABLISH A RELATIONSHIP POLICY. When you believe that someone has "done you wrong" and you want to continue the relationship, you may need to clarify the "rules" of the relationship. Remaining angry with someone may fuel your ego's agenda. You begin with an awareness that the other individual has an ego with an agenda. Instead of maintaining an angry focus on the "bad" thing the other individual did or neglected to do, define what you need or want to be different. In a friendly manner, you ask for the realistic, reasonable, and relationally fair change and wait for the their response. "From now on Ted, I'd like for you to call me if you are going to be more than twenty minutes late, are you willing to do that?" It is important to end most assertive statements with a question to clarify the other's commitment to change. In other words, you attempt to clarify the structure of the relationship.

The agreed upon commitment to change becomes what I call a relationship policy. This policy combined with their ability to follow through, will allow you to determine trustworthiness over time. The mistake most people make in relationships is to maintain an ego focus on the bad or wrong behavior of the other and then attempt to change that person through criticism, judgment, parenting, or threat. These tactics eventually cause damage to relationships and lead to a continuation of problems. If the other is willing to apologize, then you may want to ask them to specifically define why they think their behavior was wrong for them and/or the relationship. A clear response here will serve to strengthen the relationship in that there is a greater sense that you are both on the same moral page. Ideally, in the end you have asked for what you want or need, clarified future expected behavior, and let go of the anger. Forgiveness becomes more agreeable with this relational clarification. There is always a possibility that you may not get cooperation. In that case, return to the Cognitive Challenge, or consider a different feeling resolution.

> **The Belief System Formula:** I value internal-power. Forgiveness is right behavior. I expect myself to forgive as appropriate. I am a forgiving person.

> **The Perceptual Challenge:** I see anger as an opportunity to become more forgiving. I see anger as an opportunity to develop relational trust.

COMPROMISE. In using this resolution for anger, you would want to consider the big picture, and determine what is in *Your Best Interest*. Compromise means being able to appreciate and consider someone else's point of view along with their needs and wants. You will want to be aware of ego stubbornness as you relax your natural desire for control. Can you remain open to consider compromise and/or negotiation? How much are you willing to depart from your values and/or moral code in order to maintain a relationship? It is more tolerable to compromise in a relationship when there is a balanced history of give and take from both parties, or when both clearly gain from the arrangement. In other words, "My experiences with you over time allow me to trust that it's ok to compromise with you." Still, sometimes it is hard to give up what you want so very much. There is integrity in being able to say, "I am willing to compromise, even though I experience some loss of what I wanted, because there is a gain for us." For help with this, take a look at sad resolutions in the next chapter. After your careful consideration (the cognitive challenge), perhaps some things cannot be compromised. There is also integrity in being able to say, "This is very important to me (*YOBI* valued), so I'm afraid I just can't compromise in this case."

> **The Belief System Formula:** I value compromise that is in my best interest. Compromise is right behavior. I expect myself to compromise when possible. I am fair.

The Perceptual Challenge: I see anger as an opportunity to learn about compromise.

BREAK IT UP. (*Procrastination Part 1*) "I don't like having to do this." "I'm afraid I'll do a bad job." These are two different types of thoughts, which produce two different feelings. As you can see, the feeling origin of procrastination could be based in either ego anger or ego fear. Procrastination as a behavior is seen as the avoidance of a certain task. Fortunately, almost any task, big or small, can be broken down into a number of smaller, organized, and prioritized tasks. At some point, the smaller tasks become tolerable, and therefore approachable. You could also mix in some enjoyable (perhaps ego gratifying) activity in-between the tasks. So, when you face what appears to be an overwhelming task of gigantic proportions, and your "I don't like this" angry ego thinking has brought you to a screeching halt, remember—think "BOP'EM" : break it down, organize it, prioritized it, and ego mix it up. Then celebrate the completion of each small victory toward the big victory at the end. I have worked with many clients who are looking for a magic solution to the problem of procrastination. If there is a magical solution, it is related to how you perceive the problem and the outcome. The problem is the ego thinking too big; the solution is to think smaller from a different perspective.

> **The Belief System Formula:** I value the "BOP'EM" resolution. Putting work first and play later is a healthy approach for me. I expect myself to effectively approach big tasks and break them down. I am effective.

> **The Perceptual Challenge:** I see anger as an opportunity to become more effective and experience a proud outcome.

➤ **INTERNAL RESOLUTIONS FOR MAD.**

UNDERSTAND AND PRACTICE FORGIVENESS OF THE HUMAN RACE.

Expect that everyone out there has an ego with an agenda just like you. Some are more aware of this fact than others. Some attempt to transcend or go beyond their ego, and some do not. Staying angry with people in general for being human and following their nature will only fuel your ego's agenda and decrease your level of trust in the world. Challenge yourself to be ready to forgive. This form of forgiveness doesn't mean that you tolerate bad behavior from others. It means that you are able to understand human nature, set limits where appropriate, and move on.

So, realistically expect that *some* people in *some* circumstances on *some* occasions will want to use you to:

1.   Relieve their pain.

2.   Increase their gratification.

3.   Increase their sense of power and control.

4.   Create or confirm a sense of their ego-ideal such as overall superiority, intelligence, attractiveness, bigger, better, faster, stronger, etc.

When this happens, remember to respond from your belief system. Practically speaking, you may want to establish an overall belief (expectation) that just like you, others around you will follow their ego's agenda, and on those occasions when they don't, celebrate!

> **The Belief System Formula:** I value forgiveness of others. It is right to forgive others whenever I can. Practicing forgiveness increases my inner-peace. I am forgiving.

> **The Perceptual Challenge:** I see anger as an opportunity to become compassionate.

MAKE A RULE. You may need to establish a rule for yourself that says, "I don't act on intense anger until I have given myself time to fully consider my options in a moment of calmness." If you are prone to acting out your anger impulsively, your ego may put up a fight against this rule. Some might say that rules are meant to be broken, this one is not.

> **The Belief System Formula:** I value self-control. Thinking before I act is right behavior. I expect to exercise self-control over my anger. I am responsible for my behavior. I am my behavior.

> **The Perceptual Challenge:** I see anger as an opportunity to grow into peacefulness.

YOBI REALIGNMENT. You may determine that the origin of your anger is due to an expectation that is no longer realistic and is not aligned with *YOBI*. This kind of anger may be maintained at a subconscious level of awareness. In that case, you will need to do some conscious work to establish a new and more realistic belief, and then go about finding evidence to support it. You might find help with this in Chapters 9, 10, and 11, or by using the Establishing A New Value worksheet in Appendix B.

> **The Belief System Formula:** I value being realistic. It is right for me to maintain realistic thinking. I expect myself to monitor my cycle-logical functioning. I am grounded in reality.

> **The Perceptual Challenge:** I see anger as an opportunity to become more realistic.

"OH WELL..." An entire solution summed up in two powerful words. What does this solution really mean? "I didn't get what I wanted, oh well, it's really in my best interest to move on." This is only healthy to the extent that you really believe what you are saying to yourself. In contrast, using "oh well" as ego maintenance to cover up a specific continuing disappointment will do more harm than good in the long run.

> **The Belief System Formula:** I value the ability to move on. It is right for me to detach from outcomes that are no longer in my best interest. I expect to detach as necessary and appropriate. I am seeking out my own best interest.

> **The Perceptual Challenge:** I see anger as an opportunity to learn about detachment and moving on.

TRANSFORM YOUR ANGER. Transforming the feeling of anger requires you to look *beneath* your anger-based thinking to a subconscious level. Beneath anger you will discover a desire for change. The fact is that some things in life we cannot change. Therefore, you may need to consider acceptance of what you cannot change (go to resolutions for sad solutions below to deal with the loss of your expectation). As you explore your anger you may determine that it is actually related to a possible negative consequence. That is, "I don't like what could happen." It would be far more helpful to deal with this situation as fear rather than anger (go to fear solutions below). If you determine that your anger is due to how you behaved, "I'm not happy with how I did that, it was wrong," you will want to explore your guilt at some point rather than to beat up on yourself for too long (go to resolutions for bad solutions below).

> **The Belief System Formula:** I value self-discovery. It is right for me to think through my feelings. I will explore my feelings in search of greater meaning prior to acting on them. I am in search of a deeper self.

> **The Perceptual Challenge:** I see anger as an opportunity to become more insightful.

FORCE AN EMOTIONAL CHANGE. Take a temporary break from your anger and force a positive emotional change until you can make a cognitive change. This resolution is about doing something predictably enjoyable to help you get your mind off of whatever you are mad about. This will give your brain and the rest of your body a temporary break from the stress, and allow you to look at the problem later with a fresh perspective. I often recommend doing something that will completely grab your perception and hold it there, such as seeing a movie at a theater (with snacks). Another good idea for some is the combination of taking a warm bath with music, something tasty to eat or drink, something pleasantly aromatic, and low lighting. Either of these environments considerably stimulate your senses at the same time, and give you a temporary break. Of course, you will eventually want to return to a cognitive form of problem solving.

> **The Belief System Formula:** I value self-nurturing behavior. Sometimes, the right thing is to take a break from my feelings. I expect myself to take a break as appropriate. I am flexible.

The Perceptual Challenge: I see anger as an opportunity to learn about adaptability.

THE VIRTUE OF PATIENCE. In many ways, the opposite of anger is patience. As you look beneath the feeling of anger to its subconscious origin, you may find a desire for results to happen on your time schedule. The resolution here is simple. "Things (self, others, world) will not always go my way or according to my time schedule." This resolution is about learning to delay gratification when appropriate. How do you know what wait time frame is appropriate? You apply the cognitive challenge, or the *expectation test*. In other words, "What is a realistic, reasonable, and fair time frame for this situation?" Believe it or not, an effective way to learn the value of patience is to simply practice it. For example, if you practice appropriate patience while driving in rush hour traffic, you may find that your experience is much more pleasant than if you maintain a focus on the idea that the person in front of you isn't going fast enough. So you choose to focus your attention on something pleasant. With this resolution you create peace of mind through your choices.

> **The Belief System Formula:** I value patience. Practicing appropriate patience is the right thing to do. I will practice patience whenever I have appropriate opportunities. I am patient.

> **The Perceptual Challenge:** I see anger as an opportunity to learn the value of patience.

WELCOME CHANGE. At this point you probably know that a fundamental and critical action step involved in effective anger management is to monitor your expectations. This resolution challenges you to maintain a global expectation, or belief, about the reality of change. You cannot anticipate every little possible change that life has to offer. However, you can develop a realistic acceptance that you change, other people change, the world will change. Expect that change will be part of life, and that will never change. To the extent that you understand the nature of change, you will be less angry as you encounter it.

> **The Belief System Formula:** I value the potential benefit that comes from change. It is right for me to welcome appropriate change. I expect myself to be open to change and engage in adaptive behavior. I am open-minded.

> **The Perceptual Challenge:** I see anger as an opportunity and means for my own transformation.

APPLICATION OF THE METHOD

Henry was really struggling with his weight situation. Upon further exploration we determined that on a subconscious level Henry was feeling quite angry with himself, and the world in general. "I am so angry that I can't get myself to stop my out-of-control feeding-frenzy." We did some work to identify his specific angry thought and then applied the steps of the Cognitive Challenge. Step 1) My eating is out of control. Step 2) I want to have complete control over my eating from now on. Step 3) It is not realistic to have complete control. It is not reasonable to expect a person to perfectly follow a plan. It is not fair to expect myself to be perfectly controlled all of the time in how I eat. This is very important to me. What Henry wanted did not pass the challenge.

We determined at that point that Henry needed to revise what he wanted and develop a new expectation of himself. The new belief system entry needed to be consciously developed and then regularly brought to his conscious awareness until it became subconsciously maintained. The new expectation needed to pass the challenge. From then on, he expected the following: "I will eat according to a healthy dietary plan. There will be days that I won't follow my plan perfectly, but I can continue when I want. This will be a lifestyle change to include a healthy exercise program."

Exercise 13-1: Use the cognitive challenge and choose the appropriate resolutions to manage your anger and/or stress. Then, go to appendix F and write down the values, morals, expectations, or self-image statements that honor and support your resolutions.

14   Managing 'Sad'

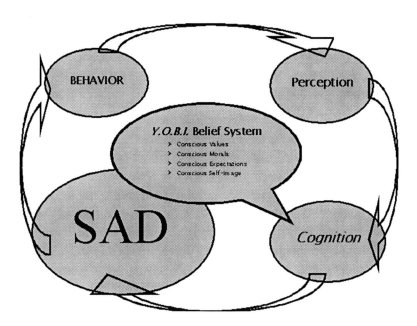

The Desire for Same

The feeling of sadness is related to the experience of loss. Sadness is experienced when you anticipate loss, imagine loss, or when you have actually suffered a loss. There are qualities of helplessness and hopelessness that accompany sadness, which can develop over time into full-blown depression. Loss occurs in the *macro* and the *micro* levels of our lives. There are big losses such as death, divorce, and termination from a job. Then there are smaller losses like broken vases, stolen bicycles, and favorite sunglasses thrown out by accident with the garbage. Sadness can be experienced on any level of awareness. There are also the *intangible*, or *conceptual* losses in life. Not only can we experience the loss of things or people we value, we can conceptually feel the loss of hope, freedom, future dreams, and trust in others. Regardless of the magnitude, level of awareness, or form, the origin of sad still has to do with loss.

To the extent that mad is about wanting change, sad is about wanting things to stay the same. Sadness and anger are opposites in this respect. Underlying the experience of sadness you will find that you want to maintain the status quo. Fundamentally, you become sad when you experience a loss. If you take that a step further, you would probably like to reverse the loss, and maintain the former experience. Thus, underlying the experience of sadness is a desire for things to stay the same. Understanding the concept of sadness in this manner may transform how you deal with it.

Value and timing are critical features of how we deal with loss; "how important was the loss to me, how much time did I have to prepare, and what if any other significant stress was I facing at the time?" As a general rule, the more we value something, the more intense the sadness is when it becomes a loss. Sometimes we know a loss is coming and we can prepare for it over time. The grieving involved with the loss of a loved one who had been diagnosed with a terminal illness then gradually declined over ten years, is very different from being caught off guard when a son or daughter is suddenly killed in an automobile accident.

The experience of disappointment could be looked at as a kind of cognitive bridge from mad to sad. The general kind of thinking process related to disappointment is, "I really wanted that job (or other valued outcome or possibility) but I just don't think it's going to happen, and I'm really disappointed." This cognitive transition from mad to sad is a process similar to grieving, but on a lesser scale. Disappointment might also be looked at as preparation for grieving, "I'll soon know for sure, but for now, I guess I'm really beginning to believe that this proposal is not going to turn out like I wanted it to. This may be a big disappointment." In disappointment, there is a period of time to fully consider the possibility of loss. The experience of disappointment can be a very healthy way of moving from the original expectation, to a decision or realization that what I wanted does not seem possible. Therefore, "I really need to consider it a loss."

➢ **ALTERNATIVE SAD INTENSITY WORDS.**

Hurt	Helpless	Grieving
Down	Hopeless	Devastated
Depressed	Blue	Despairing

➢ **THE TYPE OF THOUGHT THAT PRODUCES SAD.**

"This is a loss."

"I am helpless to do anything about this."

"This is hopeless."

"I think this is going to be a loss."

"I think this is a loss."

"This loss is painful."

➢ SAD PERSPECTIVES.

Ego Sad: "Things won't ever go my way."

"I never get what I want."

"I've lost power."

"I've lost control."

"Why do things always have to change?"

YOBI Sad: "This really hurts."

"This could hurt for a while."

"This really caught me off guard."

"Some things are going to change."

"It may not be easy, but I know I can get through this."

"This isn't what I wanted, but I can adjust."

➢ THE COGNITIVE CHALLENGE FOR SAD.

The challenge associated with sad is to again "apply the *expectation test*." The *expectation test* will only work when you have clearly identified the loss, and by contrast, what you are trying to maintain. When considering the challenge, keep in mind that the extent of your ability to control external conditions has limitations. If you answer yes to each of the conditions in the third step, you will most likely want to look for an external resolution. If you answer no to one or more, you may want to pursue an internal resolution, or revise what you want to maintain so that you get yes answers. The steps are as follows:

1. Identify the loss am I concerned with.

2. Identify what I am trying to maintain.

3. When I consider the big picture, is what I want to maintain integrity-based and:

    a) Realistic?

    b) Reasonable?

    c) Relationally fair?

    d) Relatively important?

➢ EXTERNAL RESOLUTIONS FOR SAD.

HEALTHY DISAPPOINTMENT. Some people have a habit of giving up too soon on what they want. Disappointment can be an important transition for people who quickly resign themselves to sadness due to *learned helplessness*. Learned helplessness is generally created in early childhood. In childhood, you are dependent on the caretakers in your environment for survival. They had the power and authority to control your environment completely. If they denied the majority of your needs or wants over time, you would eventually conclude, quite logically, that it was a hopeless cause, and that you were helpless to effectively do anything about it. You learned that you should not consider your needs or wants because they are irrelevant. This resolution is for those of us who "give up too soon." Evaluate your loss with the cognitive challenge, before you give up. The experience of disappointment can be a positive transition for those who are quick to leap into helplessness and sadness without going through an appropriate amount of problem solving. In other words, if you have been told that you "give up too soon," you may want to *try on* a little disappointment for size. Take some time to go back and look at mad resolutions for problem solving ideas while *wearing* that disappointment.

> **The Belief System Formula:** I value reconsideration of loss. It's right for me consider assertiveness as an option. I expect myself to reconsider initial sadness. I am able to reconsider lost opportunities.

> **The Perceptual Challenge:** I see sadness as an opportunity to be taught about perseverance.

TRANSFORM YOUR SADNESS. Transforming the feeling of sad requires you to look beneath the sadness-based thinking to a subconscious level. Beneath sadness you may find a desire for things to stay the same, to maintain the *status quo*. As you further explore your sadness, you may determine that it is actually related to a possible negative consequence. That is, "I am afraid to deal with the loss that I think is going to happen." It would be far more helpful to begin dealing with this potential loss as a fear rather than sadness (go to fear solutions). If you determine that your sadness is due to how you behaved, "I'm not happy with how I did that, it was wrong, I've lost my self respect and dignity," you will want to explore your guilt at some point rather than to conclude that all is lost with regard to your integrity (go to bad solutions). And finally, if you realize your sadness is due to stubborn resistance, "I didn't ask for this and I just don't want to deal with this loss," you may want to look at dealing with this as anger (go to mad resolutions).

> **The Belief System Formula:** I value being able to contemplate my disappointment long enough to consider other options. It's right for me to face emotional pain. I will face emotional pain courageously. I am able to tolerate emotion.

> **The Perceptual Challenge:** I see sadness as an opportunity to learn about tolerance.

➤ **INTERNAL RESOLUTIONS FOR SAD.**

NOTHING LASTS FOREVER. Expect that loss will be a part of life; this isn't a philosophical epiphany. It's not pretty, glamorous, fancy, or clever. Its just plain old-fashioned truth that we need to get used to. Someone whom I greatly respect and love has a way of summing this up, "Just suck it up, and move on." Now those are words to live by. The simple and undisputable truth is, *things* in life will change; *you* will change, *people* around you will change, your *environments* will change, and your *world* will continue to change. Some changes bring about loss. The question is, "Will your belief system tolerate change and accept loss as necessary?" There is no doubt that some changes and losses are extremely painful and avoidance would seem to be preferable. There is also no doubt that some losses are real and not reversible. Resistance and the persistent avoidance of the reality of those losses will prolong your suffering. Your acceptance doesn't necessarily mean that you believe the change or loss is right, it simply means that you acknowledge reality. When you experience persistent sadness about a specific loss, right or wrong, you may need to consider acceptance of what you cannot change, and move on through a process of grieving.

> **The Belief System Formula:** I value being able to detach with honor. It is right for me to detach as appropriate with a minimum of struggle. I expect myself to recognize loss when it is apparent. I am honorable.

> **The Perceptual Challenge:** I see sadness as an opportunity to be taught about honor.

BEGIN TO GRIEVE THE LOSS. With a real confirmed loss, you will want to begin a process of actively grieving. This means establishing full awareness of the loss, and dealing with it. One simple description of the process of grieving was introduced in Chapter 2 and includes the following stages: denial, anger, bargaining, despair, and acceptance. The first phase, denial, is fear-based cognition about a bad outcome or situation that has been brought to awareness. "This is not happening," must eventually become, "This is happening, and I am facing this outcome." Next phase is anger, "This is not going my way," must be transformed into, "I can't change this," or, "This outcome will not change." In the bargaining phase, associated with the feeling category bad, one attempts to change the undesired (bad) outcome through negotiation. "Have I done something wrong," must be transformed into an honest appraisal of "right or wrong, I will face this change and learn from it." Despair or sadness is central to the concept of grief, "This loss really hurts, how can I go on?" The healthy resolution is, "This really did happen, this does hurt, and this is a change." The final phase, acceptance, is most closely associated with glad, "I have survived this real loss, things really have changed, I am readjusting, moving on, and now looking forward in my life." Theoretically, with acceptance the grieving cycle is complete or resolving. If any of these phases has not been completed with a healthy resolution thought, the feeling can remain an obstacle to being able to move on. The time frame involved in this process can be minutes or years, depending on the perceived value of the object of loss.

The external form of this resolution involves going through the steps of your grieving and writing down all of your thoughts and feelings relate to the phases.

> **The Belief System Formula:** I value growth through grieving. It's right for me grieve as necessary and appropriate. I expect myself to face loss courageously. I am brave.

> **The Perceptual Challenge:** I see sadness as an opportunity to learn about the transformation of pain.

REFRAME THE LOSS. Take another look at your loss and see if you can frame it in a different perceptual way. Can you take the lemons at hand and make lemonade? Can you see the glass as being half full instead of half empty? Is it possible that you can find a potential gain that coexists with your loss? I find that when properly motivated, people can do amazing reframing. Reframing is similar to conscious ego maintenance in that you are trying to manipulate your thinking in a way to justify or rationalize a specific perceptual outcome. The difference is that the desired outcome is consistent with your belief system and represents *YOBI*. For example, divorce, being laid off at work, or death are all forms of loss. These are painful losses. It may help to tell yourself, "Along with the divorce comes the freedom to plan my own direction in life." With death, "The universe works in mysterious ways that we don't always understand, I don't like it, but maybe it's for the greater good." With other types of losses or adjustment, you may tell yourself, "What comes around goes around," "Every cloud has a silver lining," "Things happen for a reason," or "When one door shuts another opens."

These are most likely familiar sayings to you. They are familiar because they work for many people quite well. However, any of these reframing statements will only work if you genuinely believe it, or can find truth in it for you and your situation. Remember, you cannot fool yourself for long. Your feelings will bear out your most fundamental truth. If you tell yourself, "Its ok, I was dumped by my boyfriend, but things happen for a reason," and you continue to cry and remain sad for six months, you apparently do not believe your reframing statement on a deep level of awareness. In order to move on, you will need to do some additional processing of the feelings around your loss. If you are not ready to accept the reality of your loss, you will most likely not be willing to engage in the process of letting go, and subsequent moving on.

> **The Belief System Formula:** I value being able to find the silver lining with every cloud. It's right for look for positives. I expect to find positive perceptions when I look for them. I am able to create joy in my life.

> **The Perceptual Challenge:** I see sadness as an opportunity to learn about optimism.

RE-ASSESS WHAT YOU HAVE. This might simply be regarded as "counting your blessings." When you find yourself in a painful grieving process of letting go, your focus will be on "the loss" of what you no longer have. You can become stuck in a perspective of what you don't have. You may experience a perceptual snowball effect of thinking about all of the other losses you have had. It may be helpful to consider that which you still have. For some, this is a difficult task. You may have lost your job, but you do have skills to apply elsewhere. You may have not been able to get that new car that you wanted, but you do have a roof over your head and food in your home. Cases of disaster such as fire, flood, and hurricane are relatively rare. Fortunately, most of us are spared these and other horrendous situations. Anyone who survives such an event may be greatly challenged for a long time to adjust and recover; perhaps never again being fully the same. Most of us can truly count ourselves lucky to be able to live without encountering disasters. Take another look at your life to see what you may be taking for granted.

> **The Belief System Formula:** I value what I have in my life. It's right for me to acknowledge my good fortune. I expect myself to remember and acknowledge what I have. I am grateful.

> **The Perceptual Challenge:** I see sadness as an opportunity to learn about gratitude.

➢ APPLICATION OF THE METHOD.

Henry had made some behavioral changes related to his weight situation. Five weeks into his plan, he reported, "I've been feeling different lately, it seems that I cry for no reason at times, and I think I may be depressed." We started the session with clearly identifying the feeling involved; he was sad. Upon further exploration we determined that his sadness was subconscious; it happened for "no reason." I asked Henry, "What is your loss?" The immediate physical reaction was clear in Henry's eyes as they swelled with emotion. "I feel as if I've lost my best friend, food. Also, I am becoming aware of how much time in my life I've wasted in the pursuit of gratification from food. There is lost time I could have spent with friends, family, and in pursuit of some meaningful activities or hobbies. Then there's the loss of time and money spent trying out every diet or exercise machine on television that never worked. There has been more loss than I've ever considered before. I realize I can't change what I've done, the choices I've made." While tears flowed down his cheeks, I allowed some time for the reality of this pain to be experienced without interruption.

"This has been very painful for you; you'll need some time to grieve this loss. It seems that you're grieving losses. The time and money are real losses, and food can no longer be your substitute for a best friend." In time we moved on to the next series of questions. To reframe the loss I asked, "What have you gained from this loss? What do you have to be thankful for? How will you move on?" One by one we addressed these questions. Henry had much in his life to be thankful for. He made a list of his good fortune, and then made a commitment to remind himself of the list on a regular basis. The time and money were gone. Now he realized the true importance of his future choices and the impact on his peace of mind. He knew how to move on by developing new values, morals, and expectations. "Its time for me to develop real relationships with real people, and make lifestyle changes in my exercise and eating habits." We incorporated these values into his belief system and emphasized the gains from which he could expect to benefit. Henry also decided to challenge his thinking and perception, "From now on, I'm going to see my emotions as resources for learning about myself, and not as pain that I need to seek refuge from in a bowl of ice cream or a bag of corn chips."

Exercise 14-1: Use the cognitive challenge and choose the appropriate resolutions to manage your sadness and/or stress. Then, go to appendix F and write down the values, morals, expectations, or self-image statements that honor and support your resolutions.

15 Managing 'Bad'

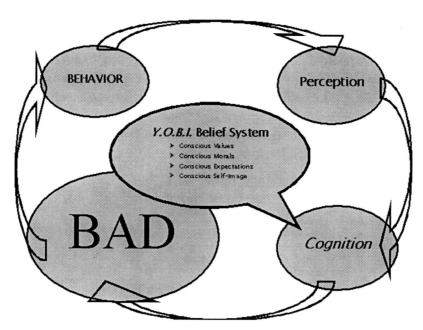

The Desire for Security

The feeling of guilt (bad) is based in noncompliance with moral code standards. Guilt can be experienced as a result of not living up to expectations established by you, someone else, or some other perceived outside authority. Resolution is partly dependent on determining the origin of the guilt in one of those three realms. In other words, "Whose moral code standards am I in conflict with?" Of course, guilt can be experienced on any level of awareness. Intense guilt that is produced from a deep subconscious level of awareness is possibly rooted in early childhood: "I feel really bad. I just can't figure out why, and it makes no sense to me."

Guilt is an unpleasant and powerful emotion. Beneath the experience of guilt you may find a desire for security. This is a simple, yet perhaps compelling way to explain the power of guilt as being related to a fear of loss of security. The subconscious mind may equate guilt with being disconnected from the group, severe hardship, punishment, or even death as a result of having done something wrong. From an ego perspective, it is dangerous to be ostracized or ousted from the group. As you experience guilt, your own ego maintenance may take over in an effort to reduce this emotional pain. In other words, you may automatically become defensive, shift blame, point fingers, or find other ways to keep power and control, and sustain an idealized public view. In a larger sense, your ego would like to maintain its value or power in the group. Essentially, a positive view of ourselves gives us a sense of security, "I'm ok." Thus, underlying the experience of guilt may be a desire for security. Understanding the concept of guilt in this manner may transform how you deal with it.

When it comes to accepting responsibility for the impact of one's behavior in relationship to others, or with the surrounding environment, some individuals underestimate their impact, while others overestimate it. That is, due to ego involvement, you may underestimate: "I'm not bad, others are…I don't act bad, others do." Or, you may overestimate: "This is all my fault, I'm probably wrong as usual…I'm in need of security and approval, so I'll take the blame." Therefore, know how your own ego maintenance generally works, monitor your guilt (or lack of), and apply the cognitive challenge accordingly.

> ## ALTERNATIVE **BAD** INTENSITY WORDS.

Guilty	Self-Reproach	Remorse
Shame	Repentant	Embarrassed
Dishonor	Wrong	Disgrace

> ## THE TYPE OF THOUGHT THAT PRODUCES **BAD**.

"That was the wrong thing for me to do."

"I really let them down."

"How could I have done that?"

"Why did I do that?"

"I can't do that any more."

"I feel horrible about this."

> ## **BAD** PERSPECTIVES.

Ego Bad: "I can't ever seem to do the right thing."

"I'll never forgive myself."

"I hate it when I can't live up to her standards."

"I gave up too much power."

"I gave up too much control."

"I should have been able to prevent that."

YOBI Bad: "That was the wrong thing for me to do."

"That wasn't the right thing for me to say."

"I approached that situation wrong."

"My behavior is against my own standards."

"I have really let myself down."

> ## THE COGNITIVE CHALLENGE FOR BAD.

Bad, or guilt, is probably the most complex of the five feeling categories. The challenge associated with bad is to "apply the *expectation test*" only after you have clearly identified the wrong thought or behavior, and the moral code responsible. The following steps will ultimately lead you toward a resolution that is external, internal, or perhaps a blending of the two. Generally speaking, if you answer yes to each of the conditions in the third step, you will most likely want to look for an external resolution. If you answer no to one or more, you may want to pursue an internal resolution or modification. The steps are as follows:

1. Identify what you think you have done wrong.

2. Clearly identify the specific moral code standard you think you are in conflict with.

3. When I consider the big picture, is the standard integrity-based and:
   a) Realistic?
   b) Reasonable?
   c) Relationally fair?
   d) Relatively important?

> ## EXTERNAL RESOLUTIONS FOR BAD.

ACKNOWLEDGE THE CONFLICT (with behavioral change). Resolving your guilt may or may not involve another person. If you challenge your guilt, you may conclude that you have indeed breached your own standards for conduct. With this resolution, you further conclude that the standard is in *Your Own Best Interest*, and choose to maintain the standard exactly as it is. Finally, you vow to yourself to change the conflicted behavior. "I did something wrong according to my own moral code. I believe I was wrong, and because I believe in this standard, I make a commitment to myself to change the behavior."

> **The Belief System Formula:** I value integrity. It's right for me to be responsible to myself. I expect myself to behave in a responsible manner. I am responsible.

> **The Perceptual Challenge:** My experience with guilt can teach me about integrity.

APOLOGY OR CONFESSION (with behavioral change). When you conclude that your misbehavior has done harm to a person or a relationship, there is an additional step to take. You complete the above acknowledgement resolution, and include an apology or confession of wrongdoing to the other person. An appropriate and effective method includes: 1) a genuine verbalization of being sorry, 2) a description of how you disregarded you own standard, 3) why in your own opinion it was wrong, and 4) your specific plan for behavioral change. In order to create or maintain trust in the relationship, you'll also want to be accountable for the misbehavior, and be sure to follow through with the stated behavior change. "I'm really sorry that I didn't get the laundry done last night as I said I would. It's important to me to follow our plan of keeping up with chores around here. I got caught up in a movie that I started to watch, and I didn't make time for it like I should have. It was completely my fault, and from now on, I'm going to make sure I get it done as we agreed."

> **The Belief System Formula:** I value accountability. It's right for me to be accountable to those that I care about. I expect myself to face those that I care about with honor and courage. I am accountable.

> **The Perceptual Challenge:** I see guilt as an opportunity to learn about humility.

SELF-FORGIVENESS (with behavioral change). We all fall short of living up to our own moral standards perfectly, and we have made mistakes in the past. We can be haunted by these mistakes and suffer over time with self-loathing or possibly even depression. This resolution of guilt, "I did the best I could at the time," is best implemented when you have already established it as your belief. The belief is essentially this: "I believe people do the best they can just to survive at any moment, as they understand the moment, themselves, and, as they perceive life. They are engaged in this survival within the context of balancing pleasure and pain, and with respect to their own values and morals in that moment." This belief can be maintained in the expectations component of your belief system. If you can find meaning and truth in this belief, then you can apply it not only to other people, but to yourself as well.

Let me break this belief down into smaller pieces. On a fundamental level, we are all trying to survive. This fundamental directive may not always be clearly observable in our everyday behavior. However, it will become observable whenever you perceive your life to be in danger. The ego is clearly interested in survival. It believes that painful feelings are dangerous and will attempt to convince you to avoid them and the situations that generate them. Simultaneously, we seek out gratification and gratifying experiences. The ego would obviously like to create mostly gratification, but will settle for a balance of these first two agenda directives. Additionally, we may be attempting to follow established morals and values. Over the course of your life, morals and values can change, and what is emotionally or physically gratifying or painful may also change. Moreover, as all of these changes occur over time, our view of self, others and life also change. So a bad choice that you made eight years ago, or eight days ago, was made within a context of that time and your belief system at that time. You might not make the same choice today. Holding on to your guilt will not change the past. Concluding that you did the best you could at that time, based on your belief system and your pain at that time helps you to let go of the guilt. Follow the steps from the above Apology or Confession resolution as you essentially apologize to yourself and establish a moral standard that applies for today and the future.

You may have some difficulty with this resolution if you are not convinced that you did the best you could. In that case, recall your misdeed and the circumstances at that time, and ask yourself, "Why didn't I make a different choice?" If you have further doubt, keep this in mind: Emotions, both painful and pleasurable, when combined with the convincing nature of ego maintenance, can be powerful motivators of misguided behavior. Expect that in life you will make mistakes, or fall short of your own standards along the way. Expect yourself to follow your own moral code consistently, but not perfectly. This resolution is not to be used as disguised ego maintenance; this is a form of self-compassion. Be understanding and gentle with yourself, but firm in upholding your moral code.

> **The Belief System Formula:** I value being able to engage in self-compassion. It's right for me to be fair with myself. I expect that I will make mistakes. I am fair and compassionate with myself.

> **The Perceptual Challenge:** I see guilt as an opportunity to learn about compassion.

➤ INTERNAL RESOLUTIONS FOR BAD.

APPROVAL SEEKERS & CONFLICT AVOIDERS. Approval seeking individuals feel guilty when they perceive that someone is angry with them. Someone else's anger at you is not necessarily your problem, nor does it need to be your automatic guilt. Consider establishing the following belief for yourself: "If someone is angry with me it simply means that they do not like the way I am behaving, SO WHAT!"

1. "I did not make them mad and I do not have to make them feel better."

2. Another person can perceive, think about, have feelings about, and respond to my behavior. However, "I cannot create feelings in someone else."

3. "I may want to evaluate my behavior to see that it is reflective of my own morals and values, which generates my own approval."

4. If necessary, "I may want to make reflective changes in my behavior (reflective of my morals and values), and act accordingly, to again end up with my own approval." Self-ish-ness equals integrity.

5. "I may not want to make any changes at all."

The Belief System Formula: I value my own approval. It's right for me to seek out my own approval. I expect myself to develop self-approval. I am approved of by me.

The Perceptual Challenge: I see guilt as a means of becoming more independent.

TRANSFORM YOUR GUILT. Sometimes guilt is related to group mentality and the possibility of abandonment or being thrown out of the group. This guilt is obviously related more to security than to a breach of internal morality. Transforming this kind of bad feeling requires you to look beneath the guilt-based thinking to a subconscious level. Beneath guilt you may find that your thinking has nothing to do with morality. "I feel bad, and I determine it comes from thinking that I will displease others (**fear** of their consequences for noncompliance)." "I feel bad, and I determine that it comes from thinking that I easily succumb to the wishes of others (**mad** at myself for not being assertive)." "I feel bad, and I determine that it comes from thinking about a loss of relationship (**sad** about abandonment)." It would be far more helpful to begin dealing with this kind of guilt by *thinking it* into another feeling realm, and then problem solving it as such. Essentially, with this resolution you conclude that you have done nothing wrong according to your own standards but have misidentified your feeling as guilt. You can then take steps to resolve your feeling with other more appropriate internal and external resolutions.

The fact of the matter is, you will not please all people. The question is, "Will you please yourself; will you maintain integrity?" There are going to be times when you may need to risk some amount of security loss in order to maintain personal integrity. That is, you may need to displease others in order to please yourself. For those who are inclined toward people pleasing, this notion will seem selfish and you will likely experience guilt. However, to the extent that your belief system has been consciously developed by you, *"self-ish-ness"* will be equal to integrity. You may need to consciously remind yourself of this "self-ish-ness equals integrity" belief for some time until it is subconsciously maintained.

> **The Belief System Formula:** I value being able to look at guilt as a desire for security. It's right for me to explore guilt. I expect myself to face emotional pain courageously. I am emotionally healthy.

> **The Perceptual Challenge:** I see guilt as an opportunity to learn about personal integrity.

RESOLVE EXTERNAL CODE CONFLICT. To the extent that you are in conflict with someone else's moral code or some other system of morality, you may want to take a look at the external resolutions for mad, sad, or fear. For example: Susan was 38 years old, recently divorced, and living in a new city on her own for the first time in her life. She had entered therapy to help her in adjusting to her new situation. Last week, she found herself feeling bad after a phone call with her mother. Her mother was coaxing her to get a different job, "That one's not good enough for you." Susan loved her job and wanted to stay, but she felt bad about not having her mother's support.

In our next session, Susan explored her thinking related to her initial feeling of guilt and discovered that she had done nothing wrong. The bad feeling was not about a current moral code conflict, but suggested a different kind of thinking: she was not doing as her mother told her. Susan is now in a position to resolve her problem as we explore the next question: "How do you feel about not doing what your mother is telling you to do?" "Mad, because I'm tired of her not supporting me in what I want to do." "Sad, because I know that if I don't do as she says, she will withdraw from me emotionally, that's a loss." "Fear, because I think something bad will happen, I'm just not sure what." We concluded that Susan had mixed feelings about her situation, and moved into a problem-solving mode by addressing the feelings one by one, and the possible resolutions for each.

At the end of the session, Susan had decided to make some external changes. Although she would have liked her mother's support, she did not need it. The most likely worst outcome would be temporarily losing connection with her mother. This would be a chance worth taking to transform their relationship toward something healthier. From then on, prior to engaging in conversations with her mother, Susan intended to give herself a reminder to see herself as a grown and responsible adult. Also, she planned to take an assertive approach toward her mother in their future conversations.

With this resolution, you essentially have concluded that you have done nothing wrong, do not need to feel guilty, and take steps to resolve your feelings with other more appropriate external resolutions.

> **The Belief System Formula:** I value living up to my moral code. It's right to live my moral code. I expect myself to live according to my moral code. Having free will, I am ultimately accountable to me.

> **The Perceptual Challenge:** I see guilt as an opportunity for transformation.

MORAL CODE CHANGE & MODIFICATION. Is there an exception to the rule? Some of your moral code standards can be traced to early childhood. You or someone else may have developed rules for you that are based on early childhood dynamics that are no longer applicable today. For example: Jimmy was raised in an environment with very little parental supervision or involvement. He was required to take care of his younger siblings. Early on in his life, he was operating on a moral code standard that said, "Take care of others, that is your job." As an adult, he will need to modify this moral code standard when it comes to the adults in his life. At a minimum, he will need to decide whom in his life it is appropriate for him to care for, and to what extent. If he doesn't modify and establish clear parameters, Jimmy will no doubt get caught up in the position of caretaker for most people in his immediate environment and possibly become obsessive about it.

You may have been raised in an aggressive and hostile environment. In such a place, you developed subconscious standards or fundamental rules that said, "Protect yourself from others at all times, don't show weakness, and never let your guard down." As an adult you may want to modify these standards. In other words, "There are exceptions to these rules…there are some situations, times, places, when it's safe and in my best interest to be vulnerable."

> **The Belief System Formula:** I value growth and flexibility. It's right for me to look at my life in the big picture perspective. I expect to change and develop over time. I am dynamic.

> **The Perceptual Challenge:** My experience with guilt may be an opportunity for personal growth.

➢ APPLICATION OF THE METHOD.

Henry was four months into his improved lifestyle. He had established a regular workout routine and had vastly changed his dietary intake. He was feeling better both physically and emotionally, and although he had not lost a tremendous amount of weight, he felt confident about the future, "This is the best thing I could have done for myself."

It was eight-thirty on a Friday night, and Henry was finally getting home. His wife was out with her friends that evening. Having finished a stressful and longer than usual day at work with a new software program, he was wondering what to do with his time. An e-mail had arrived earlier that afternoon from his buddy. He was invited for bowling at nine-thirty. However, it was also Henry's regular workout night at the gym. He was facing a difficult decision. He knew that if he went bowling, he generally ate some junk food along with it. Henry was beginning to feel the pressure of the decision. He felt a sense of guilt as he was torn between what his ego would like to do and a course of action already determined by his belief system. He had become much better at accepting his feelings as they were and did not want to rely on ego maintenance to deal with them. He knew this was guilt, and he was willing to deal with it consciously.

The manner in which this conflict was resolved could set a precedent for how he managed any future guilt. Henry made a decision to examine his guilt through the cognitive challenge. As a result, he decided to establish an additional moral code entry that said it was basically acceptable for him to take a break from his exercise routine and healthy diet as long as he resumed them as soon as it was reasonably possible. He needed to honestly consider how he felt and make a commitment to himself to follow this additional code. He needed to be on the lookout for any ego maintenance or interference. Moreover, he needed to continue to be consciously aware of his values, morals, expectations, and self-image related to his health. In the end, Henry decided to honor his new values, and engaged in a compromise with himself:

"I'll do my workout first, have a healthy meal after, and then join my buddy at ten. When I get there, I'll have a small bag of pretzels and ice water." This was pleasing to him, his ego, and his buddy.

Exercise 15-1: Use the cognitive challenge and choose the appropriate resolutions to manage your guilt and/or stress. Then, go to appendix F and write down the values, morals, expectations, or self-image statements that honor and support your resolutions.

16 Managing 'Fear'

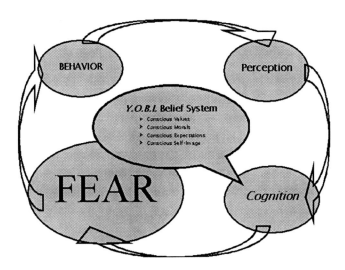

The Desire for Control

The feeling of fear is based in the anticipation of real or possible negative consequences. Similar to anger, fear can be experienced as a build up (of unresolved worries over a course of time), as a surprise (caught off guard), or anything in-between. Fear, like other feelings, can be experienced on any level of awareness. Regardless of the level of awareness, it originates from the idea or perception that something bad may happen. Fear can be experienced at any point along your cycle-logical functioning. You can think fearfully, behave with caution, and you can perceive in such a manner as to look for things to worry about. Those who believe that they need to control life will certainly look for and find things to worry about. In doing so they believe they will reduce fears and increase control.

Thanks to a survival-based ego agenda, we are compelled to establish and maintain control in an effort to reduce or eliminate our fears. Ironically, those who attempt to control others, environments, or situations may be prone to experience anxiety, panic attacks or anger over time as they discover that they cannot control everything around them. This can result in producing an equal and opposite reaction. When you are in fear of people or situations, you may try to reduce your fears by attempting to gain control. As you gain what you believe to be control, there also exists a possibility of losing it, thus the greater the amount of potential anxiety. When it comes to control, the more you perceive you have, the more you fearfully perceive you can lose—increased worry equals anxiety.

Underlying the experience of fear, you will find that you have identified some type of eventual negative consequence, or danger ahead, and on that level of awareness you are preparing for that eventuality. Fundamentally then, you believe that you are in danger and need to eliminate it. Thus, underlying the experience of fear is desire for control. Understanding the concept of fear in this manner may transform how you deal with it.

Unlike the other emotions, some would say that fear is a true primary emotion and therefore at the root of all other painful emotions. This concept was introduced and briefly discussed in Chapter 2. Again, while it is perhaps an interesting academic debate, for the purpose of problem solving I believe that working with five basic emotions is much more helpful in determining course of resolution. At any rate, it is quite possible that once you have successfully resolved other feelings you will find fear waiting for your attention and resolution. Below, you will find several possible resolutions to assist you in your efforts.

➢ ALTERNATIVE **FEAR** INTENSITY WORDS.

Scared	Nervous	Apprehensive
Afraid	Anxious	Alarmed
Terrified	Worried	Concerned

➢ THE TYPE OF THOUGHT THAT PRODUCES **FEAR**.

"Something bad is going to happen."

"I'm really worried about this."

"I think that this could really turn out bad."

"I'm feeling pretty scared."

"This is going to be horrible."

"This might get pretty bad."

➢ **FEAR** PERSPECTIVES.

Ego Fear: "I can't lose control of him."

"What if I just go crazy?"

"What else can go wrong?"

"I'm losing power over her."

"What if I lose everything?"

"Everyone will see that I'm weak."

YOBI Fear: "This is a frightening situation."

"I'm afraid I'm losing integrity."

"I'll lose self-respect if I keep doing this."

"I'm afraid that I created this bad situation."

"I'm afraid I'm not maintaining my values."

"I just don't know what to do with my life."

➤ THE COGNITIVE CHALLENGE FOR FEAR.

The challenge associated with fear is to once more "apply the *expectation test*." The *expectation test* will only work when you have clearly identified the negative consequence or danger ahead, and by contrast, what you want to control. As has been previously mentioned, "Your only real control is related to how you chose to think, what you say, and what you do." Therefore, when considering the challenge, keep in mind that your ability to control external conditions has limitations. If you answer yes to each of the conditions in the third step, you will most likely want to look for an external resolution. If you answer no to one or more, look for an internal resolution or modification. The steps are as follows:

1. Identify the danger or negative consequence I am concerned with and degree of likelihood that the negative consequence will happen.

2. Identify the extent of control (influence) I would like to have.

3. When I consider the big picture, is the extent of control (influence) I want integrity-based and:

    a) Realistic?
    b) Reasonable?
    c) Relationally fair?
    d) Relatively important?

➤ EXTERNAL RESOLUTIONS FOR FEAR.

PROACTIVITY. With this resolution, you have evaluated your worry/fear via the cognitive challenge and have determined that your fear needs external attention. Proactively managing fear means that you consciously engage in realistic problem solving while either soothing or ignoring the interference of your ego. "I see some problems emerging at work, which leads me to think our office will be shutting down." In this case, ego interference might tell you, "Don't worry, let's hope for the best, this problem can wait, this can't happen to me." By contrast, ego interference could say, "Those bad people, you can't trust them, you need to get another job as soon as possible. If I lose my job, I'm going to get even with this place somehow." Acting in *YOBI* might look like this: "You have some time to plan proactively for this possibility. You can't afford to ignore this, start networking, put your resume together, and begin to put out some feelers." In other words, "What can I do proactively to deal with this?"

> **The Belief System Formula:** I value proactively managing problems. It's right for me to proactively manage my problems. I expect myself to develop a proactive management style. I am proactive.

> **The Perceptual Challenge:** I see fear as an opportunity to become a more efficient problem solver.

SOLVE THE WORST CASE SCENARIO. "What's the worst thing that could happen?" Some individuals engage in this type of thinking automatically and regularly. They identify a possible problem, immediately imagine the worst possible outcome, and then become stuck in that fearful feeling without resolution. Any worry that remains unresolved will be left to grow in the depths of their subconscious mind. Over time, this can produce various anxiety disorders, and affect their physical well-being. The adaptive version of this thinking goes more like this, "What's the worst thing that could happen, and what could I do in that case?" Here is the alternative and adaptive method:

1. Identify the fear feeling.

2. Identify the fearful thought.

3. Apply the cognitive challenge for fear.

4. If appropriate, identify the worst-case scenario.

5. Then, identify possible solutions. The vast majority of problems encountered in life are not life threatening, and have effective solutions. The solutions oftentimes involve dealing with uncomfortable feelings, change, or confronting the object of fear which may be essentially what the ego wants to avoid.

6. As you identify a solution(s), make a solid mental note of it, or better yet, write it down including any plan of external action. With this or any other feeling solution, you will only experience a reduction of feeling if you believe what you are telling yourself. To the extent that you can commit your realistic solution to memory and/or take action you will effectively reduce your fear and potential for anxiety or future panic attacks.

This resolution might be developed into an ongoing list or journal of worry resolution. It may be of great service to your over-stimulated brain and nervous system to essentially remove these worries from your everyday thinking and write them down on paper. Writing down worries seems to be a magical process, transforming subjective brain activity into objective reality. In this form, worries are much easier to deal with. You can describe them using as much detail and depth as you wish, which can help you to see them realistically. Also, you can now begin the next two critical steps of brainstorming potential solutions for each worry, and then prioritizing the order in which you will begin to address and resolve them.

> **The Belief System Formula:** I value developing solutions for worries. It's right for me to be solution focused. I expect myself to recognize fear and resolve it with a good plan. I am a problem solver.

> **The Perceptual Challenge:** I see fear as an opportunity for learning to worry less, and experience more peace.

BACK IT UP. Make a backup plan, also known as a contingency plan. Let's say that you have come up with a great strategy for resolving a problem that has been causing you to be fearful or to worry. However, even the greatest of plans are not guaranteed. This resolution suggests having at least one additional solution to employ in the case that some unforeseen event prevents your first solution from working. "If not plan A, then plan B." Your may even want to create more than one contingency plan. This solution can really provide some peace of mind.

> **The Belief System Formula:** I value a back-up plan. It's right for me to establish a back-up plan when necessary and appropriate. I expect myself to find a back-up plan when I need it. "I've got my back."

> **The Perceptual Challenge:** I see fear as an opportunity to become self-reliant.

BREAK IT UP. (Procrastination Part 2) "I'm afraid I'll do a bad job." Again, the feeling origin of procrastination could be based in either anger or fear. Procrastination Part 1 was about the anger of not liking a task and then avoiding it. Here procrastination as a behavior is seen as the avoidance of a certain feared task outcome. This resolution is virtually the same. Again, many tasks can be broken down into a number of smaller, organized and prioritized tasks. At some point, the smaller tasks become less frightening, and therefore more approachable. So, when you are facing what appears to be a task with potentially dangerous outcomes of gigantic proportions, and your "I'm afraid of what might happen" fearful thinking has brought you to a screeching halt, remember—think "BOP'EM": break it down, organize it, prioritize it, and ego-mix it up. Then celebrate the completion of each small victory toward the big victory at the end.

> **The Belief System Formula:** I value the "BOP'EM" resolution. Putting my fears in perspective is a healthy approach for me. I expect myself to approach big tasks confidently and break them down. I am confident, "I can do this!"

> **The Perceptual Challenge:** I regard fear as a confidence builder.

CREATE WIN - WIN SITUATIONS. To reduce fear about a bad outcome, try creating your own *win-win* strategy. In this resolution to fear, you create two separate outcomes that are both favorable to you. These outcomes are non-ego, and *YOBI* in nature. To the extent that you genuinely like either outcome, this can be an extremely effective method of fear reduction. For example, let's say you are unhappy in your job because you don't like your immediate supervisor, and you feel you should be paid more. You might avoid doing anything about it because of your fear that you don't want to "rock the boat" and you need to continue to earn a living. Creating a *win-win* outcome means that you begin looking for another job on your own time. When you find one that you believe you would like, and that pays what you believe you are worth, you ask for an offer of intent in writing. You then ask your current employer for the changes that you believe are realistic, reasonable, and relationally fair. In your mind, you know that you have a *win-win* outcome. You set up the circumstances so that either you get the changes you want, or you accept the job offer that you have in writing and would like. Regardless of how the current employer responds, you win either way.

> **The Belief System Formula:** I value creating *win-win* scenarios. Self-preservation is right. I expect myself to engage in self-preservation strategies. I am a winner.

> **The Perceptual Challenge:** I see fear as an opportunity to be taught about self-preservation.

➢ INTERNAL RESOLUTIONS FOR **FEAR.**

STOP 'WHAT-IF' THINKING. As an internal belief system resolution, perhaps this is a sub-category of the Worst Case Scenario. Many people have a habit of looking for potential problems in life to worry about. Essentially, your ego is attempting to micro-manage life. The origin for this habit may date back to early childhood experience, which makes it a hard habit to break. So often, the beginning of a worry thought begins with "what if…" "What if I lose my job?" Even if you don't specifically say the words "what if…" this resolution is for the worrier. There is a simple strategy resolution for this tendency. Simply stated, you add an important word to the worry thought, "so." "So what if that happens… if that happens, this would be my solution…" You say to yourself, "So what if _____ happens, in that case I could _____." In other words, you reduce the intensity of the worry/fear by minimizing the significance with a realistic and reasonable solution that you believe in. "So what if I can't finish this project, I can ask for an extension, it's happened before?" "So what if I can't find my way to their house, I can always call and ask for directions?" "So what if I lose my job, if that happens, I can always look for and find another one, I've done it before." Obviously, this is not the solution for all fears, but it can be effective with minor nagging worries. The Worst Case Scenario resolution encourages an external proactive nature, whereas this resolution is attempting to reduce your negative inner dialogue.

The Belief System Formula: I value a "so what if…" inner dialogue. When appropriate, I maintain a "so what if…" policy regarding worry. I expect myself to uphold this policy. I am a worry reducer.

The Perceptual Challenge: My experiences with fear might be opportunities to develop peace of mind

CREATE FLEXIBILITY. Some individuals have difficulty in making decisions. One common reason for this difficulty is due to a basic (subconscious) fear of making the *wrong* choice. As a result, they tend to overanalyze the situation. Because they tend to regard choices as being either right or wrong, they tend to worry themselves into anxiety and panic. They tend to put off making decisions due to getting lost in the details, leaving them morally confused, bewildered and hopelessly bogged down in fear. They tend to ask others what to do, going from one opinion to the next in search of some perfect answer. Lacking in direction, these individuals would very much like to have a crystal ball. They say that there are no guarantees in life. That is, there are no guarantees that any choice you make will produce an outcome just exactly like you want. The best any of us can do is to make informed choices and regard outcomes as being "more or less in my flexible life path direction" (instead of right or wrong). If you have already done the work of consciously establishing your belief system, then this fear resolution will work well. The right choice for any decision will be what is consistent with *YOBI*; you make choices that are right for you, and are consistent with your values and self-image. Essentially, this resolution is about being flexible with yourself. It is about being able to roll with the punches. Be flexible to the extent that you can make a *YOBI* decision and modify it later as needed.

The Belief System Formula: I value making informed choices. Flexibility is good for me. I expect myself to make some unfortunate turns on my life path, and then get back on track. I am aware of my needs and wants, and I am flexible.

The Perceptual Challenge: I see fear as an opportunity to become more flexible.

REDUCE FEAR & MISTRUST IN RELATIONSHIPS. There is an implication that a team approach to a task would benefit both parties as opposed to going it alone. There is always some amount of risk involved when you rely on and cooperate with another party. The implied fear is that the other party will stop cooperating or want to go it alone again, either with, or without you. Trust, therefore, becomes the stabilizing force of the relationship. "I trust that we will continue to work together cooperatively toward the conditions of this union."

Trust is arguably the most important component of any relationship. By contrast, when there is mistrust, it seems to affect all other components, and carries the most potential for painful feelings. To reduce this potential, change your concept of trust from being an all or nothing judgment about someone, and instead concern yourself with observations of their behavior in your experiences over time. Let the basis for your trust reside mostly in your perception of experience, and rely minimally on statements of intent. Simply put, hear the talk, but trust the walk.

Still, to be able to function relationally, you must be able to predict compliance with the conditions (expressed needs and wants) of the relationship. "I need to know what to expect from you." Without a sense of trust, the relationship will eventually experience imbalance, chaos, sabotage, or failure. When trust is doubted, fear is generated, "If they don't comply, there is danger ahead in terms of the success of this relationship, and I could get hurt." Reducing your risk/fear in any relationship means that you do these things:

1.   Assertively establish the conditions of the relationship (initially and ongoing).

2.   As a result of those conditions, clearly establish the rules (policies).

3.   Trust according to your observation of compliance with the rules over time.

Expect that building any kind of trust will require time and experience. The amount of time and the amount of experience will vary from circumstance to circumstance, however the formula remains the same:

$$TRUST\ =\ EXPERIENCE\ +\ TIME$$

The Belief System Formula: I value relationships. Trust experience. I expect myself to behave with honor in any relationship. I am honorable.

The Perceptual Challenge: I see fear as an opportunity to be taught about healthy trust. Trust is experiential, not personal.

KNOW REAL CONTROL.   Somewhat similar to "what if…" thinkers, controlling individuals want high amounts of control over life around them—situations, environments, and other people. When controlling individuals experience "what if" thinking, they resolve their worry/fear by trying to establish ways to control life. What can we really control in life? This question was addressed in the cognitive challenge, and in Chapter 3. We have ultimate control over how we choose to think about things, what we say, and what we do. Any other kind of complete control we think we have is an illusion. We simply do not have ultimate control over life. To the precise extent that we believe in the illusion of external control, we eventually become enslaved to the illusion. The more we think we can control, the more we want to control, and the more we worry about how to maintain control. This eventually leads to—things not going your way (mad), the perception of loss (sad), and much worry about keeping control (fear). With this resolution, I suggest that in order to reduce your worry/fear, you come to a realistic conclusion about the issue of control. "What can I realistically and reasonably do, and what can I not do?" (Perhaps use the cognitive challenge for fear.)

The Belief System Formula: I value self-control. I prioritize self-control over external control. I expect myself to maintain self-control at all times. I am realistic.

The Perceptual Challenge: Fear is an opportunity to learn about serenity.

➢ APPLICATION OF THE METHOD.

Henry arrived at work just before 8 a.m. like any other day. On this particular Friday, he and nine other colleagues received some bad news. Due to an unforeseeable financial crisis, the company he worked for needed to let go of ten positions in the next ten months. Henry's position would be one of the ten to go. Upon hearing this news, Henry experienced what he later described at a panic attack. That night, he went home and engaged in binge eating, beginning with cold leftover pizza, and ending with a substantial amount of chocolate fudge swirl ice cream just before nodding off into a fitful night of sleep.

The next morning at his therapy session we engaged in a process of problem solving with a combination of fear resolutions. "The worst case scenario is that I could be the first to lose my job, and have great difficulty in finding another comparable one. In that case, I'd need to apply for unemployment payments while I look for at least a short-term transitional job. We may temporarily go into debt, but we can get our way back out of that with time. For now, I can proactively get my resume updated, and begin a job hunt through networking, classifieds, or Internet sites. In this day and age, a job can come and go with very little warning and may have nothing to do with your job performance.

"Basically, I have relatively little control over the big picture. I can only control how I chose to respond to it. When it comes right down to it, there are no guarantees about most jobs. I cannot trust that a job will be there forever for me. In beginning to look for a new one, I need to keep in mind that I am not looking for the perfect or right job, I am looking for a job that is generally in sync with my career direction. Because of the severance package we are entitled to, I do have some amount of bargaining power with any potential employer so that I can create a win-win outcome. I am not in a desperate situation right now such that I have to take the first thing offered to me. I figure that between the severance package and my savings I have the financial means to look for a good job over the next five to six months. If I am one of the last to be let go, I can add an additional four months.

"My backup plan is that five months from now, if I haven't gotten a good job, I'll begin to consider moderately good transitional jobs. Additionally, we could begin a process of cutting back on our inessential expenses. Finally, I continue to remind myself that I've made it through tough times before, and I can do it again. There will possibly be some changes, but this won't be the end of me, or what I can become." As he walked out the door of my office, Henry proudly remarked, "I think I'm getting this now. My feelings aren't my enemy. From now on, I'll actually be able to grow through my feelings if I don't panic, stay committed to challenging them, and stay positive."

Exercise 16-1: Use the cognitive challenge and choose the appropriate resolutions to manage your fear and/or stress. Then, go to appendix F and write down the values, morals, expectations, or self-image statements that honor and support your resolutions.

17 Managing 'Glad'

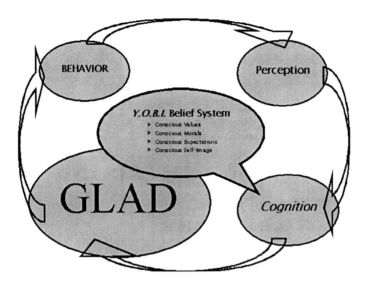

The Desire to Feel Good

Feelings of gladness are based on the opposite of the other feeling categories. In other words, gladness can be experienced when you:

- Think things are going your way. (*Not Mad*)
- Think that you are fortunate. (*Not Sad*)
- Think about being proud. (*Not Bad*)
- Think about a positive future event. (*Not Fear*)

At first glance, you may think that this looks like ego based thinking, "Yeah I got my way, I'm really great, just look at what I have, and guess where I'm going." This may indeed be the case at times. However, as with the other feeling categories, there are both ego and *YOBI* based origins for feelings; glad is no exception. *My way*, to the extent that it is a fit to my belief system, can be a positive experience. *My way*, as a result of ego agenda involvement, could become an addictive problem. The same comparison could be said of fortune, proud experiences, or future events. Knowing the origin of your glad feelings is critical for developing peace of mind. To assist in determining the origin of your thinking, you may want to use the five questions provided on p. 121.

Each of the other feeling categories have been described as having an underlying desire—change, sameness, security, and control. If there is an underlying desire associated with glad, is simply to feel good.

➢ **ALTERNATIVE GLAD INTENSITY WORDS.**

Joyful	Anticipation	Peaceful
Happy	Fortunate	Contented
Excited	Serene	Blissful

➢ **THE TYPE OF THOUGHT THAT PRODUCES GLAD.**

"I really like the way the plan is working."

"I'm so lucky to have a warm, caring husband."

"I like the way I handled that problem at work."

"I am really looking forward to this weekend."

"I feel great about my plan, and how I'm following it. "

"I'm really doing well with this new assignment."

➢ **GLAD PERSPECTIVES.**

Ego Glad: "I look pretty tough today."

"At least I look like I'm in control."

"I'll bet I can take charge of this place."

"From now on, I'm in control around here."

"I'm better than him/her for these reasons…"

"Glad I'm not that ugly, stupid, miserable."

YOBI Glad: "I'm really pleased with my effort."

"I got the job!"

"I'm proud of how I handled myself."

"I'm looking forward to this event."

"This peace and quiet feels good."

"I'm lucky to have good friends."

➤   THE COGNITIVE CHALLENGE FOR **GLAD**.

The cognitive challenge associated with glad is very different from the former challenges: answer each of the following questions with at least five genuine responses, and then evaluate those responses with the last question. (See appendix E worksheet) To the extent that you have an abundance of favorable *YOBI* based responses, you probably experience much gladness in your life. To the contrary, as you lack favorable responses, you may experience much anger, sadness, guilt, worry, depression, apathy, confusion, indecisiveness, remorse, or emptiness. Regardless of your responses, the external and internal resolutions can provide structure and guidance for creating a more meaningful and satisfying experience in this life. The cognitive challenge is:

1.   What is going my way in my life?
2.   What do I have in my life that I am pleased with or grateful for?
3.   In what way am I proud of me?
4.   What am I looking forward to?
        and
5.   Are my above responses supported by my belief system?"

➤ EXTERNAL RESOLUTIONS FOR **GLAD**.

COMPLETE THE GLAD COGNITIVE CHALLENGE. This resolution involves completing the glad cognitive challenge with at least five responses. If it seems as though nothing is going your way in life, look for the little things in your life that are going your way. Consider things that you may be taking for granted. If you feel as though you have nothing of value in your life, avoid comparing yourself or your situation with others because there are always those around you who are less or more fortunate. Do you have a roof over your head, food in your home, clothing to wear, health, employment, transportation, this book to read? If you feel bad about yourself, begin to create proud moments in your life. You have the power to make these moments happen through your choices each and every day. Open a door for someone. Engage in unconditional acts of kindness towards others. Develop and follow your moral code. If you don't see any fun in your future, create something to look forward to. Grab a calendar and do some activity planning. Make something happen. This doesn't necessarily mean that you need to plan a grand scale expedition to Europe. A mix of simple and easy plans with something more complex included periodically works just fine. You want to be able to look forward to the future with gladness.

If you have difficulty with any of the glad cognitive challenge questions, ask someone in your life who is generally optimistic to help you take a look at each of these questions, and then try not to argue with or minimize their responses.

The Belief System Formula: I value gratitude and creating joy in my life. I take responsibility for my joy. I expect to create and find joy in my life. I am joyful.

The Perceptual Challenge: I experience joy to the extent that I create it.

FIRM UP YOUR RELATIONSHIPS. Relationships with others can be fantastic. The experiences we have with other people in our lives can be a wonderful source of joy. On the other hand, when a relationship is not working, it can become a significant source of emotional pain. There are no guarantees of satisfaction that come with a relationship. Nor are there any guarantees that they will work to achieve any specific results. I believe that the best way to minimize a potentially painful outcome is to establish an assertive agreement with the other person. The agreement might go something like this: "I value assertiveness, and you can count on me to behave assertively with you; therefore, I ask that you behave assertively with me. Can I expect that from you?" In such a relationship, the conditions (the needs and wants of each person) are clearly expressed.

Bear in mind that the needs–wants conditions represent the best interest of a relationship chosen by you. The emotional pain (anger, sadness, guilt, fear) is reduced (not eliminated) for both individuals as they engage in an ongoing honest expression of what they need and want in the relationship. Each person has the opportunity to make choices along the way to accept, decline, or negotiate the conditions. There is minimal guesswork, minimal surprise, and minimal buildup of unrealistic expectation. Relating to others in this way takes thought, energy, and courage. Approaching relationships in this manner helps to reduce the overall pain, increase the joy potential, and provide structure for the development of trust. This should appeal to your ego on some level.

The Belief System Formula: I value assertiveness in my relationships. Behave assertively as a rule. I expect myself to behave assertively in my relationships. I am assertive.

The Perceptual Challenge: I see my level of assertiveness as a predictor of joy-happiness-success in my relationships.

CREATE GENUINE JOY. People, places, or things, cannot *make* you happy. These are outside of you, and therefore ultimately outside of your control. In seeking out immediate gratification, your ego may want to control all that is external. This can eventually lead to painful ego based feelings. True and lasting joy does not depend on someone or something, but is created internally by you perceptually and relationally. In order to experience Genuine Joy—Happiness—Gladness you need to be determined to find it in your perception of life, and through relating with everything around you. This resolution suggests an approach that differs from relying on your environment to *make* you feel happy. I don't rely on my spouse to make me happy; I do experience joy in relating to her, through the process of creating with her, and through what we create. I don't rely on my guitar to make me happy; I experience joy in my relationship to it, and through what is created via the relationship. The same can be said about my relationship with my children, my family, music, nature, and my job. "I create peace of mind internally—perceptually and relationally." Theoretically, with this resolution I can live on a park bench and find joy in my life. On the other hand, I might live in luxurious wealth and be miserable because I look for negatives, problems, and losses in my life. If I have created my joy by possessing things or people, I will be in pain when they are gone. Find a way to create joy in your life with, or without specific need of someone else or something else. Begin to look for joy in your life; if it is scarce, begin to create it.

> **The Belief System Formula:** I value creating joy in my life perceptually and relationally. My joy is created by me. I expect to create and discover joy in my life. I am joyful.

> **The Perceptual Challenge:** I see myself as the creator of glad-ness both perceptually and relationally.

SEEK HEALTHY GUIDANCE. In life, there are big decisions and small decisions to be made. There are going to be occasions when you have great doubt and indecision, and when you go to your belief system for guidance you are still confused or not entirely satisfied. Occasionally, you may need to seek out the healthiest belief systems around you. So then, seek out the belief system perspective of those emotionally healthy people around you who care about you and are interested in your best interest. With no one immediately available to you for guidance, rely on the perspective you believe they would suggest to you. As an additional resource, rely on your intuition about how the universe works, and go with that perspective. Simply put, this resolution says, learn to go with the healthiest version of life whenever possible. Seek direction from your consciously established belief system for life decisions whenever possible, and in whenever you feel doubt, permit yourself to trust other perspectives; those who are healthy, those who care about you, those you trust.

> **The Belief System Formula:** I value my belief system direction, and the perspective of those who care about my best interest. My belief system is the compass for my life. I expect myself to live my life by that compass, and ask for assistance as necessary. I am going in the right direction for me.

> **The Perceptual Challenge:** I see that as I determine the course of my life, I become my own directional compass.

KNOW YOUR BOUNDARIES & SET LIMITS. These are not new concepts in the field of mental health, although they have rather ambiguous meanings. I believe that there is a distinction between these concepts in that boundaries are your rules for how you will allow others to interact with you, or treat you. These rules are ideally developed out of, and represent, your belief system. "I don't allow others to tell me what is right for me." "I don't purchase anything from a business or store that does not guarantee their products to my satisfaction." "Because I'm committed to someone, I don't engage in sexual behaviors with anyone else." On the other hand, limits are the external expressions of your boundaries, as stated by you to others. In other words, "My boundaries are my rules, and my limits are the enforcements of my boundaries." "Greg, I won't allow you to decide what's right for me to do, I'll have to figure it out on my own." "Sir, if you aren't going to guarantee your product, I will not be back to do business with you." "Sorry Brenda, I am involved with someone and in a committed relationship, so I can't do that." The essence of this resolution is this: Know your rules, let others know your rules as appropriate, and from this comes integrity.

(Related glad resolutions for additional help: Chapter 13 – Get Assertive, Chapter 15 – Approval Seekers & Conflict Avoiders, and all solutions in Chapter 16.)

> **The Belief System Formula:** I value my integrity. I do the right thing for me. I expect myself to courageously enforce my boundaries. I am an effective in meeting my needs.

> **The Perceptual Challenge:** I believe that integrity is mine—one choice at a time.

USE YOUR GLAD HISTORY. This resolution begins with a simple question, "What have I learned about joy in my life?" When you look back over your life experiences, what has brought genuine joy to your life? Make a list. Could you or do you create that joy now in your present set of circumstances? (See p. 166 Create Genuine Joy, for additional information.)

> **The Belief System Formula:** I value learning from the past. I make use of past experiences and expect to learn valuable lessons from them. I am my own best teacher when it comes to my joy.

> **The Perceptual Challenge:** I see past joy as a representation of future joy.

> ### INTERNAL RESOLUTIONS FOR GLAD.

DEVELOP PEACEFUL SOLITUDE. One of the central themes of this book is to learn to develop peacefulness in your internal dialogue. A powerful and effective method for increasing your peace of mind involves developing comfort in solitude. When you create alone time with no distractions, you are forced to get to know yourself and how your mind works. You can get to hear how your ego-self talks and have an opportunity to develop a unified love-based relationship to that perspective within you. To the extent that you enjoy spending time with yourself in solitude, you not only increase peace of mind, but also improve the potential quality of all other relationships. There are a variety of ways to carry out this resolution including: silent meditation, yoga, relaxation techniques, peaceful solo hobbies such as painting or sculpting, quiet exercise routines, writing poetry or in a journal, spending quiet time in nature, or simply turning off external noise doing nothing for a while. Allow yourself to get lost in moments of time. This resolution says: You can learn to monitor and maintain a nurturing relationship with yourself, and others.

> **The Belief System Formula:** I value peace of mind. Integrity brings peace of mind. I expect myself to be a monitor of my internal dialogue. I am involved in creating my peace of mind.

> **The Perceptual Challenge:** Peace of mind is my choice.

MAINTAIN HUMILITY. Avoid engaging in ego-based criticism, judgment, authority, control, and power. Approaching experiences such as peace of mind or integrity means carefully monitoring your thinking with regard to your perception of others. Consider the following beliefs. Instead of criticizing of others, "I believe that there are many ways of thinking about things, saying things, and doing things. I simply do not know what is best for everyone. I know what's best for me." Instead of judging or assuming authority over others, "I believe that I am not an expert on how everyone should live their lives. I know what is right for me. In essence, I am not superior to anyone else, nor is anyone superior to me. Superior or inferior levels of people simply do not exist except in my ego-based perception and/or thinking." As you recognize and leave behind the perspective of ego-based superiority, each person you encounter may show you something new about life and relationship.

> Fearlessly, as you open your mind to other perspectives, you discover there is a fantastic unlimited potential for learning and growth.

By contrast, attempting to gain power or control, assuming authority, or parenting in relation to other fully functioning adults usually leads to painful feelings. Pained emotional outcomes may develop such as anger when they don't cooperate, sadness when they leave, or fear of losing control and/or power. Instead, "I interact with others in a cooperative relationship."

The act of parenting is of course required in actual age-appropriate parent-child relationships. However, when parenting is based on a model of results through power and control, teenage rebellion can become intensified and extreme. Positive results can be achieved when a parent chooses to motivate a child's behavior through gentle realistic encouragement, loving authority, and modeling of appropriate behavior.

The Belief System Formula: I value my acceptance that others will choose to live as they wish, and that I am no better or worse than anyone else. I believe it is right to practice non-judgment. I expect others will live as they desire. I am accepting.

The Perceptual Challenge: I see that my value neither exceeds nor is diminished in relation to the value of others. Value, when referring to a person, is like attempting to assign importance to one drop of water in an ocean compared to any other.

EXPERIENCE INNER-POWER. A sense of power derived through ego-means is ultimately limited. The limitation becomes apparent whenever environments or people stop cooperating with your ego's agenda. The limitation is experienced whenever they stop helping you to be gratified on demand, disregard or break from your control, or become unimpressed with you. The limitations are also brought to light when you experience painful emotions that you are unable to resolve, feel powerless against the outside world, or regard yourself as inferior to someone else. The resolution is to experience inner-power. A sense of inner-power comes though *becoming* your consciously developed belief system.

The Belief System Formula: I value the experience of inner-power. Inner-power is my truth. I expect to find that inner-power is preferable to external power. I am truly powerful.

The Perceptual Challenge: Real power comes from me.

CLEARLY KNOW YOUR VALUES. Let's break this down:

1. **Clearly:** I establish my values in a way that they are clearly and precisely stated. The best way to do this is to write them down and prioritize them.

2. **Know:** I commit the prioritized list to memory. I am able to identify my values quickly and without any doubt. This will come in handy when I need to make quick decisions in difficult situations.

3. **Your:** I take ownership of my values; my values are chosen by me, for me. Problems are inevitable when I allow others to determine what should be important to me. Ownership means I am fully responsible for my failures and my successes. Defining success and failure is also up to me. Rather than to make "the perfect life" my standard for success, I say, "This is my life and it is unfolding, more or less, in a way that I choose."

4. **Values:** All that is important to me. I know them. I live them. The values of my choosing give meaning to my life and I become a unique individual, with value to myself. I value, I become, I am.

The Belief System Formula: I value having a direction for my life. It's right for me to establish that direction in a conscious manner. I expect myself to live my life in a conscious manner. I am awakened!

The Perceptual Challenge: I see that consciously choosing my values leads to an awakening of who I am.

MAINTAIN A BALANCED FOCUS. Balance is the key to success in many areas of life. To live with a focus primarily on the past, or the present, or the future, creates its own set of problems. A focus on the past creates stagnation. A focus on the present creates a problematic future. A focus on the future creates a lack of day-to-day enjoyment. Balance is the resolution. Live your life with an ability to maintain your focus on that which requires your attention in the moment, but balance it with the entire realm of time.

The past is in the past; you cannot go back and change it. Notwithstanding, many people become perceptually stuck in the past. The best you can do is to develop a realistic perspective of the past, learn from it, and move on. Make time to remember the good times, wax nostalgic as they say, "Do you remember when…wasn't that a blast!"

Many people get perceptually stuck in the future, "This will be better when…if we could just…someday when…" Plan for the future, but avoid living for it. Many people become apathetic or are overcome by inertia, "I just don't feel like it right now (or ever)." Make fun happen, "Hey, how about this weekend we…"

Many people become workaholics to avoid the pain of the present. Take breaks from your busy day to relax, meditate, experience quiet, or do something fun just for yourself, even if you can just get a hold of five minutes, "I'm going to take a little break now, this couch looks good." This resolution is all about taking a balanced approach to life in terms of your perception of time, and your place in it. It's your time, make the best of it! Get lost in moments.

The Belief System Formula: I value a balanced perspective of focus. Make time to value past, present, and future. I expect myself to maintain a balance. I am aware.

The Perceptual Challenge: I see time as a seamless continuum where no one realm has more value than any other.

KNOW THE FREEDOM OF RESPONSIBILITY. Anger is of course based on the notion that "things are not going my way." It stands to reason that as long as you maintain the problematic expectation of your way, you will maintain your anger. You are ultimately responsible for the manner in which you think about things. Therefore, you are ultimately responsible for your feeling experiences. Feelings are choices made by you.

If I choose to maintain angry feelings, I will eventually conclude, "I have become an angry person." If I choose to maintain sad feelings I will conclude, "I am a sad person." If I consistently choose to act irresponsibly, "I have become an irresponsible person." It seems that I become what I consistently choose over time. "I am responsible for my choices, what I choose, I become." To this extent, self-image is a decision made by you. When you acknowledge and accept these ideas about responsibility, there can be freedom in knowing that you are not stuck. You can create your own joyful feeling experiences, and a self-image of your own choosing.

I may be treading on thin ice as I suggest that a person is choice. Oftentimes, we hear from the field of psychology and religion that we should, "Separate the person and the deed," "Hate the sin, not the sinner," or "It's not you that I dislike, it's your behavior." I would suggest that as human beings we are all capable of making some bad decisions from time to time and can unfortunately wind up hurting people along the way. These are perhaps forgivable individual acts and therefore do not represent the character of entire person. However, when behaviors are repeated, and increase with frequency over time, I believe that at some point, the person is accurately associated with their behavior; they essentially become their behavior—reputationally.

> **The Belief System Formula:** I value my choices. Responsibility for peace of mind is mine. I expect myself to choose wisely. I am what I choose.

> **The Perceptual Challenge:** I see self-image as an outcome of my choices.

DISCOVER NEW TRUTHS. Perception is a choice. Do you see the glass as half full, or half empty? How you perceive external reality is ultimately up to you. "The *truth*" as such becomes a matter of perception, and therefore relative to your perspective. As I have said previously, if you want to see the world with skepticism, potential pitfalls, or pessimistically, then you will surely find yourself living in a very dangerous world. As you think about most things, you can challenge yourself to "see if there is another way of looking at this." Will you discover that there is *"truth,"* or information, to be found in the other perspectives?

> **The Belief System Formula:** I value alternative perspectives. I maintain an open mind. I expect myself to consider alterative ways of looking at life. I am an open-minded realist.

> **The Perceptual Challenge:** I know that the potential for peace is in all things around me and within me.

DON'T FORCE YOUR WAY. After you have completed any cognitive challenge and feel confident about what you want, you still may encounter resistance. As you live out your belief system, pay attention to external resistance. One of the biggest problems in relationships occurs when one person attempts to force their belief system onto the other. Allow others to be themselves, to live out their own version of life. Expect that they will see things in their own way and in their own time. It is when you force your version of reality onto the world that you can eventually encounter painful outcomes. If your ego gets involved, you may fool yourself into stubbornly persisting well past the point of wisdom. When you continually encounter painful feelings, recognize this as a signal for you to reevaluate what you want. Get a second opinion, or simply do an additional cognitive challenge. Get to know when enough is enough. Know when it is time to go with the flow of the universe that is around you.

> **The Belief System Formula:** I value the flow of the universe. Cooperation is good whenever possible. I expect myself to be a monitor of resistance in my world. I am cooperative.

> **The Perceptual Challenge:** As I encounter resistance, I reassess who I am; thus, there is a continual merging of my belief system with the flow of the universe around me.

➤ APPLICATION OF THE METHOD.

Henry arrived for his appointment with news that he had made it through his transitional employment period without any additional panic attacks. He found a job with a different company in his third month of searching, and increased his overall salary slightly. He also announced that he had lost an additional twenty pounds and was planning on joining a walking club.

"I've been in clubs before, and really enjoyed the interaction. My wife is going to join too. And speaking of my wife, we have been doing better. We discussed our problems and set up some relationship policies. We also created a calendar for planning walking trips with our new walking friends. She has begun to address her alcohol use with a therapist and has even gone to a couple of A.A. meetings. I'm feeling better about my life now. I decided that I have much to be thankful for. And I have come to a conclusion that it was through my experiences with being overweight and isolated that I can now greatly appreciate the new interest I have in people and activity. I guess I never fully understood until now that I can create my own joy without abusing food. I'm now doing this by genuinely relating to others and finding meaning in the experiences that we create. In the past several months, I've made some big decisions, created new values, and fought through feelings that were painful. I found an incredible sense of power within me as I discovered that I could influence how I feel and think by establishing my belief system in a conscious way. I believe I have also begun to experience a greater sense of peace as my inner conflict decreases. My perspective of the world has become more realistic and positive, and I discover that I am my own greatest source of joy."

Exercise 17-1: Use the cognitive challenge and choose the appropriate resolutions to manage your gladness. Then, go to appendix F and write down the values, morals, expectations, or self-image statements that honor and support your resolutions.

---

*This is a quick version of the basic formula for managing feelings:

This is my feeling/situation: _____.

The outcome I would like is: _____.

Does that outcome require an internal or external change _____?

Is the outcome and my approach a fit for my belief system _____?

Revise or identify the resolution approach and implement.

Part 4. THE CHOICE

18 Integrity – One Choice at a Time

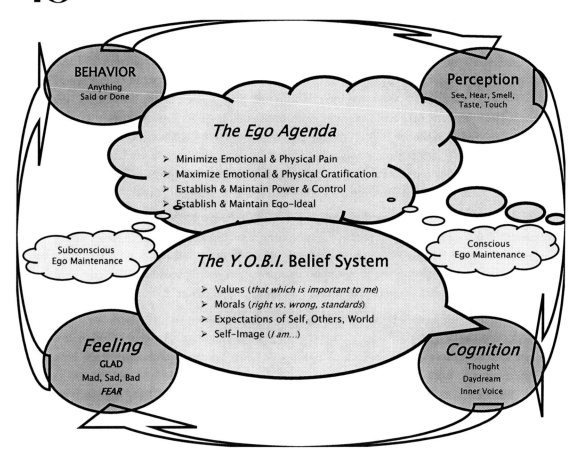

Who's Leading the Way?

You do have a choice about how to live your life. That choice is ultimately yours, no matter what your situation is. Your attitude in any given set of circumstances is your choice. Obviously, some circumstances are more extreme than others. Some individuals are born with the proverbial silver spoon, and others are victims of atrocities perpetrated by madmen. There are many silver spooners who make a lifetime of decisions that lead them into a prison. Conversely, there are decent people who are unfairly treated but go on to make choices to maintain their own heroic integrity (Rosa Parks, Victor Frankl, Ann Frank, Mahatma Gandhi, and Nelson Mandela to name just a few). Most of us won't ever find ourselves in extreme circumstances. We are, nonetheless, faced with painful and difficult choices in our lives. Over time, the choices you make will reveal the direction of your life. Who's leading the way? Whose agenda do you follow in making choices? By now it is obvious that you will follow either the agenda of your ego, or some other consciously determined agenda. When it comes to your life, which agenda is primarily guiding your way? Your *way* is a choice. Recognition of this choice is critical to those seeking peace of mind through integrity.

As much as your ego may disagree, the only thing you have control over in life is your choice of how to live it. You can control: 1) how you choose to think about things, and 2) your choice of behavior (what you say or do). With time and a good plan, you can also greatly influence your perception, feelings, and subconscious cognitive processing. You cannot, however, completely control people, things, events, or environments around you. Eventually, the natural flow of the universe around you will let you know that you are not as powerful as you think. Suffice it to say that if it were possible for people to completely control anything outside of themselves, we would live in a very different world right now.

It's your universe; are you are in charge of it? In your universe, you can be your own hero, your own villain, or your own victim. Again, some life circumstances are more challenging than others. Some of us are silver spooners, and some of us are innocent victims. I think that regardless of the difficulty or challenge, you are at the center of, and like it or not, you are in charge of your universe, always with choices of how to construct it.

From the big decisions of your life, to the even more important little daily ones, you are in charge. As you seek out *YOBI*, you will likely find that you have to, in essence "micro-manage" your ego's involvement in your decision-making. At first, this may take a significant amount of your attention and energy, but with practice and time, it will get easier. This chapter is about choice. In order to consciously and effectively assess your choices in life, you need to:

Recognize, Know, Predict, Evaluate

1. Recognize that ultimately, everything you do involves a choice.
2. Know your agendas.
3. Recognize the cycle-logical functioning associated with each agenda.
4. Recognize levels of awareness.
5. Recognize ego maintenance.
6. Predict the potential outcomes of the choices you have considered.
7. Evaluate the outcomes and alignment with *YOBI*.

Then...

8.   Choose.

9.   Value the choice.

10.   Act on the choice.

11.   Manage resistance against the choice.

12.   Re-evaluate the choice; go back to the first step as needed.

13.   Recognize yourself on the *YOBI* path.

Bob's Boss

Bob's wife made an appointment for his first therapy session. "She pretty much insisted that I do something about these episodes." He began the session by saying that he had no experience with therapy and didn't really think that it would help. Bob was thirty-six years old and worked for a successful radio station in their sales department. A year ago, Bob and his wife of eleven years had their first child, and he accepted a promotion to a senior sales position. Shortly after that, the manager of his department resigned and a new one came on board. "I can't stand her," Bob told me. In a matter of several weeks, Bob reported that he was feeling some "emotional changes" in the form of what he called "anxiety episodes." He was having trouble getting up for work in the morning, and was starting to drink alcohol at night after arriving home from work. The "anxiety episodes" generally happened on the drive to work, though lately he was having them on the weekends as well. Bob wanted to eliminate these episodes, reduce his stress, and get his life "back to normal."

Mary's Men

Mary, a single, thirty-three year old, arrived for her first appointment thirty minutes early. She spent the first ten minutes of her first session apologizing for being "such a mess." She wanted to be clear that she was not looking for any quick fix to her problems. Mary continued on to acknowledge that she had been in therapy before, and "some of it" had been helpful. She was however "in trouble again." Mary had been involved in a series of "really bad" relationships with men over the past fifteen years. "I guess these guys just know how to find someone like me that will fix all their problems." She described a history of troubled relationships that began in her senior year of high school, and continued to the last relationship that ended a week previously. She discovered him cheating on her "as usual." She went on to relate that she seemed to do well in starting relationships, and knew how to attract a man. "I give all of myself to them, I just don't understand how they can do this to me." It was her hope that therapy would help her to make sense of what she was "doing wrong" with men, and figure out how to go forward.

1. RECOGNIZE CHOICE

Everything we do involves a choice. The recognition of choice is equivalent to taking responsibility for the behavior you produce. At the point that you acknowledge your choices, there is bad news and good news. The bad news is that you may experience painful feelings of guilt, sadness, fear, or anger toward yourself. Moreover, you may need to make some different choices and/or then behave differently. These changes may be uncomfortable. The good news is that you may eventually experience something positive, and be able to lead the way in establishing a direction for your life.

Application to Bob: Bob had some difficulty in seeing his part in the anxiety he felt. He wanted to blame parenthood and his new manager for his problems. In order for Bob to be able to move on and improve his life, he needed to accept the fact that he and his wife chose to have a child, and that he chose to apply for and accept a promotion. These things didn't just happen to him. Later, he would need to acknowledge his belief system choice in how he regarded women who were in a position superior to him.

Application to Mary: Initially, Mary's perception was, "All these men just changed on me, I really think men just can't be faithful." Mary would need to take a good look at how she chose unfaithful men.

2. KNOW YOUR AGENDAS

Knowing the content of the agendas put forth in this book gives you an advantage in being able to quickly assess your cycle-logical functioning and figure out your motivation. The differences in these agendas should be pretty clear by now. The agenda of the ego is to minimize pain, maximize gratification, have power and control, and establish ego-ideal. A consciously developed agenda (belief system), involves clearly determining your own values, morals, expectations, and building a self-image as a result.

Application to Bob: The following recent behavioral changes suggested that Bob's ego was leading the way in his attempt at problem solving: an increase of alcohol consumption to reduce his emotional pain, a desire to remain in bed to avoid the emotional pain of work, avoidance of the change/work required with therapy, and irrational fear on the way to work.

Application to Mary: Mary was not able to see her motivation right away. However, by the second session, she knew that she sought out comfort, self-esteem, and validation of her worth through relationships with men. If they could minimize her emotional pain, she was willing to tolerate their misbehavior and put aside most of her own needs and wants in the relationships. Through our discussions, she was becoming aware of her ego's voice, and its influence in her choices.

3. RECOGNIZE THE CYCLE-LOGICAL FUNCTIONING ASSOCIATED WITH EACH AGENDA

You can learn to recognize the ego's agenda in your decision-making. When you experience any intensified feeling, you will want to be able to identify the thinking behind it along with the perspective origin of the thinking. In other words, you need to recognize the thinking as originating from either your ego, or from your belief system. Any changes needed are made at the point of the thinking and/or the behavior, not the feeling. You could attempt to will a feeling to go away or ignore it, but you run the risk of the feeling persisting or resurfacing without resolving the thought behind the scenes.

Application to Bob: With a just a little work, Bob was soon able to identify the thinking-feeling connection behind his behavior. He could then acknowledge the irrationality behind his fear: "Nothing bad is really going to happen to me at work, I guess I just don't want to go." The real reason for his avoidance was in his intense dislike of his new female manager. "Although I don't know her very well, I think I really hate her." He had some difficulty in identifying anything specific in her behavior that would account for such anger; he only knew how he felt. Bob also acknowledged feeling sad about the birth of his son and the resulting changes in his life.

Application to Mary: After she recognized her ego-based behavior, and the motivation for it, Mary could begin to see a pattern emerging in her history with men. The pattern had started in high school with her first serious relationship. Prior to that time, the only significant men in her life, her father and brothers, generally ignored her, or pointed out faults in her choices and her appearance. As a result, she was "emotionally starved" for male attention, acceptance, and value. As she put it, "Men are emotional nourishment for my starving ego." Her ego perceived men as the solution, they will "take away my pain." She would go on to recall specific thoughts such as, "If I could just find the right guy, everything would be good in my life."

The first few months of any new relationship were generally extremely gratifying for Mary. She enjoyed the emotional high of the new man in her life, which included a great deal of hope for her future, comfort of "having someone," and a sense of worth as someone else valued her. Conversely, she also experienced a huge decrease of fear, self-loathing and self-doubt. The ego gratification of a new relationship was very powerful to Mary, and made for an efficient superficial fix for her emotional pain.

Her obsessive pleasing behavior throughout her relationship history became apparent to her as we talked. The overall goal of her ego's agenda was to control the relationship by being a constant source of pleasing behavior for her current man. She could tolerate much of their misbehavior as long as she was able to "keep them." The cycle-logical functioning was clearly ego based, and she needed to make some changes.

4. RECOGNIZE LEVELS OF AWARENESS

"Why do I do that, it just doesn't make sense?" Recognize that many problematic feelings and behaviors are generated subconsciously, making them seem mysterious. If you look for patterns of behavior, you may find the ego agenda as an explanation. Also, look for problematic feelings and behaviors as making sense at a certain time and place in your history. Challenge yourself to look for explanations of cycle-logical functioning beneath the level of conscious awareness.

Application to Bob: Bob was experiencing subconscious anger toward his manager. He was eventually able to establish a link from his sadness to his new responsibility as a father, which made it subconscious. Also, he was able to see that he was frustrated with his new job responsibilities and getting what he believed was "very little guidance and support, she just doesn't seem to care." His wife brought his gradual increase of alcohol consumption to his attention. He couldn't believe it at first, but she was able to show him the evidence in the recycle bin from the week.

Application to Mary: Much of Mary's problematic behavior was produced from a subconscious level. The tendency to control through pleasing was a fundamental part of her personality, with origins in her early childhood. Recognizing this tendency was difficult for her until it was seen from her ego's point of view. Her ego knew from early experience that "the pleasing strategy" simply worked, at least for a short period of time. In adult relationships, Mary would determine what was pleasing to each man she was with, and then engage in the behavior. This dynamic was subconscious; it became a routine part of the relationship. She would need to watch her thinking and behavior carefully to recognize when she was behaving in pleasing ways. Additionally, she had to figure out how to behave in a healthy exchange of needs and wants with people.

5. RECOGNIZE EGO MAINTENANCE

As presented in Chapter 5, in order to begin or continue some ego-based behaviors, you will engage in certain patterns of perceiving and processing information. These patterns may occur on both levels of awareness. These patterns are called ego maintenance. The primary objective of such maintenance is to bypass the belief system and carry out the ego's agenda. Recognizing your own patterns of maintenance is critical to creating integrity and peace of mind in your life.

Application to Bob: Bob was able to maintain his own sense of control and power by blaming his sadness and reduction of free time on his wife, "You just had to have a family."

Instead of consciously recognizing a need to adjust to parenthood, his ego took the lead to avoid the pain of sadness, and anger about not having his previously free time. Also, he used alcohol to numb his pain, and feel temporarily good. He did not want to recognize the increase of his alcohol consumption until proof was offered.

Though now deceased, Bob's mother was an alcoholic. She was both verbally and physically abusive to him in his childhood. The new female manager reminded Bob of his mother in many ways, but especially in the tone of her voice, and in the way she looked at him as they were discussing potential new sales leads. Bob had a lot of left over anger at his mother, and he had never been able to confront her in real life. Although he did not recognize this for some time into therapy, he finally determined that it was not fair to use his boss as a target for his pent up anger.

Application to Mary: Mary's subconscious ego maintenance was evident in using relationships to reduce her pain and to create her own idealization. We determined that this pattern must have started early in life as she struggled to feel good about herself. Hope for the future, being valued, and self-esteem enhancements all became sought out through men. She was willing to put up with or fix their problems and eventually try gain control of the relationship, and therefore gain control of her life. Immediate gratification for the first few months, and a quick fix for her own poor self-image were powerful motivating features of her patterns. In high school, she remembered a "revelation" she had one day, "If I just do what a guy wants at first, later I can get what I want, now that's power." Over time this eventually faded into subconscious ego maintenance. It became a routine part of relationships that seemed to work, "But I guess it never worked for very long." Quite consciously, Mary figured out what was pleasing to each man she was with, and then engaged in that behavior. "I would tell myself I was being a good girlfriend, and they would always agree."

6. PREDICT THE POTENTIAL OUTCOMES OF THE CHOICES YOU HAVE CONSIDERED

Each and every day, you make choices that either bring you closer to or further away from integrity and your own peace of mind. In order to make *YOBI* decisions, you need to be able to predict the potential outcomes of available choices. Of course, no one has a crystal ball brain that can see the exact results of our choices. The best we can do is to predict potentials. That is, "If I do ALPHA, then BETA is the most likely outcome." Predicting has to be done honestly, which means you need to watch out for ego maintenance.

Application to Bob: Bob had to make some changes at work and at home. This included acknowledging that he had made a joint decision with his wife to start a family. If he maintained his anger at his wife and son, he would develop resentment and further avoidance. Although he was not absolutely sure about the connection between his manager and his mother, it made some sense to him. He needed to make daily choices to see his work environment in current reality, and not as a reminder of his past pain. It was also necessary to get organized about his approach to work, and choose to see his manager as an ally instead of an enemy. Bob was predicting that if he made these changes, he would be gaining in integrity, "These are tough changes, but I'm pretty sure I'll be happier."

Application to Mary: In many respects, Mary's choices had to do with the future. She needed to choose relationships in a different way than she ever had in her past. In her future, compatibility needed to be valued, and she needed to make choices about compatibility that represented her own best interest. "I guess I need to choose to value my own best interest by valuing my needs and wants. If I don't, there's a good chance that they will go unmet. I'll need to determine what my needs and wants truly are in a relationship, and then choose to communicate them even though I think it's going to be frightening at first." These choices needed to be made on a daily basis, and were going to be very difficult for her because of the subconscious nature of her tendency to please.

7. EVALUATE THE OUTCOMES AND ALIGNMENT WITH *YOBI*

When you are determining your choices in any set of circumstances, at a minimum you will have a choice to do, or not to do something. You can't ever really say, "I had no choice in the matter." However, you can say to what degree any choice is, or is not, in *Your Own Best Interest*. A robber holds a gun to my head and says, "Give me your wallet or I'll shoot you." I have a choice to live or die. I don't have to give it to him, but it represents my own best interest to do so. If the robber then ties me up, I can still choose if and when to struggle, or not to struggle. Know that you have choice and can choose whatever works best for you.

Application to Bob: After evaluating his choices, it all became pretty clear to Bob. He made a choice to acknowledge his original participation in family planning even though he was unprepared for the changes that it would bring to his life. He also made a choice to see his work environment in a positive realistic manner. Much later, he decided to begin a process of forgiving his mother. In doing so, he eventually reduced much of his anger toward her, the past, and the women in his current life.

Application to Mary: Mary was convinced that if she was ever going to experience a happy and healthy relationship, she was going to need to follow her plan. It required making difficult choices that might go against a lifetime of habit, but she knew that the potential for a positive outcome was there in those choices.

Then…

8. CHOOSE

Believe it or not, this can be one of the most difficult steps to take. Why? If you attempt to behave in a way that is contrary to the agenda of your ego, you may feel something painful: you may feel fear, sadness, guilt, or anger. These feelings may be subtle, unmistakable, or anything in between. These feelings are likely produced by the perspective of your ego. However, *if* you have done the work to consciously establish your belief system, *and* have fully determined that the choice you are about to make is clearly within *YOBI*, *then* you can conclude, "There is nothing to fear, there is nothing to lose, I am safe, and it's ok if things don't completely go my way."

Being on the threshold of choice can produce fears about: 1) doing the wrong thing, 2) failure, 3) loss, 4) change, 5) taking a risk, 6) making a commitment. For some of us, these fears are avoided, or put off whenever possible by not choosing. There are ego gratifying outcomes in not choosing: at least momentarily we can stay safe, lose nothing, stay in control, and do nothing wrong. When things go bad, we can blame others, or the circumstances, and not have to take responsibility for a bad outcome. Some people make a habit of not choosing, and leave the choice up to the situation to choose for them.

On the other side of choice, there is relief, challenge, adventure, and growth. The way to reduce your risk in choosing is to know your values and morals and let them guide your way. The decisions you make will not be perfect, but more or less in accordance with *YOBI*.

Application to Bob: This was indeed a difficult transition for Bob to make. The plans for change made good sense to him. However, he fought his ego's need to act out. In our sessions, he recalled how as a teenager he had developed a great amount of rage toward his mother for being emotionally absent for so many years, "She gave us very little guidance or support, she just didn't seem to care, but she knew how to criticize and slap us around." Although his rage was real to him, he was never able to express it, and instead avoided her whenever he was able, which worked well in reducing his pain.

Each day Bob had to consciously choose to not act out his old rage. His very simple, very effective, but very difficult choice was this: "I need to choose to go to work each day, that's all there is to it."

Application to Mary: Mary decided to make a few lists. First, she made a list of the personality characteristics she would like in a partner. Next, was a list of the characteristics in a partner that she thought would be clearly incompatible with her. And finally, there was a list of the characteristics that she believed would be important to her in a healthy relationship. Until she was happy with her lists and was able to do some work on herself, she chose to forgo dating.

9. VALUE THE CHOICE

One way to develop value in your choice is to use the Establishing A New Value worksheet, and review it on a regular basis. In addition to that, you could make it a daily habit to notice the value in your choice. This will help you to experience an ongoing conscious connection with your choice and with change along the way.

Application to Bob: Bob completed two worksheets for Establishing New Values that he called "working independently," and "increasing quality parent time." These valued behaviors were intended to replace "wanting approval from my boss," and "avoiding parenting." He also started maintaining a daily journal to keep track of his new behavior and the outcomes.

Application to Mary: Mary completed a worksheet for Establishing A New Value. The unwanted behavior was, "Pleasing partners while ignoring my needs and wants," and the valued behavior was, "Choosing to value my consciously established needs and wants through clear communication." Each day on her drive home from work, Mary would make a conscious note of how her new choices were working for her.

10. ACT ON THE CHOICE

Trust is based on, and created through, time and experience. The only way that you can really trust, or know, that your choice is in your best interest is to act on it for an amount of time determined by you. That is, you need to have some experiences involving your choice to know if there is a good fit.

Application to Bob: Bob continued to work on "increasing quality parenting time" in our sessions. This was difficult for him due to his own unhappy and abusive childhood experiences. However, he knew that it was important not only to him, but to his son. The more he got on the floor to play with his son, the more he knew that his decision was good one.

Bob was able to get himself to work on time for three months in a row. He decided to give himself eight months to adjust to his job environment. If he wasn't adjusting satisfactorily by then, he would begin the search for a new job.

Application to Mary: Four months after Mary began therapy, she met someone new at work. Michael was an attractive man, nearly her age, and had transferred to her office from a different department in the same building. She had noticed him in the lunchroom on several occasions. After a couple of days of light conversation, she began to notice something about her thoughts. She was fantasizing about asking him if she could help him with the new job he was doing. This type of thinking was now familiar to her. She had been doing this for many years. She was following a long history of establishing a relationship by coming to someone's rescue. This behavior represented her ego's way of determining if Michael was a "catch." If he took the "bait," and responded with "yes, I could really use some help," it would be just the opportunity that her ego thrived on. However, because of the conscious work she did in developing her lists, she knew that there was something more important than immediate ego gratification with Michael. She made a conscious choice to disregard this fantasy. She reviewed the lists that she made, and reviewed her Establishing a New Value worksheet.

Mary needed to continue to monitor the old thinking patterns of her ego, and choose differently. She made a policy for herself to wait at least one month to go on a date with someone she was attracted to. In that month she could get to know the person as a friend and monitor the give/take balance of needs and wants. She could also monitor their ability to follow up on their word as a measure of trustworthiness.

11. MANAGE RESISTANCE AGAINST THE CHOICE

Your ego (not to mention the egos of others) may offer considerable resistance to your choice. This is especially the case when you are choosing to steer away from very gratifying behavior. Making the choice to delay the gratification, ignore the impulse, and perhaps experience temporary painful feelings will be very challenging. Your ego will likely resist any change that goes against its agenda. In order to help manage the resistance, review your motivation, and know that sometimes change takes time. As mentioned previously, you may reduce some of this resistance when there is some amount of acceptable ego gratification involved.

Application to Bob: Bob experienced much resistance in following his plan. We discovered that he subconsciously perceived his manager as having little emotional input, "She expects me to figure things out with very little guidance. Whenever I find myself mad at her, I explore my thoughts, and that's the expectation I find." As we non-judgmentally and realistically assessed his manager's style, we determined that she had a "hands-off" method with everyone who worked for her. We concluded that she wanted people to work independently, had confidence in people to get the job done, and trusted that if anyone needed guidance that they would ask for it. Bob was accustomed to a different management style. Now, he needed to readjust his expectations to a current reality on a daily basis, "She's not my mother." Instead of getting angry or ignoring the problem, he proactively requested weekly meetings with her to reduce his anxiety and worry about not meeting her expectations, and she was glad to accommodate him.

Application to Mary: Much of Mary's unhealthy relationship behavior had been produced from a subconscious level of awareness. Therefore, she needed to monitor her feelings very carefully, as they were the first signs to her that she needed to review her choices and behavior.

In her relationships with men, she needed to be on the lookout for intense feelings of anger ("He isn't doing anything for me"), guilt ("I'm not doing enough"), and fear ("If I don't do more, I'm going to lose him"). Whenever she experienced such feelings, her ego wanted to carry out its agenda as a fix, "Engage in more pleasing behaviors." Instead, Mary needed to recognize the agenda, make a choice to not act on the feelings immediately, and give herself a chance to review her lists, and her worksheet. With much time and effort, this newly established conscious process became more routine, more subconscious.

12. RE-EVALUATE THE CHOICE; GO BACK TO THE FIRST STEP AS NEEDED

With any choice, or with change, you monitor the results, looking for a positive outcome. With ample time and experience, you may decide that the change is not in *YOBI*. You may need to go back to step one, and start over again. Doing so is not failure; it is adjustment, or fine-tuning toward an outcome that you know is consistent with *YOBI*.

Application to Bob: There were a couple of setbacks for Bob along the way. On two occasions during the weekly meetings with his manager, Bob needed to excuse himself from the meetings when he became "overwhelmed" with the discussion. He was able to identify the feeling as anger or frustration, "She just sat there and let me do all the work, and there's this critical sound in her voice." Bob made some fine-tuning of his plan to ask for direct feedback whenever he perceived criticism. As it turned out, his manager had some of her own difficulty in giving direct feedback, which they were then able to work out in the meetings. Over time these meetings improved, "We did better than I expected, I guess she's not so bad after all, just kind of cold, oh well, she's my boss, not someone I have to like." He had a couple of "rough mornings" that he was able to work out through reviewing the values worksheets that he had written out. All in all, he continued to demonstrate to himself that he was doing the right thing; he felt a greater sense of integrity.

Application to Mary: Each time that Mary met someone, especially a man, she needed to monitor her feelings and her thoughts. When she chose to have ongoing contact with someone, she carefully observed her interaction, reviewed her lists, and reviewed her worksheet as needed. Periodically, Mary reported having doubt about her plan and wondered if she was doing the right thing. "Should I deny myself the pleasure of being pleasing to someone I really like?" In therapy, we identified this thinking as a form of conscious ego maintenance based in anger (things were not going her way or fast enough). The issue was not really a question about being pleasing to someone; it was about timing and finding a healthy balance. This was a concept that she needed to continue to remind herself of whenever she engaged in this type of conscious ego maintenance.

13. RECOGNIZE YOURSELF
ON THE *YOBI* PATH

With time and experience, you will see yourself behaving consistently within the boundaries of *YOBI*. You will participate in the development of a self-image that you can be proud of. You will build self-respect. You will make choices within a belief system of your design. You will create integrity, one choice at a time.

Application to Bob: In time, Bob was able to see how his behavior was critical to achieving his own peace of mind. He eventually went on to make other values changes as it made sense in order to create integrity. Bob's wife attended one of his last sessions. She noted, "Bob has become, quite a big fan of his boss. And, our son has become quite a big fan of Bob. I don't know what has happened to him, but it is good. There is no doubt that he's also become more of his own boss, in more ways than one."

Application to Mary: Each time she reviewed her values, and the other materials, Mary's conclusion remained the same; though difficult, the choice was clear, the path was hers to choose, and she was gaining faith in the outcome.

Mary decided to diversify her free time activities. She joined a couple of social clubs, and began to practice yoga at a local studio on a regular basis. Toward the end of therapy, Mary had met a man from a business club she joined. She remained faithful to her belief system, and after dating for a year and a half, they got engaged.

19 Nature Meets Nurture – The Peace of Mind Perspective is Born

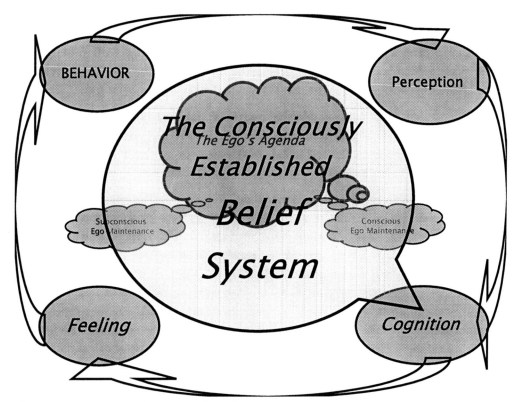

Making Friends With the Enemy

Tom Anderson appeared to be in much better spirit for his next appointment with me, "So Tom…how are things going?"

"Well, I guess things are slowly getting better at home. It's been about a month now since I told Laura about the gambling debt. I think that was just about one of the toughest things I've ever done. This has been a pretty hard thing for her to deal with. I did a lot of damage to our relationship. I understand that the trust has been broken, and that is going to take some time to fix. As far as my father is concerned, I had a talk with him. I told him that he was welcome to stay with us, but that he had to be nicer and stop ordering everyone around. He took it well, better than I expected. So far, it seems to be making a difference. I am finding out that being assertive with people in my life is scary at first, but overall, I can see how it's a good thing for me. I just have to slow down long enough to assess the situation first, and then sort of ignore any fears I have about it. I had no idea how much fear and anger I had inside me. I really thought I'd gotten past that years ago."

"Lately I've been remembering more of what happened when I was growing up. I'm trying to put it all in perspective though. I'm doing the work we've discussed of processing the anger, and coming up with resolutions that fit the current situation. I still have a lot of work to do, but it's worth it. The ego part of me is stubborn. When I get frustrated with myself, I can hear my father's voice from the past, and that's not good. So, I'm learning that it's better if I make a conscious effort to sort of talk nice to myself. Strange huh?"

Is your ego the enemy? Is it possible that as you continue seek out what your ego wants, you provide it with a means of dominating your life, leading to your own self-destruction? Perhaps that is a bit dramatic. Nevertheless, pursuing your ego's agenda is a form of self-destruction, in that you decrease your chances of experiencing peace of mind.

If you are reading this book, you are more than likely fortunate enough to live in a society where our basic survival is virtually assured. Social programs and government assistance to help those in need of food, shelter, clothing and health care are well established. Notwithstanding disease, accident, or suicide, you should live to be in your eighties. It would appear as though your originally designed instinct toward *physical* survival is, for all intents and purposes, obsolete. I believe that this primitive instinct to avoid physical pain and seek out physical gratification, is no longer operating on just a physical level. It would appear that over time, human beings have taken a further developmental step; we are now also trying to survive emotionally. In other words, we are trying to eliminate *emotional* pain, and seek out immediate *emotional* gratification. This was most likely not a part of the original design. There may have been a time when we needed to worry about running into saber tooth tigers or wonder if we'd gathered enough food to make it through the winter. This is no longer the case. We are not trying to avoid life-threatening tigers on a daily basis any more. We are simply trying to avoid stress in our jobs and in family life. We are not going to die from the stressful situations, but on some level of awareness, we equate it with dying. Just ask someone that suffers from panic attacks. They will tell you that they thought they were going to die, and have even spent thousands of dollars in Emergency Rooms to guard against it.

> On a subconscious level, it seems that we have erroneously come to equate our physical survival with emotional survival. In other words, your ego wants you to believe that painful emotions will kill you. Therefore, it only makes sense to your ego that you should try to eliminate all painful emotions in order to survive.

The ego is not necessarily your enemy. It may or may not have your best interest in mind. Clearly, ongoing stress is not healthy for you, and may shorten your lifespan. However, when was the last time you read an obituary that identified stress as the cause of death? You will not be able to completely destroy or eliminate your ego, or its perspective. That leaves few options. If you can't get rid of your ego, maybe you can learn to live with it harmoniously. A very wise person once said, "Know thy self." I would like to add something to that: "Know thy self, and thy ego, for you will be joined for a long time." Know and understand the agenda of your ego. Additionally, if you can develop a friendly self-to-ego relationship, that would be icing on the cake.

The Ego's Solution?

Your ego thinks that it has the solution to the problems of life. Subconscious ego says, "I know how to please you best. I know what is important to you. I know what is right for you." It begins to implement its solution from day one of your life. It starts with an attempt to survive through reducing pain and increasing pleasure. In these first days of living, we instinctively search out the breast for reducing hunger, cry to be held, and cry to signify pain, all in an attempt to survive. We make a connection in an infantile way: "When I don't like this pain, I make the need known, it gets taken care of, and I am gratified." Eventually, your ego moves on and attempts to establish and maintain power and control over people and environments. We have all seen the three year old in a grocery store or in their home crying out, "I want that candy, I want it, give me, I want it." Over time, your ego attempts to control everything and everyone. This attempt is carried out on all levels of awareness.

In what it believes is the solution, the ego attempts to control the uncontrollable. The fact of the matter is that ultimately, life is uncontrollable. I use the word *"uncontrollable"* because there is a force in the universe that is more powerful than your ego, called entropy. This force of nature is described in physics as one of the laws of thermodynamics.

Any Ordered System

We live in a universe that is in a continuous state of *breaking down* in terms of its complexity. The term used in physics to describe this natural process is entropy. Technically, entropy could be simply defined as: organization becoming disorganization. On a large scale, this occurs because the universe is in motion. It is expanding, cooling, and becoming less dense. Entropy describes the eventual outcome of all matter/energy, resulting from the uni-directional flow of energy in space-time toward disorganization. You could call entropy an instinctual directive toward the equilibrium of energy systems. This movement involves energy going from highly heated motion to completely stable cooled inactivity. Entropy occurs on all levels of reality from the very large to the very small; it is a universal law. Any ordered system from galaxies to families to fish tanks is subject to, and will follow entropic law, unless there is a more powerful ordering system to temporarily influence it. For example, left to itself, a fish aquarium will transform from a clean and healthy environment to a green mess. The green mess would eventually dry up, and the green dust would be blown away leaving no trace of what used to be a thriving tank. Without a more powerful ordering system, such as the fish owner maintaining the aquarium, the aquarium would change and become increasingly disorganized moving toward green slime dust. The same goes with the gravity holding together a solar system, the rules holding a relationship together, and my brain maintaining my body. To remain functional, or recognizable, a system must be ordered by a force more powerful than itself. Your body is an energy system, and as such, requires ordering so that you don't succumb to the force of entropy. If you did not eat or drink, in a matter of days you would dry up like the fish tank, and eventually become human dust. There is no doubt that you need some sort of ordering system to guide you away from death and toward life. There must be some urge to eat, drink, avoid wild tigers, and engage in other survival behaviors.

From the first day of you life, your ego has influenced your behavior by following an instinctually ordering system to produce survival. Simultaneously, you were influenced by whatever was the most powerful or compelling ordering system around you. As you grew up, the parental figures in your environment taught you what they thought was important, what was right and wrong, what you should expect (yourself, others, and the world), and who you were. You were exposed to their belief system by their verbal instruction and their actions. That particular ordering system may or may not be in your best interest now. With the conscious establishment and maintenance of your own belief system as an ordering system, your life could be different. That critical question once again is, what ordering system will you choose, your ego's instinctual agenda, or a system of your own conscious design?

Thanks to the dynamic of entropy, we find ourselves in a rather difficult situation. Without an ordering system, everything around you, including you, is involved in a process of becoming more disorganized—this is the nature of life. On the other hand, we and other earthly creatures are trying to build up life around us. At a minimum, this build up generally requires our time, our energy, and an effective plan. We are involved in a continual struggle against nature. Your ego follows instinctual directions toward a process of survival. Essentially, your ego is implementing what it believes is an effective plan—a *solution* for the problem of entropy. If we follow the survival plan of the ego, then we attempt to reduce all pain, increase all gratification, gain control over nature, and attempt to predict the future in such a way to ensure our continuing survival and gratification.

Not only do we fight against the natural inclination of matter around us, but also we build and manufacture things out of raw materials. Then over time, we watch as it eventually all falls apart; buildings, clothing, homes, cars, and even relationships. We establish and build some relationships with the hope that they will forever be the way they were in the beginning. This is impossible, yet we try our hardest to maintain them as they were, and in our efforts, we can destroy them. Change is going to happen, this is uncontrollable; it is only a matter of time. The only remaining question with regard to change is, how do we deal with it?

I feel compelled to contradict myself with this next statement. At present, I know of no reliable information to suggest that the second law of thermodynamics (entropy) will change. In other words, according to this law, no matter what you do to try to build up life around you, the natural force of life will maintain its movement toward disorganization. Entropy is a fact, and it will *not* change. Theoretically, entropy will stop when all matter has reached a stable cooled equilibrium. Until then (many billions of years from now), you cannot fight Mother Nature; you will have to learn to work with her.

It seems that the ego always wants more. It values the notion that more is always better; more immediate pleasure, more power, more predictable control. Realistically however, life is unpredictable, and is constantly changing around us. Everything we build up will eventually succumb to decay and gravity. Every organic and inorganic thing will follow the laws of thermodynamics; all things will break down to lesser-organized states of existence. Surely then, this earthly reality is an *ideal* environment to have regular experiences of anger or frustration from not getting what you want, how you want it, and when you want it. On the other hand, what if you chose a nurturing response to life? In spite of the continuous frustrations, you adjust your perspective, learn patience, become more realistic, and maybe even learn how to have peace of mind in what could be an otherwise chaotic environment. Ironically then, you have the Peace Of Mind Perspective:

> **THIS PHYSICAL REALITY MAY BE
> THE MOST SENSIBLE (*OR EVEN THE PERFECT*) ENVIRONMENT
> IN WHICH CONSCIOUSNESS WILL EVOLVE
> TOWARD BEING PEACEFUL.**

Our time was almost up for the hour, as Tom continued, "I realize now, I did a bad thing, well maybe a few bad things, but I'm not a bad guy. I am more sure of that each time that I make better choices. I think I'm really starting to get this now. My ego is always going to be ready to step up and take the lead in my decision-making. After all we've talked about, if I let it happen now, it's basically my choice. I do have options that we've talked about here. I've worked hard to make my belief system my own. I'm not living in the past any more. Having that discussion with my father was tough, but the decision came right out of my new values. I really expected myself to follow my standard of being assertive with him, and it worked. And not just to get him to behave differently, because that could change any day. What makes the difference is how I feel about myself. And, knowing that I like these changes. I guess its not really too late to teach an old dog like me new tricks."

"Lately, I'm noticing a problem with this guy from work. He's one of these guys who always has to be right about things. You know, it has to be his way or the highway. What do you think I should do?"

"Tom, I think you might already know the answer to that question."

"Yeah, you're right, I do actually, 'the *expectation test* and a resolution.' But that doesn't make it easy."

"No it doesn't Tom."

Conscious Awareness Revisited

According to physics experts, theoretically, matter and energy are indistinguishable on a sub-atomic level. That is, you cannot tell the difference between matter and energy on a very small scale. They essentially turn out to be the same thing, made of the same stuff. So if all things in the universe are a form of energy, does that include your consciousness, or what you know as *your mind?*

I think that consciousness is neither matter, nor energy but is an experience. Consciousness is experienced as a phenomenon of perception. As an experience of perception, consciousness is not subject to physical laws, and therefore is not subject to entropy. Our consciousness does not break down over time per se, although you might say that a psychological breakdown is a matter of entropy *getting the best of us.* In that case, the ability to organize and make sense out of life around us is impaired because entropy has reared its ugly head. For some people this is temporary, and for others it is for a lifetime. Generally speaking however, perception is fully functioning even in the middle of any disorganized mess we find ourselves in. On the other hand, our physical bodies, including our brains, are subject to and are clearly affected by entropy. As the physical senses and the brain deteriorate with age, your perception is altered, but not completely ended. You continue to take in information and try to organize it in a meaningful way. You might say that consciousness is *anti-entropic*, and operates in spite of the natural flow of the universe around us. As an anti-entropic experience, your consciousness is not a part of the physical universe per se; it is more like a window that allows you to observe *it*, and your *self.*

Physical reality is subject to entropy, which makes it ultimately and completely out of your control. Fortunately, as an experiential window of sorts, your consciousness is not subject to entropy. This is the good news:

> Your behavior and your belief system are matters of conscious choice and therefore ultimately under your control. In fact, they are the only things you do have control over. Your belief system can be (re)established, and then maintained by you. Your belief system can be geared toward whatever agenda you choose. The agenda of the ego is clearly about survival and gratification. An agenda of higher consciousness is concerned with creating integrity and experiencing peace of mind. The choice is yours; which agenda will you choose to direct your attention and energy?

"So it looks like making choices to follow my belief system instead of my ego's agenda will be an ongoing effort. I know each agenda, and I know how to manage the painful feelings," said Tom as we both stood up and walked toward my office door, "Does this ever get any easier?"

"Yes it does. As you begin to consistently live out your belief system, one choice at a time, your trust in the outcome of integrity will be the incentive to continue. Positive results will prevail, and you will be evolving. You won't ever be rid of your connection to your ego, after all, it's the original representative of your body. But, you can have a compassionate and nurturing relationship toward it, and toward life itself."

Beyond Ego: The Real Entropy Solution

What is the real solution to entropy? The ego's solution is to follow its agenda; control all aspects of life to ensure that feeling immediately good is powerfully maintained. This agenda is maintained in spite of a universe that constantly and irrevocably changes in the direction of disorganization. It seems to me that fighting against a powerful force that will never change is ultimately self-defeating and a waste of energy. I believe that the real solution lies in going beyond the agenda of the ego. What is beyond ego? To get beyond ego you need to value something other than its needs and/or goals. This idea was first introduced in Chapter 9, Conscious Values. Again, you value and pursue something similar to the following agenda:

➢ A tolerance, and/or, acceptance of, appropriate painful feelings as a necessary as part of problem solving, instead of ego maintenance.

➢ A delay of immediate gratification when appropriate, thus the development of patience.

➢ Inner-power, not power over others.

➢ Self-control, not control over others.

➢ Self-acceptance, in favor of other-acceptance or idealization.

➢ Consciously developed values, morals, and expectations.

➢ The establishment and on-going development of your own self-image.

➢ Acceptance of a realistic, reasonable, and fair amount of influence over life, combined with the ability to adapt.

➢ A *Functional Anger* Style.

➢ Peace of mind instead of "feeling good."

➢ The experience of integrity.

Valuing these ideas represents a way of living that goes beyond your ego's instinctually driven agenda. A fancy way of saying this is that those ideas *transcend* the nature of the ego. If you were able to live this way, *you* would go beyond, or transcend, your ego. You could simply call it living a life of higher consciousness. I call it living a consciously developed belief system and living according to *Your Own Best Interest*. I can tell you this: the ego is generally not interested in a higher consciousness and will fight you tooth and nail to have its own agenda followed. Your ego has been around for a long time and will not be eliminated from your life easily, if ever.

Much of its agenda is carried out on a subconscious level, making it difficult for you to detect. Often you will discover that the agenda has already become involved in your cyclelogical functioning before you are even aware. "The chocolate cake that I just ate was meant to soothe my nerves from a stressful day. It was not necessarily in my best interest to eat it. I noticed it in the refrigerator, instantly thought that it looked good, felt some glad anticipation, and without any additional thought grabbed it for my pleasure. After the third highly gratifying bite, I realized that there could be other methods of stress management such as mediation, exercise, talking it over, etc.; but the cake still tastes good, and the ego perspective in me knows it for sure. Maybe tomorrow I will run an extra ten minutes?"

The critical question to ask yourself is: "What's in it for me if I decide to not follow my ego's lead?" At first glance, this appears to be a lot to ask of yourself—a scary proposition indeed. It may seem as though you give up control, the feeling of power, and physical and emotional satisfaction as quickly as you can get it. Maybe that has been a lifetime of a lifestyle that seems right. Maybe giving up all of that doesn't feel right. Ask yourself, "Is living an ego-based lifestyle leaving me with the peace of mind that comes from integrity?"

The ego always wants more. If you primarily follow its agenda, you will always want more. It is only a matter of time before what you have is no longer enough. This may result in your experience of increasing or continual frustration, anger, fear or anxiety, as you perceive that things are not going your way, or that you are losing control. The ego's agenda advocates that if you just get angry enough, or just worry enough, that you might be able to change reality when you don't like it.

Entropy essentially tells us that it is the tendency of physical matter to fall apart. The big question is, "While all of life around you is falling apart, what is going on inside of your head?" Remember the good news—your consciousness is not affected by entropy. Fortunately then, you have a choice to establish your own method for living in entropy, and to hopefully keep your inner-life from falling apart.

Who is leading the way to establish the direction for your life? When your approach to life is based on conscious design, you can know the value of managing anger without external power or control. You can know the value of a functional anger style. You can know the value of self-control instead of other-control. So, the question I mentioned was, "What's in it for me if I don't follow my ego's lead?" The answer is, "Peace of mind, the freedom to be me, inner-strength, and a satisfaction based in integrity."

Still, there is ego.

There is no doubt that the ego follows an agenda. That agenda may be the basis for much of your cycle-logical functioning. By knowing the agenda and how it operates, you have a good chance of being able to recognize its influence in your life, and make changes if you choose. Your best chance for change and growth toward peace of mind is to establish your own agenda—a belief system of conscious choice. It's up to you, the individual, to create your own belief system. You might borrow from someone else's completely, or perhaps grab on to bits and pieces from a variety of resources. Ultimately, the choice is yours. You are responsible for the integrity of your universe—one choice at a time. *May you choose wisely then.*

The Big Picture of
Cycle–Logical Functioning

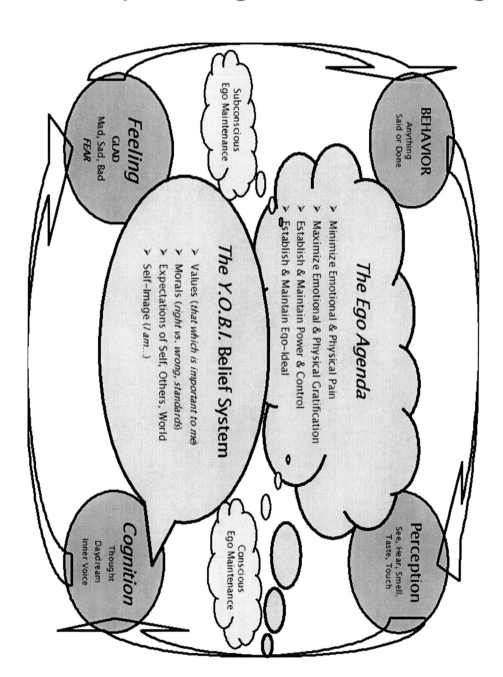

B Establishing A New Value

This is a tool to be used for a variety of situations (problems, beliefs, thoughts, ideas, behaviors). As such, some questions may not apply to all situations. The repetition is by design for the purpose of covering all perspectives and levels of awareness. Best results are possible when you challenge yourself to avoid a quick, "I don't know" response.

Identify the **unwanted** behavior (or belief) specifically: _____

_____

_____

Identify the **wanted** behavior (or belief) specifically: _____

_____

_____

The Ego Agenda

1. How does your ego value the **unwanted** behavior? In other words, what are the ego-based gratifying outcomes that result from the **unwanted** behavior? For clarification, answer the following questions.

How does this behavior eliminate or minimize painful ego-based anger, sadness, guilt, or fear? _____

_____

_____

_____

How does this behavior create an ego-based gratifying experience? _____

_____

_____

_____

How does this behavior create a perception of ego-based power and control? _____

_____

_____

_____

How does this behavior create a perception of ego-idealization? _____

_____

_____

_____

Ego Maintenance

2. How have I used ego maintenance to engage in the ***unwanted*** behavior? (Get real honest with yourself, and think from an ego perspective).

I have ignored the negative outcome(s) of this behavior by: _____

_____

_____

I have told myself this behavior is OK because: _____

_____

_____

I have told myself this behavior is not bad because: _____

_____

_____

I have told myself this behavior is good because: _____

_____

_____

I have told myself this behavior is smart/clever/superior because: _____

_____

3. What are the additional defending or supporting ideas, thoughts, feelings, and gratifications of the **unwanted** behavior?

It's okay for me to get *my way* through this behavior because: _____

_____

_____

It's okay for me to reduce my *sadness/loss* with this behavior because: _____

_____

_____

It's *right* for me to engage in this behavior because: _____

_____

_____

It's okay for me to reduce my *fear/worry* through this behavior because: _____

_____

_____

It's okay for me to feel *good* through this behavior because: _____

_____

_____

Belief System Solution

4. Correct the above defending or supporting ideas, thoughts, feelings, and gratifications of the **unwanted** behavior? Why is the **unwanted** behavior wrong? Refer back to the specific ways that you just made it "ok', and refute them.

It is wrong for me to get *"my way"* like this because: _____

_____

_____

It is wrong for me to reduce my sadness/loss like this because: _____

_____

_____

It is wrong for me to reduce my *fear/worry* like this because: _____

_____

_____

It is wrong for me to feel *good* like this because: _____

_____

_____

5. How does the ***unwanted*** behavior **conflict** with my Belief System?

This is how the unwanted behavior conflicts with my *values*: _____

_____

_____

This is how the unwanted behavior conflicts with my *morals*: _____

_____

_____

This is how the unwanted behavior conflicts with my *expectations* of myself: _____

_____

_____

This is how the unwanted behavior conflicts with my *self-image*: _____

_____

_____

6. These are the current, eventual, or potential negative **consequences** of the ***unwanted*** behavior.

Emotional consequences:

Mad – my anger is: _____

Sad – my loss is: _____

Bad – my guilt is: _____

Fear – my fear or worry is: _____

Consequences to self: _____

_____

_____

Consequences to others: _____

_____

_____

Other consequences: _____

_____

_____

_____

_____

7. Refer back to the ***above*** conflicts and negative consequences as needed. If and/or when you engage in the ***wanted*** behavior, describe how those consequences and conflicts are eliminated.

This is what I *gain* when engaging in the wanted behavior: _____

_____

_____

Conflict with my *morals* is eliminated by (*"I now feel proud because"*): _____

_____

_____

This is what I look *forward* to: _____

_____

_____

This is who I *become*: _____

_____

_____

Other positive outcomes: _____

_____

_____

8. These are the specific Belief System entries I establish or emphasize in support of the *wanted* behavior.

Values: _____

_____

_____

Morals: _____

_____

_____

Expectations: _____

_____

_____

Self-Image: _____

_____

_____

The Conscious Management of Feelings

9. I would need to establish the following methods of feeling management related to the *unwanted* behavior. This feeling management would support and maintain the *wanted* behavior.

This is how I manage feelings of *anger* that would interfere with maintaining the *wanted* behavior: _____

_____

_____

This is how I manage feelings of *sadness* that would interfere with maintaining the *wanted* behavior: _____

_____

_____

This is how I manage feelings of *guilt* that would interfere with maintaining the **wanted** behavior: _____

_____

_____

This is how I manage feelings of *fear* that would interfere with maintaining the **wanted** behavior: _____

_____

_____

The Choice

10. Take all this new information and name the **wanted <u>new</u>** behavior. (Give the wanted behavior a name that is relatively brief, easy to remember, and catchy).

_____

Now read over the information until you have clearly concluded that the new behavior is in your best interest!

Appendix

Case Examples

Case Example – Jerry

(See Jerry's case in Chapter 9 under *The Development of Values*, 4. *Using Your Feelings*.)

Establishing A New Value

Identify the ***unwanted*** behavior (or belief) specifically: **When I get into a conflict with my wife, I get mad, yell at her, and feel like I have to win so that I'm not controlled by her.**

Identify the wanted behavior (or belief) specifically: **Having a calm and reasonable discussion about conflicts, and establishing a compromise outcome when needed.**

The Ego Agenda

1. How does your ego value the ***unwanted*** behavior? In other words, what are the ego-based gratifying outcomes that result from the ***unwanted*** behavior? For clarification, answer the following questions.

How does this behavior eliminate or minimize painful ego-based anger, sadness, guilt, or fear: **I vent frustration and anger by yelling. I avoid dealing with the loss of what I want very much. It's an active way of dealing with my fear instead of worrying.**

How does this behavior create an ego-based gratifying experience: **I get what I want. I like winning.**

How does this behavior create a perception of ego-based power and control: **By yelling, I feel like I have a better chance of getting control of the situation. I feel a sense of power over the situation.**

How does this behavior create a perception of ego-idealization: **I feel like I am right in getting what I wanted. I know what's best. I tell myself I'm in control.**

EGO MAINTENANCE

2. How have I used ego maintenance to engage in the ***unwanted*** behavior? (Get real honest with yourself, and think from an ego perspective).

I have ignored the negative outcome(s) of this behavior by: **I avoid thinking about negative outcomes. I tell myself that I won't compromise or lose out on what's important to me no matter what.**

I have told myself this behavior okay because: **Couples yell at each other all of the time, my mom and dad did, I'm supposed to be the boss, you can't get what you want unless you fight for it.**

I have told myself this behavior is not bad because: **I'm usually right, and she knows it.**

I have told myself this behavior is good because: **Arguing is good for a relationship. She'll never leave me, and if she does, I'll be just fine without her**

I have told myself this behavior is smart/clever/superior because: **I like winning, being right, getting my point across, and staying in control. It's a way of toughening her up.**

3. What are the additional defending or supporting ideas, thoughts, feelings, and gratifications of the **unwanted** behavior?

It's okay for me to get *my way* through this behavior because: **Someone has to be right and guide things.**

It's okay for me to reduce my sadness/loss with this behavior because: **Sadness is weakness, and I can't have that.**

It's *right* for me to engage in this behavior because: **You should take control, or someone else will.**

It's okay for me to reduce my *fear/worry* through this behavior because: **It gets it out of my system, I can't afford to have all this stress.**

It's okay for me to feel *good* through this behavior because: **I feel like I'm a winner when I win the argument, and yelling is just what I have to do.**

BELIEF SYSTEM SOLUTION

4. Correct the above defending or supporting ideas, thoughts, feelings, and gratifications of the **unwanted** behavior? Why is the **unwanted** behavior wrong? Be honest. Refer back to the specific ways that you just made it "ok', and refute them.

It is wrong for me to get *"my way"* like this because: **It hurts our relationship, and deep down, I know it.**

It is wrong for me to reduce my *sadness/loss* like this because: **Sadness is not really a weakness, it's a feeling I need to start dealing with.**

It is wrong for me to reduce my *fear/worry* like this because: **I wind up creating more stress in the long run.**

It is wrong for me to feel *good* like this because: **My wife doesn't deserve to be treated like this.**

5. How does the ***unwanted*** behavior **conflict** with my Belief System?

This is how the unwanted behavior conflicts with my *values:* **I value my marriage more than anything else in my life. And I'm mean to her.**

This is how the unwanted behavior conflicts with my *morals*: **I know its wrong to yell and scream, no one likes that, and neither do I.**

This is how the unwanted behavior conflicts with my *self-image:* **I am generally a loving husband; this doesn't fit with who I am, or who I really want to be.**

6. These are the current, eventual, or potential negative **consequences** of the ***unwanted*** behavior.

Emotional consequences:

Mad – my anger is: **I can't control myself, and everything is going wrong.**

Sad – my loss is: **I'm losing her. I will eventually lose her.**

Bad – my guilt is: **I can't stand that I am hurting her, I feel terrible afterward.**

Fear – my fear or worry is: **I'll continue to hurt her. I will be alone.**

Consequences to self: **I feel stress afterward, and I feel bad about what I've done to her.**

Consequences to others: **I can tell that she feels bad, and I think that she is becoming afraid of me and walks on eggshells.**

Other consequences: **Our friends and extended family members are starting to worry about this, and I am afraid of what might happen if this goes on.**

7. Refer back to the ***above*** conflicts and negative consequences as needed. If and/or when you engage in the ***wanted*** behavior, describe how those consequences and conflicts are eliminated.

This is what I *gain* when engaging in the wanted behavior: **I gain my own self-respect and we gain a peaceful household.**

Conflict with my *morals* is eliminated by (*"I now feel proud because"*): **I feel proud because I was frustrated and was able to control myself instead of wanting to control her or the situation.**

This is what I look *forward* to: **We can get along much better, and can look forward to many years of a happy *marriage*.**

This is who I *become:* **A respected husband.**

Other positive outcomes: **A reduction of stress and problems with my health.**

8. These are the specific Belief System entries I establish or emphasize in support of the *wanted* behavior.

Values: **Respectful conflict resolution. Assertiveness.**

Morals: **Make attempts to compromise with those I love whenever possible.**

Expectations: **I expect myself to engage in a peaceful and rational discussion with my wife. I expect myself to be able to control my anger.**

Self-Image: **I am a reasonable, calm, and fair husband.**

The Conscious Management of Feelings

9. I would need to establish the following methods of feeling management related to the *unwanted* behavior. This feeling management would support and maintain the *wanted* behavior.

This is how I manage feelings of *anger* that would interfere with maintaining the *wanted* behavior: **Remind myself that I don't need to be in control. Take a time out as needed. Remind myself that even if she becomes angry and loud, I expect myself to remain calm, make attempts to stay on the topic, and attempt to compromise as needed.**

This is how I manage feelings of *sadness* that would interfere with maintaining the *wanted* behavior: **Remind myself that there is no loss in not being in control. I don't need to be in control of my wife. There is gain in engaging in the wanted behavior.**

This is how I manage feelings of *guilt* that would interfere with maintaining the *wanted* behavior: **Remind myself that there is nothing bad or wrong with cooperation in a loving caring relationship.**

This is how I manage feelings of *fear* that would interfere with maintaining the *wanted* behavior: **The former fear is that if I didn't take control, I would be controlled by her. I now know that is not valid. I am committed to fairness in my relationship, and I will ask for that.**

The Choice

10. Take all this new information and name the *wanted **new*** behavior. (*Give the wanted behavior a name that is relatively brief, easy to remember, and catchy:* **"Mr. Calm Compromiser."**

Now read over the information until you have clearly concluded that the new behavior is in your best interest! **There is no doubt that this is in my best interest, and in the best interest of our relationship.**

Case Example – Helen

Establishing A New Value

Identify the *unwanted* behavior (or belief) specifically: **Eating junk food late at night when I'm alone.**

Identify the wanted behavior (or belief) specifically: **Eating a healthy evening meal, and having a light healthy snack two hours before bedtime.**

The Ego Agenda

1. How does your ego value the *unwanted* behavior? In other words, what are the ego-based gratifying outcomes that result from the *unwanted* behavior? For clarification, answer the following questions.

How does this behavior eliminate or minimize painful ego-based anger, sadness, guilt, or fear: **When I'm mad about work, it helps me get my mind off it. When I'm alone, I feel less sad when I eat good tasting things. I don't worry when I'm eating.**

How does this behavior create an ego-based gratifying experience: **I love to eat food, it feels good, and it's what I want. It helps me to deal with a loss of companionship. I feel proud that I don't drink, smoke, or do drugs. It gives me something to look forward to each night. I like getting my way, feeling gratified, being in control of feeling good.**

How does this behavior create a perception of ego-based power and control: **I feel like no matter what bad things happen, I can make a good meal and make my bad feelings go away like magic.**

How does this behavior create a perception of ego-idealization: **That's a tough question, I'm not sure. Maybe on some level, I think that while other people are struggling with life's problems, I've found a way to deal with it.**

Ego Maintenance

2. How have I used ego maintenance to engage in the **unwanted** behavior? (*Get real honest with yourself, and think from an ego perspective*).

I have ignored the negative outcome(s) of this behavior by: **Not looking in the mirror. Buying increasingly larger clothes over time. Telling myself I will be okay eventually.**

I have told myself this behavior okay because: **I deserve to feel good at the end of day. Don't worry, I'll exercise double tomorrow.**

I have told myself this behavior is not bad because: **I've got nothing else to do anyway, I'll be just fine. Most of this country is overweight anyway.**

I have told myself this behavior is good because: **I don't think about being alone.**

I have told myself this behavior is smart/clever/superior because: **It feels good to eat, who needs to be so skinny.**

3. What are the additional defending or supporting ideas, thoughts, feelings, and gratifications of the **unwanted** behavior?

It's okay for me to get *my way* through this behavior because: **It's my business, and I can do whatever I want to.**

It's okay for me to reduce my *sadness/loss* with this behavior because: **No one cares about my health or me anyway.**

It's *right* for me to engage in this behavior because: **At least I'm not using drugs or alcohol, now that would be wrong!**

It's okay for me to reduce my *fear/worry* through this behavior because: **Life's too short to worry about what my weight will do to me. I could die tomorrow on my drive to work.**

It's okay for me to feel *good* through this behavior because: **I'm not hurting anyone.**

Belief System Solution

4. Correct the above defending or supporting ideas, thoughts, feelings, and gratifications of the **unwanted** behavior? Why is the **unwanted** behavior wrong? Refer back to the specific ways that you just made it "ok', and refute them.

It is wrong for me to get *"my way"* like this because: **It's a temporary fix doesn't really solve any problems, and in the long run, creates problems. I don't feel good afterward, or the next day, and that's not what I want.**

It is wrong for me to reduce my *sadness/loss* like this because: **While I don't think about being alone, I feel sad about my loss of self-respect later.**

It is wrong for me to reduce my fear/worry like this because: **I don't like the feeling that comes soon after or the next morning.**

It is wrong for me to feel *good* like this because: **I don't feel proud about what I'm doing with food. In the big picture of my life, this is not going my way, and I feel out of control with this eating habit.**

5. How does the ***unwanted*** behavior **conflict** with my Belief System?

This is how the unwanted behavior conflicts with my *values*: **I actually value good health, and I would like to buy my clothes off the rack.**

This is how the unwanted behavior conflicts with my *morals*: **By ignoring the potential consequences, I am not being honest with myself. I believe in honesty with all people in my life. That should include me.**

This is how the unwanted behavior conflicts with my *expectations* of myself: **I expect myself to behave in a respectful manner; I'm not respecting myself. I expect to live to see my grandchildren, at this rate, I won't make it. I expect myself to be real, not self-deceptive.**

This is how the unwanted behavior conflicts with my *self-image*: **My self-image says to me: you have integrity, with this behavior, I am experiencing a breach of that integrity.**

6. These are the current, eventual, or potential negative **consequences** of the ***unwanted*** behavior.

Emotional consequences:

Mad – my anger is: **I don't like the weight I'm gaining, or how my clothes fit too tight.**

Sad – my loss is: **I'm losing self-respect, and that becomes very clear to me each day I engage in this behavior.**

Bad – my guilt is: **I feel guilty when I eat like this, it's not right for me to overindulge eating.**

Fear – my fear or worry is: **If I continue this behavior, I continue to gain weight, risk developing health problems, and need to spend money to buy new clothes.**

Consequences to self: *Many* **different health problems related to being overweight or obesity. Loss of self-respect. Deep down inside, I know that this behavior feels good in the moment, but leaves me empty overall.**

Consequences to others: **My friends see me less often over time. I am afraid that I will die before I can see my grandchildren.**

Other consequences: **As I continue in my current patterns of eating, I find that I isolate myself more and more, creating more feelings of sadness.**

7. Refer back to the ***above*** conflicts and negative consequences as needed. If and/or when you engage in the ***wanted*** behavior, describe how those consequences and conflicts are eliminated.

This is what I *gain* when engaging in the wanted behavior: **Health. Self-respect. Freedom.**

Conflict with my *morals* is eliminated by (*"I now feel proud because"*): **This is a no-brainer; I am feeling quite proud and glad that I can live life to the fullest. I am being honest with myself.**

This is what I look *forward* to: **Spending more time with my friends and family. Buying clothes off the rack. Being healthy again.**

This is who I *become*: **A healthy woman, honest with myself, a woman of integrity.**

Other positive outcomes: **Physical attractiveness to others. I would rather have a healthy sense of self-respect, and peace of mind at the end of the day, than a physically gratified body.**

8. These are the specific Belief System entries I establish or emphasize in support of the ***wanted*** behavior.

Values: **Healthy eating. Wellness lifestyle. Healthy snack two hours before bedtime. Internal honesty. Gain of self-respect each new day**

Morals: **Eat a healthy evening meal, and have a light healthy snack two hours before bedtime**

Expectations: **I expect myself to eat a healthy evening meal, and have a light healthy snack two hours before bedtime. I expect that I will find acceptable ways of dealing with the days frustrations, and maintain a healthy evening eating pattern. I expect that I will feel proud and a sense of integrity as I follow my new plan.**

Self-Image: **I am becoming a healthy woman. I am joyful.**

The Conscious Management of Feelings

9. I would need to establish the following methods of feeling management related to the **unwanted** behavior. This feeling management would support and maintain the **wanted** behavior:

This is how I manage feelings of *anger* that would interfere with maintaining the **wanted** behavior: **When I feel angry about not being able to eat junk food at night, I will remind myself that this is my choice, and that if I want different results, I need to make different choices. I expect to be glad by experiencing this new lifestyle.**

This is how I manage feelings of *sadness* that would interfere with maintaining the **wanted** behavior: **I'm going to learn how to grieve my losses. When I experience feelings of sadness, I will learn to think through the process of loss and remind myself of what I gain specifically in the end. I'm also going to start to keep a feeling journal to help me deal with my feelings.**

This is how I manage feelings of *guilt* that would interfere with maintaining the **wanted** behavior: **I am going to refer to the ideas on guilt management I have learned about in this book. I will remind myself of how proud I will be with maintaining new choices.**

This is how I manage feelings of *fear* that would interfere with maintaining the **wanted** behavior: **At night when I am most likely to eat junk food, I am avoiding the worry based thinking I begin to get caught up in. I think my feeling journal will help with this. When I start to worry during this time, I am going to write down my worries and make a promise to myself to problem solve them the next day. I look forward to a healthy and new change in my behavior.**

The Choice

10. Take all this new information and name the **wanted <u>new</u>** behavior. (*Give the wanted behavior a name that is relatively brief, easy to remember, and catchy*): **I'm going to call this, "Helen's future is looking good."**

Now read over the information until you have clearly concluded that the new behavior is in your best interest! **There is no doubt that this is the right thing for me, and I am sure of the YOBI'ness of these changes.**

Case Example – Janie

(See Janie's case in Chapter 5 under Conscious Ego Maintenance.)

Establishing A New Value

Identify the *unwanted* behavior (or belief) specifically: **Having an affair.**

Identify the *wanted* behavior (or belief) specifically: **My effort toward increasing the stability and quality of my relationship.**

The Ego Agenda

1. How does your ego value the *unwanted* behavior? In other words, what are the ego-based gratifying outcomes that result from the *unwanted* behavior? For clarification, answer the following questions.

How does this behavior eliminate or minimize painful ego-based anger, sadness, guilt, or fear: **I feel wanted and cared about by someone, it feels good, and it's what I want. I don't feel so alone when I have someone else's attention. I feel proud that I can attract someone to me. It gives me something to look forward to each day at work.**

How does this behavior create an ego-based gratifying experience: **I like the feeling of getting what I want, feeling desirable, being in control of feeling good.**

How does this behavior create a perception of ego-based power and control: **I don't feel like I can do anything to change my situation at home, so I'm taking matters into my own hands and getting a response I want. Being sexually attractive feels powerful to me.**

How does this behavior create a perception of ego-idealization: **I'm attracting sexual attention. I'm sexually attractive, wanted.**

Ego Maintenance

2. How have I used ego maintenance to engage in the *unwanted* behavior? (Get real honest with yourself, and think from an ego perspective).

I have ignored the negative outcome(s) of this behavior by: **I've told myself, I'm not going to get caught, I'll just be careful.**

I have told myself this behavior okay because: **I hate my marriage, and I deserve to be happy.**

I have told myself this behavior is not bad because: **I'm not hurting anyone; everyone does this at some time. Sometimes, marriages end, oh well.**

I have told myself this behavior is good because: **It feels good, I've got nothing else to lose, everything's going to be okay.**

I have told myself this behavior is smart/clever/superior because: **If he's not going to solve this problem, I will.**

3. What are the additional defending or supporting ideas, thoughts, feelings, and gratifications of the **unwanted** behavior?

It's okay for me to get *my way* through this behavior because: **I deserve to be happy too; I'm tired of being angry all the time.**

It's okay for me to reduce my sadness/loss with this behavior because: **I've had enough loss in my life, I put up with this for years, now it's my turn to be happy.**

It's *right* for me to engage in this behavior because: **Everyone else does this, why not me.**

It's okay for me to reduce my *fear/worry* through this behavior because: **It gives me something to look forward to, if not this, I'm sure it could be worse.**

It's okay for me to feel *good* through this behavior because: **I'm a normal human being who needs love and affection.**

Belief System Solution

4. Correct the above defending or supporting ideas, thoughts, feelings, and gratifications of the **unwanted** behavior? Why is the **unwanted** behavior wrong? Refer back to the specific ways that you just made it "ok', and refute them.

It is wrong for me to get *"my way"* like this because: **I don't really want someone else, I want my husband, I'm just mad at him. My marriage and self-respect are more important than feeling good about being attractive to someone else.**

It is wrong for me to reduce my *sadness/loss* like this because: **I feel sad about my loss of self-respect, and at the end of the day, I still feel alone.**

It is wrong for me to reduce my *fear/worry* like this because: **I don't like the feeling that I get soon after I come home from work.**

It is wrong for me to feel *good* like this because: **I'm not really getting what I want in the big picture of my life. What I really want is true intimacy with my husband.**

5. How does the ***unwanted*** behavior **conflict** with my Belief System?

This is how the unwanted behavior conflicts with my *values*: **Marriage is important to me. So are commitment and honesty. My behavior is clearly in conflict.**

This is how the unwanted behavior conflicts with my *morals*: **Deep inside, I know that this is wrong, it's just that I'm so hurt. No matter what my situation might be, I still believe in my own sense of honesty, and I'm feeling guilt when I really think about what I'm doing.**

This is how the unwanted behavior conflicts with my *expectations* of myself: **There is no doubt that I expect better behavior from me, and I wouldn't ever find it acceptable for my husband to do something like this.**

This is how the unwanted behavior conflicts with my *self-image*: **I am much smarter, and better than my behavior lately. I know that something has got to change. I can't be this kind of person.**

6. These are the current, eventual, or potential negative **consequences** of the ***unwanted*** behavior.

Emotional consequences:

Mad – my anger is: **I don't like the person I'm becoming, or how I'm treating the person I love. It's wrong for me to cheat, even if I hate the marriage. I need to work on being content with my behavior, so I can know I've done my best.**

Sad – my loss is: **I'm losing my sense of self-respect, and whatever sense of connection that I felt with my husband. This marriage still has a chance.**

Bad – my guilt is: **I feel guilty because I know my behavior is wrong. I'm hurting myself, and potentially him. Not everyone does this. Deep inside, I know that this behavior is wrong for me.**

Fear – my fear or worry is: **If I continue this behavior, I may eventually begin an affair and lose my husband and our life. No matter how careful I am, I know what I'm doing. Each day of continuing this behavior, I think something bad is going to happen to me.**

Consequences to self: **It's negative that I feel glad about any part of this behavior. I've got a lot to lose, I'm afraid I'm really ruining my life with this selfish behavior.**

Consequences to others: **If my friends, or my family were to find out what I am up to, I would be hurting them with out a doubt. If my husband were to find out, I'm sure it would harm him, and do damage to any future relationships he may have.**

Other consequences: **If I have an affair, and I am able to get away with it, then I would be doing damage to my own sense of trust of others. If I can do it to someone else, surely then someone else could do it to me, and how would I ever know.**

7. Refer back to the *above* conflicts and negative consequences as needed. If and/or when you engage in the **wanted** behavior, describe how those consequences and conflicts are eliminated.

This is what I *gain* when engaging in the wanted behavior: **I live a life closer to what I want for myself.**

Conflict with my *morals* is eliminated by (*"I now feel proud because"*): **There is no doubt that working on our marriage is right for me.**

This is what I look *forward* to: **I give our marriage a better chance of working, even if it doesn't in the long run.**

This is who I *become*: **I trust that I will experience a different more fulfilling life with my new choices.**

Other positive outcomes: **I will develop a greater sense of self-respect and connection with my husband. I increase my peace of mind.**

8. These are the specific Belief System entries I establish or emphasize in support of the **wanted** behavior.

Values: **Getting help for myself, regardless if I can get my husband to go with me. Communication. Honesty. Commitment. Trust in others and myself. Dealing with painful feelings in an appropriate way.**

Morals: **Remain faithful to my marriage. Get some help from a professional when I am in over my head.**

Expectations: **I expect myself to get some help with my problems. I expect myself to remain faithful. I expect myself to discuss concerns with my husband and give him a chance to recommit to our marriage with me.**

Self-Image: **I am honest. I am trustworthy. I am faithful. I am fair.**

The Conscious Management of Feelings

9. I would need to establish the following methods of feeling management related to the **unwanted** behavior. This feeling management would support and maintain the **wanted** behavior.

This is how I manage feelings of *anger* that would interfere with maintaining the **wanted** behavior: **I will find acceptable ways of dealing with the frustrations of our relationship, and seek out a plan of restoring my own sense of worth without needing sexualized attention from others.**

This is how I manage feelings of *sadness* that would interfere with maintaining the **wanted** behavior: **I will concentrate on my effort toward the health of our relationship and focus on the potential gain of connection with my husband.**

This is how I manage feelings of *guilt* that would interfere with maintaining the **wanted** behavior: **I believe that I will experience an increase of integrity as I carry out my plan.**

This is how I manage feelings of *fear* that would interfere with maintaining the **wanted** behavior: **I look forward to a newfound sense of connection with my husband, and increased inner peace.**

The Choice

10. Take all this new information and name the **wanted _new_** behavior. (Give the wanted behavior a name that is relatively brief, easy to remember, and catchy): **A new connection with he and me.**

Now read over the information until you have clearly concluded that the new behavior is in your best interest! **I'm sure about this.**

Self–Image Inventory

Make a check beside the word that best describes how you came to think of yourself as a child.

	Superior		Inferior
	Smart		Stupid
	Good		Bad
	Brave		Coward
	Organized		Chaotic
	Attractive		Unattractive
	Special		Unimportant
	Loved		Hated
	Cared about		Tolerated
	Admired		Loathed
	Active		Lazy
	Nice		Naughty
	Independent		Dependent
	Wanted		Ignored
	Clean		Dirty
	Popular		Disliked
	Healthy		Sick
	Understood		Misunderstood
	Capable		Incapable
	Valuable		Worthless
	Strong		Weak
	Hero		Villain
	Powerful		Impotent
	Right		Wrong
	Trustworthy		Dishonest
	Competent		Incompetent
	Lucky		Unlucky

	Wise		Clueless
	Polite		Rude
	Friendly		Unfriendly
	Thoughtful		Inconsiderate
	Confident		Shy
	Empathetic		Insensitive
	Interested		Apathetic
	Fun		Dull
	Dependable		Unreliable
	Kind		Mean
	Generous		Stingy
	Giving		Withholding
	Leader		Follower
	Socialite		Isolative
	Accepting		Judgmental
	Neat		Sloppy
	Moral		Immoral

The Cognitive Challenge
Associated with 'Glad'

The challenge associated with glad is to answer each of the following questions with <u>at least five genuine</u> responses:

❖ *"What's going my way in my life?"*

1. _____

2. _____

3. _____

4. _____

5. _____

❖ *"What do I have in my life that I am pleased with or grateful for?"*

1. _____

2. _____

3. _____

4. _____

5. _____

❖ *"In what way am I proud of me?"*

1. _____

2. _____

3. _____

4. _____

5. _____

❖ *"What am I looking forward to?"*

1. _____

2. _____

3. _____

4. _____

5. _____

YOBI Profile

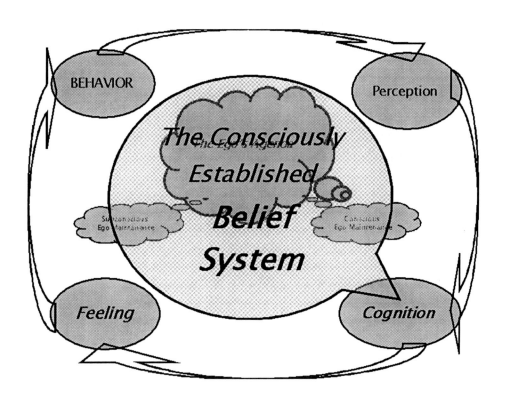

My Ego Interference / Maintenance

These are the ways I attempt to avoid legitimate **emotional pain**:

1. _____
2. _____
3. _____
4. _____
5. _____
6. _____
7. _____
8. _____
9. _____
10. _____

These are the ways I attempt to create illegitimate **emotional gratification**:

1. _____
2. _____
3. _____
4. _____
5. _____
6. _____
7. _____
8. _____
9. _____
10. _____

These are the ways I attempt to establish and maintain **power and control** over people, situations, or environments:

1. _____
2. _____
3. _____
4. _____
5. _____
6. _____
7. _____
8. _____
9. _____
10. _____

❧   My *ego's* version of **ideal** would include the following features:

1. _____
2. _____
3. _____
4. _____
5. _____
6. _____
7. _____
8. _____
9. _____
10. _____

My Evolving Belief System

❧   These are my evolving **values**:

1. _____
2. _____
3. _____
4. _____
5. _____
6. _____
7. _____
8. _____
9. _____
10. _____
11. _____
12. _____
13. _____
14. _____
15. _____

     These are my evolving **morals**:

1. _____
2. _____
3. _____
4. _____
5. _____
6. _____
7. _____
8. _____
9. _____
10. _____

     These are my evolving **expectations**:

1. _____
2. _____
3. _____
4. _____
5. _____
6. _____
7. _____
8. _____
9. _____
10. _____

     This is my evolving **self-image**:

1. _____
2. _____
3. _____
4. _____
5. _____
6. _____
7. _____
8. _____
9. _____
10. _____

Bibliography

Beck, C (1989). *Everyday zen: Love and work*. San Francisco, CA: Harper and Row.

Bednar, R, Wells, M, & Peterson, S (1989). *Self esteem: Paradoxes and innovations in clinical theory and practice*. Washington, DC: American Psychological Association.

Benson, H (1975). *The relaxation response*. New York, NY: Avon Books.

Bolton, R (1979). *People skills: How to assert yourself, listen to others, and resolve conflicts*. New York, NY: Simon and Schuster, Inc.

Bridges, W (1980). *Transitions: Making sense of life's changes*. Reading, MA: Addison-Wesley Publishing Company, Inc.

Foundation for Inner Peace, (1975). *A course in miracles*. New York, NY: Viking.

Frankl, V (1985). *Man's search for meaning*. New York, NY: Washington Square Press.

Gibran, K (1923). *The prophet*. New York, NY: Alfred A. Knopf, Inc.

Haley, J (1973). *Uncommon therapy: The psychiatric techniques of Milton H. Erickson, M.D.* New York, NY: W.W. Norton and Company, Inc.

Hawking, S (1988). *A brief history of time*. New York, NY: Bantam Books.

Kubler-Ross, E (1969). *On death and dying: What the dying have to teach doctors, nurses, clergy and their own families*. New York, NY: Macmillan Publishing Company.

Peck, M (1978). *The road less traveled: A new psychology of love, traditional values and spiritual growth*. New York, NY: Touchstone.

Zukav, G (1989). *The seat of the soul*. New York, NY: Fireside.

Zweig, C, & Abrams, J (Eds.). (1991). *Meeting the shadow: The hidden power of the dark side of human nature*. Los Angeles, CA: Jeremy P. Tarcher, Inc.

Index

Life Skills:
Improve the Quality of Your Life with Metapsychology.

Life Skills, by Marian K. Volkman, is the first ever self-help book based on Metapsychology techniques. Based on the work of Frank A. Gerbode, M.D., Applied Metapsychology makes use of one-on-one session work to achieve the individual's personal goals -- from relieving past pain to living more fully to expanding consciousness.

▫ Learn handy and usually quite fast techniques to assist another person after a shock, injury or other distress.

▫ Learn simple methods for expanding your awareness on a daily basis.

▫ Gain a deeper understanding of what a relationship is, and how to strengthen and nurture it.

▫ Learn the components of successful communication, what causes communication to break down, and how to repair breakdowns.

▫ Learn an effective tool for making important life decisions.

Praise *for Life Skills*

"*Life Skills* is replete with examples, exercises, episodes from the author's life, and tips—this is a must for facilitators, clients, and anyone who seeks heightened emotional welfare—or merely to recover from a trauma."
—Sam Vaknin, PhD, author of *Malignant Self Love: Narcissism Revisited*

"*Life Skills* is a serious, impressive, and thoughtful work with one objective in mind: teaching how to reach one's full potential in practical, pragmatic, easy-to-follow steps that will literally change one's life." —James W. Clifton, M.S., Ph.D.,

"*Life Skills* by Marian Volkman is not to be read once and then put away. It is a guide to living a full, satisfactory life, a philosophy, a challenge. If you take the trouble to do the exercises the way the author suggests, they will change your life."
—Robert Rich, Ph.D., M.A.P.S., A.A.S.H.

"I recommend this book to anyone who's setting out on their personal life's journey and adventure. I rate Ms. Volkman's book 5 stars!"
—Lillian Caldwell, Internet Voices Radio

Loving Healing Press 5145 Pontiac Trail
Ann Arbor, MI 48105
(734)662-6864
info@LovingHealing.com

180 pp trade/paper ISBN-13 978-1-932690-05-7—
$16.95

Includes biblio., resources, and index.

http:/www.LifeSkillsBook.com

Beyond Trauma:
Conversations on Traumatic Incident Reduction, 2nd Ed.

Victor Volkman (Ed.) takes the mystery out of one of the more remarkably effective clinical procedures in a way that can help millions of people revitalize and improve their lives. To those desperate people who have experienced trauma or tragedy, this process is a pathway to dealing with their feelings and getting on with their lives

In the new book **Beyond Trauma: Conversations on Traumatic Incident Reduction**, Volkman presents a series of conversations with a wide range of people from many different backgrounds and experiences. Each provides his or her perspective on Traumatic Incident Reduction, or TIR for short.

Readers will learn about how TIR has helped domestic violence survivors, crime victims, Vietnam vets, children, and others.

Praise *for Beyond Trauma*

"Beyond Trauma outlines the elements with clarity and insight as to how TIR will resolve wrestling with dilemmas, understanding your demons, and climbing out of emptiness."
 —Sherry Russell, Grief Management Specialist and Author

"Our staff therapist is finding Beyond Trauma very helpful".
 —Joan M. Renner, Director, Sexual Assault Program, YWCA of Clark County, WA

"Beyond Trauma: Conversations on Traumatic Incident Reduction is an excellent resource to begin one's mastery in this area of practice."
 —Michael G. Tancyus, LCSW, DCSW, Augusta Behavioral Health

"Not in 30+ years of practice have I used a more remarkably effective clinical procedure."
 —Robert Moore, PhD

Loving Healing Press
5145 Pontiac Trail
Ann Arbor, MI 48105
(734)662-6864
info@LovingHealing.com
Dist. Baker & Taylor

Loving Healing Press

Pub. March 2005 — 360 pp trade/paper — 7"x9"
ISBN-13 978-1-932690-04-0
$22.95 Retail
Includes appendices, bibliography, resources, and index.
For general and academic libraries.
http://www.BeyondTrauma.com

Exclusive offer for readers of *Why Good People Make Bad Choices*

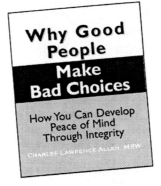

Share the power of Loving Healing Press Books
Order direct from the publisher with this form and save!

Order Form – 15% Discount Off List Price!

Ship To:

_____
Name

_____
Address

_____
Address

_____ _____
City   State

_____
District   Country   Zip/Post code

_____
Daytime phone #

_____
email address

☐ **VISA**   ☐ **MasterCard**   ☐ check payable to
Loving Healing Press

_____ _____/_____
Card #   Expires

_____
Signature

Life Skills _____ x $14.50 = _____

Why Good People... _____ x $19 = _____

Beyond Trauma, 2nd Ed _____ x $19 = _____

Subtotal = _____

Residents of Michigan: 6% tax = _____

Shipping charge (see below) _____

Your Total _$_____

Shipping price <u>per copy</u> via:

☐ Priority Mail (+ $3.50)   ☐ Int'l Airmail (+ $4)   ☐ USA MediaMail/4th Class (+ $2)

Fax Order Form back to (734)663-6861 or
Mail to LHP, 5145 Pontiac Trail, Ann Arbor, MI 48105

Printed in the United States
82387LV00004B/17

9 781932 690255